# Dialogue
# Concerning
# Contemporary
# Psychodynamic
# Therapy

Also by Richard D. Chessick, M.D., Ph.D.

*Agonie: Diary of a Twentieth Century Man* (1976)

*Intensive Psychotherapy of the Borderline Patient* (1977)

*Freud Teaches Psychotherapy* (1980)

*How Psychotherapy Heals* (1969, 1983)

*Why Psychotherapists Fail* (1971, 1983)

*A Brief Introduction to the Genius of Nietzsche* (1983)

*Psychology of the Self and the Treatment of Narcissism* (1985, 1993)

*Great Ideas in Psychotherapy* (1977, 1987)

*The Technique and Practice of Listening in Intensive Psychotherapy* (1989, 1992)

*The Technique and Practice of Intensive Psychotherapy* (1974, 1983, 1991)

*What Constitutes the Patient in Psychotherapy* (1992)

*A Dictionary for Psychotherapists: Dynamic Concepts in Psychotherapy* (1993)

# Dialogue Concerning Contemporary Psychodynamic Therapy

RICHARD D. CHESSICK, M.D., PH.D.

JASON ARONSON INC.
*Northvale, New Jersey*
*London*

This book was set in 10 pt. Goudy by Alpha Graphics of Pittsfield, New Hampshire and printed and bound by Book-Mart Press of North Bergen, New Jersey.

The author gratefully acknowledges permission to reprint lines from an untitled poem by Rainer Maria Rilke, from *Rilke and Benvenuta: An Intimate Correspondence*, copyright © 1987 by Fromm International Publishing Corporation.

**Library of Congress Cataloging-in-Publication Data**

Chessick, Richard D., 1931–
    Dialogue concerning contemporary psychodynamic therapy / Richard
D. Chessick.
        p.   cm.
    Includes bibliographical references and index.
    ISBN 1–56821–371–9 (alk. paper)
    1. Psychodynamic psychotherapy.   I. Title.
RC489.P72C48   1996
616.89'14—dc20                                        95–32111

Manufactured in the United States of America. Jason Aronson Inc. offers books and cassettes. For information and catalog write to Jason Aronson Inc., 230 Livingston Street, Northvale, New Jersey 07647.

This book is dedicated to Paula Brown

who lived on North Whipple Street, Chicago, in 1946.

. . . the unknown beloved . . . the never arrived. . . .

> Flooding toward me on this sombre voyage,
> I can feel the coursing of your heart.
> Only hours remain before I gently
> lay my hands into your gentle hands.
> Oh how long since they have been at rest.
> Can you imagine that for years I've travelled
> thus a stranger among other strangers?
> Now at last you've come to take me home.
>
> Rilke, 1987

*objet petit a*

> Lacan, 1978

Nobody sees anybody truly but all through the flaws of their own egos. That is the way we all see each other in life. Vanity, fear, desire, competition—all such distortions within our own egos—condition our vision of those in relation to us. Add to those distortions in our *own* egos the corresponding distortions in the egos of *others* and you see how cloudy the glass must become through which we look at each other. That's how it is in all living relationships except when there is that rare case of two people who love intensely enough to burn through all those layers of opacity and see each other's naked hearts.

Tennessee Williams
(Halberstam 1993, p. 262)

Writers are really people who write books not because they are poor, but because they are dissatisfied with the books which they could buy but do not like.

Walter Benjamin (1968, p. 61)

# Contents

# Preface

In this book I have borrowed from the format of Galileo, who wrote in 1629 his wonderful "Dialogue Concerning the Two Chief World Systems," in which he introduced modern physics to the world. Albert Einstein writes, in his preface to the 1974 University of California Press edition of Galileo's masterpiece, "It has often been maintained that Galileo became the father of modern science by replacing the speculative, deductive method with the empirical, experimental method. I believe, however, that this interpretation would not stand close scrutiny. There is no empirical method without speculative concepts and systems; and there is no speculative thinking whose concepts do not reveal, on closer investigation, the empirical material from which they stem" (p. xvii).

Hoping to be inspired by the spirit of the geniuses of Galileo and Einstein, I have reintroduced Galileo's three characters in a modern version. The imaginary dialogue in Galileo's day took place in the house of Sagredo, a student of Galileo. I have transformed Sagredo into "Maria," the student mental health professional. She is rather bright and quite advanced, perhaps a psychiatry resident finishing her training or a candidate at a psychoanalytic institute. Galileo's character Simplicio represents traditional thought, the physics of Aristotle. In our dialogue he becomes the student "Donald," whose defensive structures and medical training make it difficult for him to grasp psychodynamics, the concept of the unconscious, or any nonempirical aspects of psychiatry. Such a student, early in his psychiatric residency perhaps, is more at home in nineteenth-century psychiatry with its notion of hereditary degeneracy or nervous system malfunction, and in the *DSM-IV* world of psychopharmacology and neurotransmitters of the twentieth century, just as Galileo's Simplicio is more at home in Aristotle's traditional philosophy. The third interlocutor, Salviati, is the stand-in for Galileo, and as "Richard" in the present dialogue, represents my own views.

The purpose of this dialogue is the very same as that of Galileo in physics, to introduce to the mental health professional, either student or practitioner, the basic tenets of psychoanalytic and psychodynamic psychotherapeutic technique as well as current concepts and controversies in the field, with emphasis on practice rather than theory. I hope that a careful reading of this book will improve the capacity of the clinician to empathize with patients and sharpen the reader's ability to understand and interpret unconscious material. I anticipate that in pulling this all together, the reader will find herself or himself practicing an improved form of psychoanalytic therapy.

# Acknowledgments

I wish to thank my many colleagues in the American Psychiatric Association, the American Academy of Psychoanalysis, and the American Society of Psychoanalytic Physicians. I would also like to thank my other colleagues, particularly in Germany and Hungary, who have discussed the various parts of this book as they were presented in lectures and panels as well as draft form while it was being written over the past three years. Special thanks are due to Drs. Robert Baker, Ron Baron, Harriet Bursztyn, Janos Csorba, Steve Field, Richard Friedman, Seymour Gers, John Goethe, Robert Gould, Douglas Ingram, Alfred Kraus, Hermann Lang, Christoph Mundt, David Sloven, Bhaskar Sripada, Teresa Sripada, George Train, and Margaret Wein for very helpful comments and many favors. It is especially gratifying that some of these respected colleagues are my former students.

I am delighted to have the opportunity to acknowledge the excellent work and uncomplaining cooperation of Ms. Norma Pomerantz, Administrative Assistant at Jason Aronson Inc.; Ms. Janice Wright, Executive Director of the American Society of Psychoanalytic Physicians; Ms. Edith Friedlander, Associate Editor, and Ms. Dianne Gabriele, Assistant Business Manager of the *American Journal of Psychotherapy*; and my most loyal and dedicated Administrative Assistant for many years, Ms. Elizabeth Grudzien.

This book could not have been written without the help of all these wonderful people, and above all, without the patience and tolerance of my dear wife Marcia. Thank you.

# To the Discerning Reader (after Galileo)

I have always wanted to go back to Venice, where Galileo frequently visited and where he met his good friend and pupil Signore Giovanni Francesco Sagredo, "a man of noble extraction and trenchant wit." And what could be more desirable for a student than to eventually become a good friend of his or her revered teacher? In the presence of Simplicio, who was unable to rise above the prevailing Aristotelian philosophy of the day, Galileo, in the person of Signore Filippo Salviati of Florence, joined in a discussion of the new science of the time. Today's new science is still psychoanalysis, and the Simplicios of our day are unable to rise above what philosophers generally now agree to be naive nineteenth-century empiricism or positivism. Let us transport ourselves, therefore, from the palace of Sagredo to the home of Maria, and allow a new dialogue to occur. Who knows, this may be the closest I will ever get to Venice again!

# 1

## The First Day: Memories and Early Experiences

*Richard:* Thank you, Maria, for inviting us to your lovely home. We have agreed to meet for about two weeks to discuss as clearly and in as much detail as possible those tenets of psychoanalytic practice that are necessary to master if one is to be a competent psychoanalytic psychotherapist. Patients deserve to have confidence in entrusting their entire future lives and their relationships to their loved ones to our professional skills and dedication. For it is a serious and enormous responsibility indeed for anyone to assume the mental burdens of another and to attempt to bring about a substantial rearrangement of their psychic structures and defensive compromise formations. These formations have protected the patient since very early in life against the overwhelming fears, anxieties, stimulations, and traumata of the helpless infant and child; tampering with them threatens the entire arrangement. It is not a task for amateurs and it requires a deep sense of the ethical obligations involved. So we will meet each day at this same appointed time and try to review the technique and practice of analytic therapy, focusing each day on a different aspect with emphasis on the practical and controversial problems involved and those clinical situations that are encountered over and over again.

*Donald:* But should we not first, like Galileo, pay our respect to the executives of the various professional organizations and the officials and chairpersons of organized psychiatry and psychology in the hope that our work will be found acceptable? As Galileo (1629) writes:

Therefore may Your Highness accept it with your customary beneficence; and if anything is to be found in it from which lovers of truth can draw the fruit of greater knowledge and utility, let them acknowledge it as coming from you who are so accustomed to being of assistance that in your happy dominions no man feels the widespread distress existing in the world or suffers anything that disturbs him. Wishing you prosperity and continual increase in your pious and magnaminious practices, I most humbly offer you reverence.

Your Most Serene Highness's most humble
and most devoted servant and subject. [p. 4]

\* \* \* \*

*Maria:* You are both very welcome to my home. Please be comfortably seated in the parlor; coffee and tea will be served . . . and now at last may we begin? I would like to start with a discussion of the basic assumptions behind all psychoanalytic practice . . .

*Donald:* Allow me to interrupt, Maria. Give me the courtesy due to a guest. Yesterday evening I was trying to prepare myself for the beginning of our discussion and I was thumbing through some rather boring copies of the *International Review of Psycho-Analysis* in the library. I came across two articles (Thomä and Cheshire 1991, Cheshire and Thomä 1991), claiming that Strachey's translation of Freud's work was misleading, a claim that has been raised by other authors also such as Bettelheim (1983) and Ornston (1982, 1985a, b). Doesn't this undermine the whole psychoanalytic project from the beginning? Furthermore, the article by Thomä and Cheshire stresses the issue of *Nachträglichkeit*. For the life of me I don't understand what it means; all I gathered is that there is an interminable argument about the proper translation of it from the German.

*Maria:* Very well, Donald, although I think this is rather rashly plunging into the middle of things. Clearly you are concerned with the very basic foundation stone of psychoanalysis that was laid down in or is constituted by Freud's texts. Richard, can you help us with this?

*Richard:* Donald has introduced a fundamental issue that is on the cutting edge of psychoanalytic debate today. We all know about Lacan's insistence that he is merely returning to Freud in his attempted refutation of the structural theory and emphasis on Freud's early topographic model. The concept of *Nachträglichkeit* is a central one in the textbooks by Thomä and Kächele (1987, 1992). Their work has great influence in German psychoanalysis and represents what is often known as the Ulm school. In a way it presents the special ambience of psychoanalytic psychotherapy and psychoanalysis in postwar Germany. These authors stress what they call the "interactional" aspects of the psychoanalytic process throughout their work. They believe their emphasis on interactional aspects to be much deeper than Sullivan's (1947, 1953) interpersonal theory, which they say neglects intrapsychic factors and does not recognize that the analyst's "participation" constitutes intervention from the very beginning to the end of treatment. For them the transference begins and is centered on the here and now. To understand transference, they believe we must identify the patient's perception of an injury in the here and now and relate it to the childhood injury and the inevitable consequent revenge fantasies. In this Ulm model, transference is seen as an interactional representation.

*Donald:* What does this have to do with *Nachträglichkeit?*

*Richard:* Thomä argues that Freud's concept of *Nachträglichkeit* represents a major problem and has been mistakenly translated by Strachey as "deferred action." This mistranslation implies a curious notion of causality, in which something that has happened a long time ago lies dormant and does not have an effect until much later. Such an attitude reduces "the history of the subject to a monocausal determinism that pays attention only to the direct influence which actual events in very early infancy may have on the present" (Thomä and Cheshire 1991, p. 418).

*Donald:* What . . . ?

*Maria:* I begin to see their point, because such an attitude represents a kind of predestination in which the individual's fate is strictly determined in the first months of life because of presumed environmental influences. I take it this is not what Freud had in mind; is that right, Richard?

*Richard:* No, it is not what he had in mind, but it's very difficult to understand exactly what he *did* have in mind! He uses the term in several ways and the difficulty in translating it is very marked. The point is that something in the present time stirs up stored reprocessed memory traces that derive originally from infantile events. So first, during development there has been a reprocessing of the infantile events that are then stored in memory traces; these are subsequently activated by the current interaction with the therapist and evoke a traumatic response in the here and now of the analytic situation. This emphasizes the importance of the analyst's input, which reactivates the stored memory traces. But these memory traces are not simply memories of an event; they are a complex combination of actual early events, the whole childhood ambience, and the fantasy process that weaves these external factors into a highly distorted set of memory traces. The distortions are produced, in my opinion, by early infantile projections and reintrojections based on libidinal and aggressive needs. The origin of these distortions is a topic of much current controversy, involving drive theory and object relations theory. We will discuss this much later (Chapter 10).

*Maria:* Could we then go on to say that *Nachträglichkeit* represents the retrospective modification or reprocessing again of memory traces of past experience in the light of later ones?

*Richard:* That is essentially correct, and it warns us that so-called preoedipal material is subject to retrospective modification, as the Lacanians as well as French mainstream psychoanalysts have pointed out. One must always explore the condensation of preverbal material with material from later levels of development. Arlow (1991b) teaches us that in this sense preoedipal material is always seen in the context of a developmental transformation under the impact of advanced oedipal relationships. This makes attempts at early genetic reconstruction of preverbal material especially difficult. Actually I think the term *Nachträglichkeit* is untranslatable; what is important is to have a clear view of what it does *not* mean. Strachey was wrong—it does not mean "deferred action."

*Maria:* I believe I am getting the idea. Basically what is under question here is the notion of linear concepts of development; the linear sequence from oral to anal to genital and oedipal is being replaced by highly individualized sequences of condensed oedipal and preoedipal structures. What are the implications of this for interpretation?

*Richard:* Kernberg (1993) puts it very nicely. He emphasizes that interpretation "should be guided by the analyst's assessment of dominant affective investment at any particular time, predominantly, but not exclusively, through the analysis of the transference, and proceeding from surface to depth, with the awareness of the existence of multiple surfaces, and the possibility that the same impulse/defense organization may be approached from alternative surfaces into a common depth" (p. 664).

*Donald:* That was a very long and difficult sentence! It seems to me that this discussion requires a certain interest in philology and the translation of German, which very few United States psychiatrists like myself seem to have. I can understand that Strachey's translation of Freud has a certain slant as others have of course pointed out, but I think that Strachey's translation actually helped in the acceptance of psychoanalysis in the United States, where "science" has a high status. The retranslation of Freud I am convinced will be just as slanted, especially because Freud is not around to say just exactly what he had in mind. As one can see with Lacan, going "back to Freud" is like going to a Rorschach card these days, with various translators finding there what they want to find. I hope we can put psychoanalysis on a firmer footing than Freud's German texts.

*Maria:* What about Thomä's insistence on the importance of the analyst's input?

*Richard:* I agree with Kernberg's (1993) statement that the reality of the analyst's personality is important only inasmuch as it serves as a kind of coat hook on which the transference may be attached. Along with Kernberg and Etchegoyen (1991), I think there is an exaggerated emphasis these days on the importance of the analyst's personality. The interpersonal approach perhaps emphasizes the analyst too much, although this is an issue of great current debate. I think the capacity to perceive the analyst accurately is a consequence of the analysis of a regressive transference; such perception is not the cause of the regressive transference. So when the patient enters into a regressive transference he or she will often attribute it to some aspect of the analyst's input, but it does not follow from such a claim that the analyst's input has produced the regressive transference manifestations at any given point in the analysis.

It is up to the skill of the analyst to recognize the transference, rather than in a countertransference manner begin a debate with the patient over the alleged analyst's input! This is a common beginner's mistake because often such transferences are archaic, demanding, aggressive, eroticized, and so on, and as such are very draining and tension-producing in the analyst, easily leading to countertransference denial and so forth. If such transferences do not occur, one should be very suspicious of the entire psychotherapeutic or psychoanalytic situation. If they occur rapidly at the onset of the treatment, one should be aware that one is probably dealing with a borderline or psychotic individual.

*Donald:* Unless that person has already had some intensive analytic treatment! In that case the patient would probably plunge right in with the second analyst.

*Richard:* You are correct! One should keep in mind that the transference is a mixture of real experiences, fantasies, and defenses against both.

*Donald:* I think you are sliding over this problem, Richard. There seems to be a very energetic debate going on among experienced senior psychoanalysts about the role of the personality and the input of the analyst in the psychoanalytic situation. In a way you are doing the same thing that Freud did in his writings, sort of sliding over the analyst's input by assuming that the analyst will be neutral, opaque, and simply reflecting like a mirror back to the patient whatever the patient brings into the treatment process. It is no longer a matter of argument that Freud in his psychoanalytic work did not practice that way, and it is probably fair to say that he was simply warning analysts not to indulge in their countertransferences, or at least I hope that is what he was trying to do.

*Maria:* I'm still having some difficulty absorbing this immediate debate about to what extent the reality of the patient–analyst interaction constitutes the transference. I would like to think matters over and return to the whole issue of the analyst's input into the transference tomorrow.

*Richard:* A good idea. Always keep in mind Lacan's *"objet petit a,"* his concept of that part of the Other that is inevitably not there and we always wish *were* there. In a sense this constitutes the core of every transference. It is sometimes extremely difficult for the analyst to become a usable object for a patient. It requires much trial and error. Some say the art of psychodynamic psychotherapy lies in the creativity needed to provide the patient with a mutative new object experience (Newman 1992). Transference, as we shall see on later days of discussion, is often conceived of as the emergence of an object relations unit from the patient's unconscious reenacted in the relationship to the analyst. Searching for transference then would not be simply searching for hidden wishes but for an identification of the predominant object relations enactment. The inability of the patient to modify this object relations pattern due to anxiety about being denuded of what seems to be an essential part of the fabric of the self is experienced by the analyst as "resistance" (Summers 1993).

*Donald:* Denudation? I'm hungry. Right now I want to have dinner. I hope you will join me as my guests.

*Maria and Richard:* With pleasure! Although these concepts are very controversial, at least we can all agree with Wolf (1992) that "the therapeutic ambience is one of the most important factors in predicting a therapeutic outcome" (p. 125).

# 2

## The Second Day:
## The Analyst's Input

*Richard:* Donald, I hope you slept well. Now that you and I are comfortably settled in Maria's house again, perhaps we can take up the discussion from yesterday.

*Donald:* Yesterday the rather controversial concept of *Nachträglichkeit* led us to at least a general idea about what Freud had in mind by it, although it is an untranslatable term. But we left it rather vague as to just what was the role of the psychotherapist or psychoanalyst in the genesis of transference, and I'm not even clear as to what distinction can be made between transference and a patient's legitimate reaction to the behavior or interventions of the psychoanalyst.

*Maria:* This is actually a theoretical as well as a clinical issue. For example, Cavell (1993) stresses the dialectic between the patient and the therapist in contrast to the traditional emphasis on the transference.

*Richard:* There are many difficulties involved in Donald's question. For example, Freud assumed that the infant could recall the object, but this is not really true because before the age of 18 months it is generally agreed that representation arises out of action patterns, not wish fulfillment. That is to say, Freud thought the mind was a sort of inner eye, before which there are presentations. He assumed that private wordless prelinguistic imagistic thinking comes first and then words provide the lens through which the thinker perceives his thoughts. This is a Platonic point of view.

*Donald:* What is a Platonic point of view?

*Richard:* Plato thought that concepts are discovered by the mind due to its previous inborn knowledge of Forms. Actually, the infant has no "thoughts" before communication takes place; concepts are forged through dialogue and not "discovered." That is to say, the mind is continually in the making and communication with another person is indispensable to the formation of the mind.

*Donald:* I don't understand how this applies to the clinical situation.

*Richard:* Cavell (1993) explains, "The analyst is interested in freeing her patients from old and rigid ideas that get in the way of his responding sensitively and with all his available resources to what is happening now. This is sometimes but not always a matter of speaking the literal truth, or unearthing something already there. There is a kind of story in between the true and the tall, the sort of illumination partaking of both creation and discovery" (p. 86).

*Donald:* I don't get it. This is still somewhat vague and I don't see a clear clinical application of what you're talking about.

*Maria:* It seems to be a middle view in which both creation and discovery operate.

*Richard:* Yes. The point is that there is no "unknowable" behind the veil of language, there is no self independent from other selves. As Cavell puts it, "What the baby learns through its interactions with its mother shapes its view of the human world, of communication, and of itself as a communicator . . . its early communications set up pathways for thoughts, set in motion behaviors—of trust, avoidance, openness, spontaneity— that thought will come to inhabit, and reinforce" (p. 128).

*Maria:* Does this not imply yet another explanation of Freud's famous "*Fort-Da*" game? Freud (1920) observed his 18-month-old grandson playing a game in which the little boy, throwing a spool connected to a string over the side of his crib, called out "*fort*" (gone). Then he reeled it back by the use of the string, crying "*da*" (there). There are at least four different interpretations (Chessick 1992a) of this famous incident. For Freud, it represents instinctual renunciation, allowing the boy's mother to go away without protest, a form of mastery "beyond the pleasure principle." For R. D. Laing, it is an attempt to establish ontological security. For Kohut, it represents an effort to maintain control over a selfobject, which, if it works, leads to a sense of cohesion of the self, triumph, and joy. For Lacan, it is an example of how the child is born into language. The desire for the mother and the frustration of this desire are expressed through verbal sounds, "gone" and "there." So man is constituted by his language, says Lacan.

*Richard:* There is a little-noticed footnote on p. 15 in Freud's (1920) "Beyond the Pleasure Principle," in which Freud mentions the child looking at itself in the mirror and then under it (the mirror did not reach to the floor), thus making *itself* disappear. Here absence and presence are being verbalized (*fort—da*), not just the desire to control the mother. This does seem related to Lacan's clever interpretation.

*Donald:* It is certainly a mark of Freud's genius that he was able to drag this ubiquitous game into his writings. There are so many versions of it; sometimes they are called "peek-a-boo" or "hide-and-seek," and so on. My little daughter loves to play "hide," where she gets under her table or under her crib and we pretend that we don't know where she is and then she emerges triumphantly, thus reversing the frequent painful separations she has to undergo when her mother goes to work.

*Richard:* This suggests, as Maria said, another interpretation of the *fort—da* game, in which it is seen as an attempt to take in the discovery of interpersonal reciprocity. Cavell (1993) explains:

> If his activity in relation to the mother consists in his ability to summon her to him, her ability to answer him is a function of a principle of activity that is not his but hers. And this implies that just as it is by her initiative that she comes, so by that same initiative can she go. His power over her, he has discovered, is limited; for the one who answers my call can do so only because she is not part of me, nor is she, like my own limbs, at the end of my will. . . . The sounds "fort," "da" mark places in a game which is essentially both spacial and erotic and in which language and thought are together in the making, along with the discovery of other minds. [p. 224]

Lacan must have enjoyed Freud's (1930, p. 91) statement that writing has in its origin the voice of the absent person; this would be an example of Lacan's "Other."

*Maria:* There seems to be no agreement on this matter. Does the infant emerge from the womb with at least some kind of virtual self or does it require something extrinsic or external to it, something from outside its brain and skin and the resultant process of interaction with an external world before it can have or be anything we can call a self? I think we all agree that a crucial part of this external world would be the mothering one and other individuals to whom the child is libidinally attached. Then, says Cavell (1993):

> Through its interactions with them the child learns a language and comes by a sense of Self and Other, acquires the capacities to generalize, to frame scientific hypotheses as well as more homely everyday generalizations, to formulate maxims of prudence and moral principles. With thought also comes self-awareness, the ability to imagine things, including oneself, different from the ways one finds them, to form ideals, to take oneself as an object. [p. 230]

*Donald:* I still don't understand the application of this to our clinical work.

*Richard:* The entire postmodern view in my opinion is rather extreme and academic. I do think the infant is born with a virtual self or some kind of potential self that is brought out more or less by the loving interaction with others. I agree with Winnicott's famous statement that there is no such thing as an infant, only a nursing couple. But I think it underestimates the incredible intrinsic human capacity to make use of whatever there is in the environment, loving or not, in order to develop and actualize psychological potential. After all, we see a lot of patients who have received very little in the way of loving interaction with parents but who still somehow manage to develop a sense of self and some kind of personality and cognitive differentiations.

*Donald:* At last we are back to something clinical!

*Maria:* Do you agree then, Richard, with Melanie Klein's theory that gratitude and mourning can occur in a very young infant, and that in the second quarter of the first year of life already the infant is capable of recognizing the wholeness both of the object and of himself as subject? And do you also believe that the infant is capable of forming an Oedipus complex in the first year of life? What about the argument brought up earlier that the first 18 months of life consist primarily of sensorimotor patterns?

*Richard:* I think Melanie Klein goes too far. The problem with her theories of this sort, as I see it, is that from her excellent observations of 3-year-olds, who already have a very rich fantasy life and are capable of quite complicated play, she made extrapolations back to the first year of life that are both unjustifiable and unprovable. So Melanie Klein's position would be the extreme opposite of the postmodern position on the issue of the existence of a prelinguistic self. My view is somewhat in the middle, stressing more the inborn potential, the adaptive capacities and the powerful capacity to unfold that potential even under the most difficult conditions.

*Maria:* I think you are referring to inborn potential for the formation of neural synapses and connections. There is considerable experimental work on this subject, the growth and migration of neurons and the formation of neural networks, that demonstrates Richard's view on a neurophysiological level (Eisenberg 1995). This has important ramifications in explaining the destruction of proper treatment for mental health by corporate managed care, "which is transforming medical visits into commodities on a production line," for the "mind/brain responds to biological and social vectors and is jointly constructed by both" (p. 1563). Also there is considerable evidence from at least one school of linguistics, headed by that charismatic Professor Chomsky, demon-strating the amazing inborn capacity of the human infant to acquire the rules of language and syntax regardless of which particular language it is taught. This is all fairly well known at this point.

*Donald:* I understand, but I would like to ask Richard again to apply this more directly to the psychoanalytic process.

*Richard:* The implication of our discussion is that in the psychoana-lytic process the material is shaped in a combination, beginning with the input from the analyst, which, as we mentioned yesterday, can then serve as a kind of coat hook or stimulus for the excitation of certain memory traces from the patient's past. This excitation leads either to an attempt on the part of the patient to reenact the traumatic situation, or through projective identification to shape the analyst into one of the characters in that situation, or to place into the analyst the unbearable emotional aspects of that situation, or to actually perceive and experience the ana-lyst as one of the characters in that situation. When the latter occurs and there is no insight, we have a psychotic transference; when it occurs and the patient realizes that it is irrational, we have the ideal type of neurotic transference. Let me warn you once again that when I talk about a traumatic situation, as we saw yesterday, I am *not* speaking of a specific external event that occurred in childhood or infancy in the fashion that Freud thought of it; I am speaking of an event or even a series of events, such as repeated exposure to the primal scene, that are then invested with the powerful libidinal and aggressive drives of childhood and woven into a basic fantasy process, the core infantile fantasies. Derivatives of these appear in dreams, in masturbation fantasies, and are even reen-acted in adult relationships. They will similarly appear in the psycho-analytic situation through either reenactment, the transference, or the material that allegedly is brought in by the patient as a discussion of something outside of the analysis. It is the task of the analyst to recog-nize the complex combination of these fantasies and the defenses against them that produce derivatives and compromise formations that appear in the analytic process. As proper interpretation takes place, these de-rivatives and compromise formations come closer to the original archaic material until, we hope, that material itself is exposed.

*Donald:* Is it your view that exposure of this material then cures the patient?

*Richard:* No, that is only one of the factors that leads to psychoana-lytic cure, but it is a very important factor. The other very important factor has to do with the interaction between the patient and the ana-lyst. The whole trend of thinking in psychoanalysis has been away from the notion of the analyst as a mirror and toward the notion of the analyst as a partner. In the analytic process there are regular attempts to force, manipulate, or seduce the analyst into taking over the role of one or another introject so that an internal fantasy drama involving an exchange between the self and an introject can be externalized and enacted. It is the way in which the analyst responds to these forces and pressures that has an important decisive effect on the patient. For example, the capacity of the analyst to "contain" the patient's hostility and libidinal excitation without retaliation or seduction in return is one of the most important contributions in my opinion ever made by Bion. Bion (1963) compares this to the mother's "alpha function" in which beta elements—unendurable chaotic extremes of affect and fantasy—are projected by the infant into the mother, who contains them and returns them to the baby via introjection in an attenuated and nondestructive form.

*Donald:* How about a brief clinical example?

*Maria:* It is really not very complicated, Donald. If a patient comes in having been severely narcissistically wounded either in reality or in imagination by either the therapist or by other significant individuals in the patient's life, and pours all this rage out on the therapist, we have the beginning of an opportunity for the therapist. He or she can either retaliate by developing a countertransference rage and punishing the patient, order the patient out of the office (which I have actually seen occur in consultations regarding failed treatments), or become very seductive and try to lull the patient by soothing and loving words and even actions. In fact, one of the main reasons for the development of countertransference "falling in love" with a patient is that the therapist cannot tolerate the chronic anger coming from the patient and wishes to convert the situation from one in which the beta elements of rage are being constantly projected into the therapist to one in which there is a mutual collusion to defend against, neutralize, or drain out the feelings by sexual activity. The properly and thoroughly psychoanalyzed therapist, however, does not get involved in such a manner, because he or she is much more attuned to countertransference and picks up the manifestations quickly. The role of the therapist in these situations is to listen carefully to the storm of affect, wait a bit until it subsides, and then articulate it back to the patient in the form of an interpretation such as, "you are feeling terribly wounded because as you perceived it so-and-so happened, which was unfair and not in line with what you feel entitled to experience. I can understand how in this situation you would have such a tremendous rage, and let us try to talk calmly about your expectations and study in detail what has happened that has produced such a storm"— something like that.

*Richard:* Yes, I think this is a good clinical example and happens very frequently. I would only add that the therapist's task is even more complicated because he or she must distinguish this situation from one in which the patient is unconsciously trying to convert the therapist into a raging retaliatory parent, or into a seductive parent, thus actualizing some internal pressure for reenactment of an earlier scene as we just discussed. So, in the face of an affect storm, like Odysseus, as Poseidon threatened to dash him on huge waves into the rocky cliffs bordering the land of the Phaeacians, the therapist must do some very fast and keen thinking in order to evaluate the situation clearly and decide on the proper articulation. It is not easy work!

*Maria:* What about the inevitable countertransference difficulties that arise in these situations?

*Richard:* Sandler and colleagues (1992) argue that both parties are involved in the formation of countertransference. The patient, as we have seen, will attempt to actualize the interpersonal interaction represented in his or her dominant unconscious wishful fantasy. This will occur through manipulation via rapid verbal and nonverbal signals and pressures to invoke a particular response. Such manipulations and pressures can lead to countertransference experiences or even countertransference enactment on the part of the analyst. They write, "Such enactments should be considered as compromises between the role the patient is attempting to force upon the analyst and the analyst's own propensities. The analyst's awareness of such role-responses can be a vital clue to the dominant transference conflict and associated transference fantasies in the patient" (p. 91). In good analytic work, therefore, the analyst must in his or her mind recognize and evaluate the interaction and the relationship that is forming between the patient and the analyst very carefully before the analyst is in any position to understand the situation of the patient and evaluate the patient's input and the reasons for it. This requires a thorough self-understanding and analysis of the analyst.

*Donald:* Many people who practice psychotherapy have had only a brief once- or twice-a-week psychotherapy of their own. Will this be sufficient to deal with such powerful pressures?

*Richard:* One of my strongest opinions, based on many years of supervision, consultations, and teaching, is that it is not sufficient. It's like asking an intern who has had one month of rotation on the surgical service to do brain surgery. If one is to do proper psychodynamic psychotherapy one is absolutely required to have a thorough psychoanalysis of one's own. As far as I am concerned, that is the minimum requirement that one must obtain before tampering with the minds of other people. In all these years of clinical experience, including a number of consultations with therapists who have become involved in dreadful and destructive situations with patients, as well as in the analysis of some of these therapists, it becomes clear again and again that their lack of a proper psychoanalysis to begin with left them blinded to their own most important infantile fantasies, which then became reenacted out of the temptations provided by the patient in the psychotherapeutic situation. Most of these therapists had a year or two of once- or twice-a-week psychotherapy, often provided by a "psychotherapist" who was also unanalyzed! In my view this is a scandalous situation.

*Donald:* So you are telling me my two years of twice-a-week psychotherapy does not qualify me to see patients?

*Richard:* No, I am not saying that. As a general rule of thumb I have advocated repeatedly that a therapist should see patients one time per week less than he received his or her own therapy and for a shorter length of time than his or her personal therapy lasted. But those who wish to do long-term psychoanalytic treatment, whether it is intensive psychotherapy or psychoanalysis, must commit themselves to a thorough personal psychoanalysis.

*Donald:* Are there special problems of psychic stress for those who do intensive psychotherapy or psychoanalysis? Is that why you are so insistent about the practitioners having a thorough personal psychoanalysis?

*Richard:* I think there are, and these special problems are coming to be increasingly recognized, and are also being utilized to explain the tendency to unfortunate schisms that has plagued the field of psychoanalysis. For example, Eisold (1994) sees the causes for institutional fragility in the field of psychoanalysis, the intolerance of diversity and schism, as stemming from "social defences against often unrecognized forms of anxiety associated with the practice of psychoanalysis" (p. 785). These sources include the isolation of analytic work, a tension between the analyst's affiliation to his or her patient and membership in psychoanalytic organizations, and participation in the culture of psychoanalysis itself, "which sees itself as apart from the world of social reality; psychoanalysts, as a result, devalue and fear the very institutions that connect them with that world" (p. 785). Of course this is a controversial point of view, but it is worth careful consideration, because the problems of diversity and schism, as well as the stress on the psyche of the psychoanalyst over years and years of practice are still very important matters of concern.

*Donald:* I understand your point of view now, and I suppose I can live with it. But I would like to address the issue of what brings about change in psychoanalytic treatment. We seem to have identified some of the elements and I think it would be wise to try to gather them together.

*Maria:* I suggest that we devote tomorrow's discussion to this issue. I have prepared a fine dinner for us, which is now being served.

*Richard and Donald (together):* How nice! Thank you, Maria.

# 3

## The Third Day: Curative Factors

*Richard:* Thank you for having us to your lovely home again, Maria. Returning to where we left off yesterday, two general points of view have developed regarding what brings about change in psychoanalytic treatment. One approach emphasizes interpretation, especially of the transference, and historical or narrative reconstruction. The other approach emphasizes the experiential and transactional aspects of a new and better human relationship. We mentioned yesterday what I regard to be the bedrock of the psychoanalytic process, the uncovering of the patient's unique, individualized core preoedipal fantasies that undergo subsequent elaboration and repression during the oedipal period, and the analysis of these fantasies as representing compromise formations arising out of early preoedipal and oedipal infantile conflicts.

*Donald:* Can you clarify your concept of these unique individualized core fantasies any more?

*Richard:* Suffice it to say that behind the fixed and organized repressed unconscious fantasies is what Dowling (1990) calls "the blurred, undifferentiated preconceptual thought of early oedipal and preoedipal life," that perhaps includes "sensory, motor or behavioral memories, which arise primarily from preverbal experience and remain influential throughout childhood and adult life" (p. 109). The first clue to such fantasies may appear in the patient's behavior rather than in his or her verbalization during the analytic process. These fantasies differ from other unconscious content in their enduring quality and their organized storylike quality, reflecting the distortions typical of primary process, and they form dynamically unconscious templates from the childhood past that are relatively impervious to new experience. This means there is a danger even in a well-conducted analysis along the lines that combine both interpretation and an ameliorative interpersonal ambience, if this core fantasy activity has not been reached and analyzed, of considering the psychoanalysis to be in a concluding phase when the patient forms what Kohut calls an empathic matrix, or seems to be more mature, successful, realistic, and less narcissistic and more loving in his or her interpersonal relations.

*Maria:* This does not seem quite consistent with Freud's mature view, which was that the establishment and resolution of the transference neurosis by interpretations and working through constitutes the crucial curative factor in psychoanalytic work.

*Donald:* Even in 1936 at the Marienbad Symposium on curative factors there were analysts who argued that for interpretations to be efficacious, a prerequisite was the attitude, especially the unconscious attitude of the analyst to his or her patient. I can understand that. But wouldn't that affect the ego rather than the superego of the patient, in contrast to Strachey's (1934) classical view?

*Richard:* Yes. A mutative interpretation may have the ameliorative function of altering the ego rather than the superego in spite of Strachey's classic paper. In this situation the patient imitates the therapist's analytic attitude of objective observing and in consequence alters his or her ego to conform to it as a model. Another way to look at this is in Loewald's (1980) conception of the new object relationship as useful in the resumption of development and the correction of reality distortion. Here the maturity of the analyst becomes crucial and represents a higher stage of integration for the patient just as the mother mediates this for the child.

*Maria:* Wouldn't this emphasize the patient's emotional attachment to the analyst as a significant facilitator of the integrating or restructuring outcome of successful analytic work? I like to think of Nacht's (1962) famous remark, "It is what the analyst *is* rather than what he *says* that matters" (p. 207).

*Richard:* One must be very careful because emphasis on the positive affective aspect of the interpersonal relationship between the patient and the analyst can make it impossible to analyze the patient's inherent sadism and aggression. The same danger occurs in self psychology, because it emphasizes the archaic self/selfobject bond that forms between the patient and the analyst as the patient experiences the analyst's empathic capacity. Of course it is difficult to argue against the view that there are crucial noninterpretive elements that must be provided in the psychoanalytic process for change to take place. There must be a proper ambience for interpretations and other interventions to be effective.

*Donald:* How does one provide such an ambience? Where does it come from?

*Richard:* This ambience is produced by what is embedded in the analyst's attitude, which must be reasonable and decent. For example, listen to the tone and rhetorical quality of the analyst's verbal interventions; observe his or her facial expression at the beginning and the end of the sessions; study the affectual tone in which reality such as hours, fees, absences, intercurrent life crises, and so forth, are dealt with. A certain kind of elasticity in the analyst's personality is also needed, and a very substantial flexibility.

*Maria:* I still think the best example of this, which is emphasized in papers by Lipton (1977, 1979, 1983), is provided by the climate of Freud's analyses. Freud preserved a real adult object relationship, although restricted, and a natural friendly and appropriate interaction between the patient and the analyst. Empathy is an extremely important factor in the psychoanalytic process, whether or not one believes with certain self psychologists that it may make up for maternal deficits. And as Winnicott pointed out, the indestructibility of the analyst is another important factor. The analyst must survive the treatment!

*Richard:* Put it this way: The psychoanalytic process begins and ends between two adults. As Stone (1981) stated, the patient has every right to ask the question, "What sort of person is this to whom I am entrusting my entire mental and emotional being?" The argument of Stone's paper is directed against "the superfluous iatrogenic regressions attendant upon superfluous deprivations" (p. 113), even if the patient is not aware of suffering from them. Whether the kind of interpersonal ambience that arises as a consequence of the healthy analyst's natural attitude toward the patient (and toward all people, for that matter) is by itself curative or not, it certainly provides an optimum ambience for effective interpretive work.

*Donald:* If you are correct, the special individual personal characteristics of the analyst apparently have an increasingly recognized importance in the analytic process. I must admit this makes me nervous; do I understand it properly?

*Richard:* The analyst's consistent interest in the patient, benign neutrality, capacity to forgo expected retaliations, ability to maintain integrity despite attacks or seductions from the patient as we have seen yesterday, and consistent and persistent curiosity about and attempt to interpret the meanings of the patient's neurotic behavior both outside the treatment and in the transference are crucial. The capacity to transform countertransference into empathy and understanding is the most important skill of the analyst, what Abend (1989) calls "perhaps the ultimate test of the gifted analytic clinician" (p. 389). A lot depends on the empathy, ability, and honesty of the analyst, who is only too prone to feel bruised and narcissistically wounded himself or herself and in subtle or not so subtle ways may tend to blame the patient. In fact, some authors (Newman 1988) insist that in the treatment of certain patients an enmeshment in the transference/countertransference experience is necessary, a drama that must be repeated with affective participation by both parties to the relationship in order for the patient to come to grips with the psychic reality of what happened in the past.

*Donald:* Isn't this a very dangerous idea? And can it not lead to collusion or mutual acting out?

*Richard:* It all depends on the skill and personal self-understanding of the analyst! In pathological development the child's disappointment and consequent rage and protest are not soothed. The parental object is viewed as both nonresponsive and unable to contain the results of nonresponsiveness, so it is seen as doubly dangerous. The character structure that results from these early developmental failures wards off the internal pain of needs and the attachment to an intrusive, critical, excessively narcissistic, and unavailable object. It also provides the illusion of connectedness to objects but controls the attachment to new objects by distancing either through compliance or control. This is sometimes called the "defense transference," which is immediately experienced at the beginning of psychoanalytic therapy as the patient uses the same characterological maneuvers toward the therapist. The analyst's reactions to this and understanding of it allow the analyst to sample the faulty objects of the patient's childhood and, if the analyst can manage and understand the countertransference, it can facilitate an authentic recognition of the patient's inner world. So the proper mastery of countertransference facilitates the process of change in psychoanalytic therapy.

*Maria:* In Freud's structural model the analyst interprets in order to ultimately help the patient achieve an alteration in his or her pathological compromise formations in the direction of less-defensive rigidity, more-realistic pleasure, less-affective pain, and the best possible conditions for adaptive and flexible functioning of the patient. Resistance from the modern structural point of view is a "compromise formation between defenses, drive derivatives, painful affects, the need for punishment, and considerations of reality" (Boesky 1988, p. 309). According to Boesky, the traditional structural view of Freud commands us to interpret the patient's conflicts, and after that nature will build the psychic structure. What really propels the psychoanalytic process, writes Boesky, is "examining, describing, and interpreting alterations in a variety of resistances" (p. 314).

*Donald:* But what about Ornstein and Ornstein's (1977) view of the "curative fantasy"? The patient begins the treatment, they say, with the wish to have the past undone and made up for. When this is activated there occurs an interaction or engagement with the therapist, and the therapist's responses to this are crucial. The therapist, according to these authors, must help curative fantasies emerge and deal with the guilt over them, allowing them to transform and mature. What is curative, then, is not the ambience or nonspecific elements in the treatment, but the increased unfolding of archaic curative fantasies, the wish to use the therapist as a selfobject and the hope for a "new beginning." This motivates the patient toward recovery out of the assumption that the treatment will compensate for everything by bringing power, skills, and success.

*Maria:* It seems to me that the interpretation of this fantasy depends on one's theoretical orientation. For example, some would relate it to infantile instinctual aims seeking satisfaction in the transference, similar to Freud's discussion of a cure by love. The self psychologists focus on the patient's new hopes, which, due to the fear of disappointment, are defended against. Such patients reorganize their vulnerable selves around a protective character armor (Newman 1992). This is experienced by the analyst as "resistance." Patients may need to set up rejecting situations in spite of their wish to be accepted, as a defense against the possibility of disappointment. Attempting to get the patient to face his or her hostility when these fantasies are disappointed and when projection takes place implies that the patient is unlovable and that something is fundamentally wrong with the patient. Such interpretations, according to the Ornsteins and other self psychologists, just retraumatize the patient. The rage must be accepted as appropriate to the patient's experienced reality, as a response to an experienced injury due to the disappointed wish for unconditional success, acceptance, power, and skills. For self psychologists, empathic acceptance, followed by understanding, followed by interpretation, remains the crucial set of factors in analytic cure.

*Richard:* You have both described these points of view correctly. However, even more goes on in the psychoanalytic process than what you have outlined, and this is the problem that faces all investigators. For example, Weiss and Sampson (1986) believe that control is possible over one's unconscious mental life and that one regulates it with respect to beliefs and external reality on the principle of avoiding danger and maintaining safety. They view much of adult psychopathology as due to the child's wish to maintain its ties with the parents out of the unconscious guilt over separation, which the child believes will hurt the parents. There are two ways such beliefs arise. In the first, the child attempts to gratify its impulse or reach an important goal and discovers that this threatens the tie to the parents, at which point parental behavior and response becomes crucial. In the second, a traumatic event occurs for which the child blames itself, believing it was caused by his or her wish to gratify an impulse or reach an important goal. These authors claim that patients who feel that they do not deserve to be loved make rapid progress when they recognize their unconscious guilt. A deficit cannot be filled by subsequent good relationships in the ordinary course of life if the individual does not feel that he or she deserves a good relationship. This is why adult patients have persistent "deficits," for otherwise they would correct these deficits much earlier through new relationships.

*Maria:* In the psychoanalytic process the patient works with the analyst to disconfirm pathogenic beliefs by testing them with respect to the analyst and by understanding them via interpretations. The motive to do this is very strong because these unconscious expectations and beliefs are very constricting and produce painful guilt.

*Donald:* How does this testing take place in the clinical situation?

*Richard:* An important form of testing is by turning the passive into the active. The patient behaves to the analyst as his or her parent behaved to the patient. This is in contrast to the transference, where the patient behaves to the analyst as he or she behaved to a parent! All patients do both of these in order to keep traumatic memories repressed. Testing by turning the passive into the active is with the hope that the analyst will not react by getting upset but will maintain the analytic stance. If so, the patient can identify with the analyst's lesser vulnerability and question the childhood belief that the trauma was deserved. This may be observed in extra-analytic situations also, for it is not unusual that later in life the grown child may treat the parent the way the child felt treated by the parent when the child was young. The more traumatized the patient was, the more likely the patient will begin the treatment with a test involving change from passive to active, as this is safer than the ordinary transference.

*Maria:* With testing and utilizing interpretation the ego controls the transference and keeps the expression of it appropriate and relatively safe. After-education or new experiences with the analyst are the key to psychoanalytic treatment for authors such as Weiss and Sampson. But at the core of every patient there resides a crucial fantasy activity, interwoven with early infantile experiences to a greater or lesser degree, depending upon how traumatic these experiences have been. I remember of course that as we discussed yesterday, "What constitutes trauma is not inherent in the actual, real event, but rather the individual's response to the disorganizing, disruptive combination of impulses and fears integrated into a set of unconscious fantasies" (Arlow 1985b, p. 533).

*Richard:* Certain object relations and self psychology theories, as well as the views of Weiss and Sampson just mentioned, tend to minimize the role of this unconscious fantasy activity and emphasize the pathogenic effect of real events and interactions. However, I agree with Arlow (1980) that the individual's experience "is usually organized in terms of a few, leading, unconscious fantasies which dominate an individual's perception of the world and create the mental set by which he or she perceives and interprets her/his experience" (p. 131).

*Donald:* I understand your emphasis on the importance of unconscious core fantasies. You have pointed it out repeatedly, and sometimes tediously. But just what is *your* position on the curative factors in psychoanalytic treatment?

*Richard:* My position is that empathy with the patient and appropriate interpretations allowing the selfobject transferences to arise is a vital way of beginning the treatment. Along with the experience of the physicianly vocation of the analyst, empathy sets up an ambience that is optimal for the integration of interpretations and for the development of a new object relationship. This object relationship, as it arises out of the proper ambience of the treatment, continuously provides the motivation for the patient to develop.

The setting of the analytic treatment, with the patient on the couch and doing most of the talking, promotes regression. The rule of abstinence, properly applied, promotes the resurgence of yearnings for old objects, the appearance of fantasy activity, and the subsequent development of the transference. If the patient is excessively gratified, the transference does not appear, but if the patient is irrationally or sadistically ungratified in the treatment, the reaction will be one of iatrogenic narcissism and rage, which cannot properly be called transference. Everything depends on the maturation, skill, and clinical judgment of the analyst.

*Maria:* If I understand you correctly, Richard, you are arguing that the interpretation of the transference and of extratransference situations should ultimately aim at focusing down on the central psychic core of the patient through the continuous analysis of derivatives of that core.

*Richard:* That is correct. The patient's observing ego must engage with the analyst and eventually take over this search, but we should keep in mind that events such as the primal scene are rarely directly remembered. What counts as the patient's psychic reality is a basic core of fantasies or traumata in some combination of intensity woven into a unique special fantasy activity; in some patients the material will be almost purely fantasy and in others the most serious kind of abuse and exposure to real horror and death has taken place. Still, no matter how great the traumata, it is the basic unique fantasy activity woven around traumata that has the primary effect on all of the patient's subsequent behavior and capacity to relate to other people.

*Donald:* What do you maintain will happen if this vital core is reached?

*Richard:* If it is reached, identified, and worked through with the patient, including the patient's need to reenact the fantasy in the treatment situation—which some authors actually call *the* transference—it allows the past to recede into the past and no longer pervade the present. The ghosts can become ancestors (Leowald 1980). This offers the ego new options and new choices and new compromises in dealing with its three harsh masters—the id, superego, and reality. So although change can occur in psychoanalytic therapy through a new object relationship or an empathic experience with an understanding analyst, a basic structural change that does not simply consist of identification with the therapist or internalization of a more benign object can only come about when there has been a thorough understanding of the early infantile fantasy activity that forms the background mental set of the patient's perceptual and motor system, the core of the patient's psychic reality. Derivatives of these fantasies can be found in every aspect of the patient's choices, behavior, and relationships in later life and they persist to an amazing degree even into old age.

*Donald:* Is it really possible to get at these so-called core fantasies? I haven't noticed them in most of my patient work, even in intensive psychotherapy under supervision.

*Richard:* It has been my experience from the reanalysis of patients, that some analyses are aborted as this core is approached; the treatment is covered over by a superficial and premature turn toward increased integration and maturation, giving the impression that the patient has made a recovery and suggesting termination. The uncovering of these fantasies is vigorously defended against, as they represent some kind of crucial compromise formation in an attempt to master infantile anxieties, traumata, and conflicts. To expose them renders the patient vulnerable to reexperiencing the intense dread of annihilation and overwhelming fragmentation the infant suffered at a time when it was as yet extremely incapable of dealing with such powerful affects. If the patient cannot bear to have this core exposed, the treatment will abort and remain a psychotherapy even though an apparently distinct but superficial improvement in the patient may take place. This leaves the patient vulnerable to continual pervasion of his or her behavior and choices by the core infantile fantasy activity, so that the improvement is maintained only as long as the internalization of the therapist continues.

*Maria:* This reminds me very much of Freud's (1918) case of the "Wolf Man." The Wolf Man internalized the gratification of being Freud's famous patient and imagined himself under the protection of the apparently omnipotent Freud until the time when he heard Freud had developed cancer. At this point his superficial improvement broke down, and his recovery took place when he was able cleverly to establish himself not as the special patient of the omnipotent Freud, but as the sort of "mascot" of the entire psychoanalytic movement, which protected him against the sickness or death of any individual psychoanalyst. This resulted in a lasting superficial improvement in his condition, although his personality remained unchanged.

*Donald:* The famous American psychoanalyst Karl Menninger (1958) produced a somewhat different version of the psychoanalytic process than you have given, Richard. In his concept, written before Kohut's self psychology, there occurs, after a suitable period of frustration of the patient's curative fantasy, a turning around that Menninger labels *kairos* from the Greek of Hippocrates, a turning around toward maturation, which takes place at a suitable or proper point in the analytic regression. How would you explain this? There is no talk of uncovering unique core infantile fantasies!

*Richard:* I was able to get into a discussion of this with Menninger unfortunately only very late in his life. We were discussing revising and rewriting his textbook, which had already once before been reissued with a coauthor. To my dismay, although I had prepared the draft of a substantially revised version of his textbook for him to consider, Menninger died before further arrangements for a rewriting could be carried out. The question is whether this turning around that he discusses at the so-called proper point in the analytic regression does not represent an *escape* from the analysis of the patient's core and constitute a reintegration motivated primarily by an attempt to avoid depth analysis. In that sense Menninger's process might be better labeled a psychotherapy because basic structural change does not occur. I believe this also accounts for the failure of many of the early psychoanalyses, in which the patient's Oedipus complex was analyzed according to the then prevailing custom and the patient pronounced cured, after which some of these so-called analyzed early analysts went on to manifest serious psychopathology, including even psychosis and suicide. There is no reason why, after the influence of the analyst has passed, the early core fantasy activity should not regain its pervasive motivating power if it has not been uncovered and worked through, leaving the ego open to new options and choices.

*Donald:* You seem to be disagreeing with the popular concept of "alexithymia" and other alleged deficits such as the inability to experience hunger that some authors have described in their study of the eating disorders. Gedo (1979) suggests that we must address and try to correct these deficits directly. He calls them "apraxias," and recommends a form of after-education therapy. He argues that if we do not do this, we are repeating the defective parenting from the patient's past.

*Richard:* My approach stresses conflicts more than deficits so that situations like alexithymia and so forth that have been attributed to primary deficits in development could at least be partly understood as existing on the basis of conflict. Such disorders would then have a better prognosis in that once the conflict over the repressed infantile fantasies was resolved, the so-called deficits, to whatever extent they are derivatives of the fantasy activity, could disappear.

I do think Gedo has hit on something extremely important in the treatment of severely preoedipally damaged patients. Such patients are usually not amenable to a traditional psychoanalysis, and the actual training in new forms of adaptive behavior provided by the therapist can be most helpful. However, it raises the thorny question of whether this is psychoanalysis or psychotherapy. Arlow (1985b) says that psychoanalysis is fundamentally a psychology of conflict. Gedo's technique is a form of after-education therapy, which, although it may be very useful for the patient, does not really constitute an investigation of the patient's unconscious. I'm sure we'll have to turn to this issue in more detail later.

*Donald:* You also seem to be disagreeing with self psychology. Can you explain this?

*Richard:* The disagreement between my views and self psychology is because I believe that after one has worked through the narcissistic transferences and the oedipal material begins to appear, the treatment is not over. Rather, the stage has now been properly set for a traditional analysis. When the walls in the roof of a house are cracked because they are resting on a faulty foundation, one must obviously first repair the foundation. Self psychologists maintain that in humans, in contrast to a house, there is an inherent developmental force that will take over and repair the rest once the foundation is secure. But can this occur without further psychoanalytic treatment of distortions due to the patient's pathological ego alterations in later childhood stages with their characteristic conflicts, defenses, compromises, and fantasy activities?

The foundation must be repaired first if at all possible. Here the method of empathy and the study of archaic transferences become central, and it is only after these have been worked through and understood by the patient, and the building of a reasonably firm tension regulation system has been established, that the patient can then tolerate the development of more traditional transferences and the frustrations and tensions that the rule of abstinence entails. In practice these days most patients seem to need some degree of foundational repair, but in less serious cases this can go on along with traditional interpretation. Some patients, however, need a very long period of restoration of the self first.

*Maria:* This reminds me of the concept of bifurcation in physics, a phenomenon whereby the number of solutions of a certain type presented by a dynamic system changes abruptly as one of the parameters defining the dynamics crosses a critical value. Since all symptoms and behavior represent a compromise formed by the ego among the demands of the id, the superego, and reality, this concept could be applied to change in psychoanalytic treatment. That is to say, change of symptoms, change of behavior, so-called structural improvement in psychoanalysis, would all represent a change in the compromise formations formed by the ego. It follows that a sudden and abrupt jump in the direction of improvement could take place if one of the parameters defining the dynamics that are at play on the ego when it has to form a compromise suddenly shifts or crosses a critical value; the same would be true in the opposite direction. This explains the common phenomenon of there appearing to be a plateau or lack of progress in a psychoanalysis for long periods of time and then an apparent sudden breakthrough where compromise formations sharply shift.

*Donald:* Physics—I get it! An abrupt negative shift may be most commonly observed if the patient develops some kind of organic disease. The bodily needs and requirements are massively increased and the ego sometimes has to deal with them at the expense of more fortunate compromises; the onset of a bodily disease can even be heralded by the appearance of such negative shifts. For example, it is well known that pancreatic cancer is often preceded by a period of depression, and other authors have reported either depressive or hypomanic behavior heralding the onset of coronary artery disease.

*Maria:* A good idea! Another such bifurcation occurs in severely damaged patients who experience disappointment in archaic selfobject expectations. Here the narcissistic rage can become so overwhelming that a critical value is crossed; previous compromise formations such as obsessional rituals or masochism are suddenly overshadowed by massive projection and projective identification. This is an emergency and can break up the treatment if the ego's capacity to respond to interpretations is lost.

*Richard:* This can also occur in psychoanalysis as the patient's core fantasy activity is approached. In those cases where the fear of revelation of this core is overwhelming, the patient may suddenly disrupt the analysis by projection in which the analyst is perceived as an intrusive malevolent monster. Although this perception itself is a derivative of the core fantasy activity, if there is not sufficient tension regulation and capacity for insight the patient cannot continue the treatment. At this point the patient may insist on sitting up or even leaving therapy on the basis of overwhelming fear of the process or of the analyst. Characteristically they go on to some other form of group or supportive therapy that does not address the core fantasy activity.

*Donald:* As you mentioned before, I think at this point we are clearly going to have to address the issue of the differentiation between psychoanalysis and psychotherapy. May I suggest this for our next discussion?

*Richard:* Certainly.

*Maria:* The issues discussed today are difficult and controversial. I intend to review them carefully in my mind; these concepts require prolonged thought.

# 4

## The Fourth Day: Psychoanalysis and Psychotherapy

*Richard:* The primordial meaning of the psychoanalytic situation lies in the reverberations of it for the preoedipal child in the patient. There seems to be general agreement (Rothstein 1988) that the more disturbed the patient the less the treatment may be called psychoanalysis and the more it involves influencing, suggestion, correction of expectations, stabilization, superego modification, and model provision for identification or introjection, as well as holding and support, with a focus on solving specific problems. Healthier patients seem to require only a reasonable modicum of these factors and can concentrate more on reliving in the transference and reconstruction through interpretation. What is paramount in any given therapy is a function of what aspect of the patient's development is being repeated with the therapist at any given time, since that developmental stage is what determines the meaning for the patient of a given intervention. Thus the context and not just the content of any intervention must be considered in judging the appropriateness of the intervention.

*Donald:* That is quite a formal opening statement as we gather together in Maria's house on our fourth day, again enjoying the warmth of her personality and the pleasure of her hospitality.

*Maria:* Thank you, Donald. It seems clear that our task as therapists is to be able in each case to identify the predominant transference and predominant mode of relationship that the patient is using at any given time, and to tune the emphasis in the therapy to those factors that are appropriate to that developmental phase, while at the same time minimizing or de-emphasizing those that are inappropriate. For example, a fragmented, psychotic, or borderline severely disturbed chaotic patient is manifesting preoedipal pathology in which defective coping operations and interpersonal invariance have determined the developmental course and were needed for adaptation. After language has been acquired, the so-called defenses that we experience from the patient are secondary reworkings of this. But the original problem of severely preoedipal disturbed patients is coping with reality; the core fantasies in such patients reflect the sensorimotor memories and the fear of a recurrent preverbal holocaust.

*Donald:* Last evening after our discussion I reread some of the work of Gedo (1979, 1986), which appeals to me. Gedo emphasizes the failure of such severely disturbed patients to develop normal skills. This is "beyond interpretation" and the psychotherapist must deliberately demonstrate these adaptive skills to the patient. If the therapist refuses to educate the patient, Gedo claims, then there has simply been another parental failure. These preverbal patterns are the hardest to modify because they were crucial in tension relief. Gedo believes there is no correlation of self and object representations with the patient–analyst exchange, in direct opposition to the views of Kernberg. The transference depends on the therapist's personality, specific issues that are brought in by the personal qualities of the therapist, and the technical choices dictated by the therapist's psychoanalytic convictions.

*Maria:* There seems to be a lot of disagreement about all this; what do you say, Richard?

*Richard:* In the management of archaic transferences, the therapist is often "forced to do something," a reluctant compliance without which the patient develops an unmanageable rage that threatens to fragment the patient and break up the treatment. The skill of the therapist is to do just enough so that the patient has some sense of the therapist's recognition that words alone will not suffice, but not to afford so much gratification that the patient has no motivation to change, which would engender an artificial need for more and more gratification. Later in the treatment words alone *do* suffice, and the patient, we hope, is able to tolerate the psychoanalytic process involving interpretations, the pain of reliving early childhood experiences, and the analysis of core fantasies. Gratifying or educational behavior on the part of the analyst at this point is now inappropriate and represents seduction and countertransference acting out; if it takes place the result is an interminable treatment. The presence of this latter situation can be spotted by a sufficiently trained analyst through the recognition that no depth is being achieved in the development of various transference phases; the material becomes increasingly boring and repetitive. This represents analyst failure, not patient failure. Shall we discuss impasses and interminable treatment?

*Maria:* I would prefer not to at this point, but rather to go on with our discussion of psychotherapy, how it is differentiated from psycho-analysis and how one approaches the variety of psychoanalytic theories.

*Richard:* Spira (1988) explains that our very choice of a specific psy-choanalytic theory and rejection of others has a defensive function. Simi-larly, our choice of which factors we consider paramount in the psycho-analytic process also represents a compromise formation made by our ego in an attempt to balance the demands of our id, our superego, and our reality. The rigidity with which one clings to a given theoretical system is a measure of how important that choice has become as a means of reducing the therapist's anxiety; the greater the therapist's personal self-knowledge and the greater the maturation of the therapist, the more open the therapist can be to the reception of data that might lead to a gradual shift in theoretical position or a bifurcation jump. Such changes in theo-retical position, then, could be either mature if based on the accumula-tion of experience, an interchange of ideas enabling the ego to make better judgments because it has better information, or neurotic and pri-marily dominated by the therapist's need to avoid signal anxiety. Chessick (1990) tried to illustrate how the therapist's continuing self-analysis leads to a better understanding of his or her shifts in theoretical orientation over many years of practice.

*Maria:* Yesterday we agreed that two general points of view regard-ing what brings about change in psychoanalytic treatment are prevalent today. One set of conceptions emphasizes interpretation, especially of the transference, and historical or narrative reconstruction. The other set emphasizes the experiential and transactional aspects of a new and better human relationship. Clearly future investigation is needed to dis-tinguish the role of correction of painful expectations (generated out of the psychic elaboration of actual infantile experiences) through the new relationship to the analyst, from the role of interpretation of early fan-tasy activity and reconstruction of how this was developed and then con-gealed in the patient's childhood. The danger of avoiding the analysis of core infantile fantasy activity and its effect on the patient's current per-ception, thinking, and behavior, by a premature termination of the treat-ment when the relationships of the patient seem to be more successful, mature, and realistic were stressed by Richard.

*Richard:* I also pointed out that one must be careful not to utilize self psychology or object relations theory beyond foundational repair in psy-choanalytic therapy without considering the consequences. One must always ask oneself whether one is utilizing such theories and practices and the interpretations based on them defensively, in a collusion to avoid facing the patient's unique core childhood oedipal and preoedipal fantasy activity and the reverberations of it in the analyst's core fantasy activity. Continuing self analysis is required in every treatment process, which is why the analyst always learns and matures from every case. The openness of the analyst permits insight through interpretation, meliorative noninterpretive aspects of the new object relationship or experience, regression due to the analyst's reliability, which gives the opportunity to undo developmental arrests through the analysis of core fantasies, a symbolic holding environment, and the collaborative creation of a narrative, all of which are known to have therapeutic effects and to work together to produce change in psychoanalytic treatment.

*Donald:* We agreed today to discuss psychoanalysis and psychotherapy, and what differentiates them. Richard, would you please at last get to the issue. Perhaps we should start with this question: What are the assumptions behind all psychoanalytic practice?

*Richard:* The best beginner's introduction to the assumptions behind all psychoanalytic practice still remains the classic *Introductory Lectures on Psychoanalysis* by Freud (1915–1916). It is amazing to consider that he delivered these lectures without notes. The first two sections, which constitute Volume 15 of the *Standard Edition*, deal with parapraxes, dreams, and the general evidence for the existence of the unconscious. Indeed, the power of unconscious drives and fantasies (which are the embodiments of these drives) to dominate a person's life is one of the first and foremost underlying assumptions behind all psychoanalytic practice. Perhaps the most extreme example of this was presented by Groddeck (1961). In his extraordinary work, which unfortunately is no longer read by residents in psychiatry, the power of the unconscious to express itself through the body and even various physical diseases is vividly outlined by this intuitive and charismatic internist.

*Donald:* Although Groddeck was an internist, he called himself a "wild analyst," and most physicians find his views on psychosomatic medicine hard to believe indeed. Also, the issue of "drives" in Freud's sense certainly remains a subject of great debate to this day, both among biological psychiatrists and psychoanalysts themselves.

*Richard:* Arlow (1985b) explains that much of an individual's life is determined by the unconscious and expresses derivatives and reenactments of unconscious fantasies at various levels. Also, one should never underestimate the power of unconscious processes and fantasies to affect the physiology of the body and produce the most remarkable, almost unbelievable, physical conditions! A whole variety of physical symptoms, disorders, and diseases are the consequence of, or at least are profoundly determined by, unconscious psychic factors. We can discuss later what else besides Freud's "drives" determines these unconscious fantasies, but for now let's stay with clinical issues.

*Maria:* Isn't it true that the fantasies of children and infants depend on what developmental phase they are in?

*Richard:* We also postulate that children undergo certain developmental phases, although there is disagreement as to what constitutes these phases. There is general agreement that at least one of these phases in the little boy is Freud's renowned Oedipus complex and of course its opposite in the little girl, although Kleinians and Freudians disagree on when this begins and Kohut (1984) considers it a phase rather than a universal complex.

*Donald:* How are these postulates about the developmental phases in children and infants arrived at?

*Richard:* There are two ways we have come to view infant and child development. The first of these was introduced by Freud (1905) in his retrospective studies of adult neurotics. So in one of his two most fundamental works, *Three Essays on the Theory of Sexuality*, he develops an entire theory of infantile and childhood development with respect to the vicissitudes of the libido, the energy of the sexual drive. Although this was published in 1905, considerable sections on the sexual theories of children and on the pregenital organizations of the libido were added only ten years later. But many of the elements of Freud's theory of sexuality were already present in his mind by 1896. More recently there has been an upsurge of research on infant development, but it is very controversial because every research program contains in it certain preliminary hypotheses causing the investigators to tend to view the data in the light of these hypotheses, making it very difficult to interpret what is going on in the mind of an infant. At this point it is probably fair to say that there is no agreement on what infant research has contributed to our understanding of infant and child development. Kohut (1971) argues that it is in the psychoanalytic situation alone that our method of prolonged empathic immersion works, and that the findings of research in infant development and other fields of the human sciences are not germane to the practice of psychoanalysis. This is a very controversial issue, and it generates more heat than light.

*Donald:* I read (Jones 1953) that Freud's early associate, the internist Breuer, was very frightened because the famous patient Anna O., who he hypnotized repeatedly, developed a pseudocyesis possibly naming Breuer as the father—whereas Freud, when a patient threw her arms around him, realized that it was a misrecognition that he named "transference." This enabled him to deal with the feelings it aroused in him and to continue working with the patient. Isn't this also important in psychoanalytic practice?

*Richard:* You are correct. A crucial underlying assumption! All psychoanalytic therapists are indebted to Freud's discovery of the transference, in which psychic representations of the analyst are invested with features that belong to the representations of the parents. In this situation, if one follows drive theory, the drives that were originally aimed for discharge at the representations of the parents cross the repression barrier and are now aimed for discharge at the representations of the analyst.

*Maria:* I have never been able to understand what various authors mean when they differentiate between *representations* and *objects*. The use of *object* and *object representation* as well as *introject* seems to be different by every author. Can you explain?

*Richard:* There is a lot of confusion in the literature between the use of *representations*, which are intrapsychic, and the use of *objects*, which are outside the individual. This is a distinction of great importance, because if one speaks primarily of internalized object representations being the target of drive discharge, one has a wholly solipsistic or narcissistic theory. In actual psychoanalytic practice what the analyst experiences is the expression of these pulses or drives at the person the analyst is conceived to be in the psychoanalytic dialectical exchange. This conception implies the projection of a representation of the parent onto the analyst, who then becomes the object of drive discharge.

A variant of transference is constituted by the so-called selfobject transferences of Kohut (1977). In this situation there is not a crossing of the repression barrier in which the analyst is "cathected with object libido" but rather the amalgamation of unconscious narcissistic structures, the grandiose self and the idealized parent imago, with the psychic representation of the analyst in the service of the need to resume development. This contrasts with the previously mentioned classic transference that involves the amalgamation of object-directed repressed infantile wishes along with the analysand's preconscious wishes and attitudes toward the analyst.

*Donald:* What about countertransference?

*Richard:* The countertransference, which like transference we need to eventually discuss at greater length (Chapters 6 and 8), is another important basic assumption behind all psychoanalytic practice, and ignoring this factor in psychoanalytic practice invariably leads to serious difficulties.

*Maria:* What about dreams? Is the interpretation of dreams still an important part of psychoanalytic practice, or has that become obsolete?

*Richard:* In my psychoanalytic practice, I still think of dreams as the royal road to the unconscious. I also have a definitive conviction that all parapraxes, daydreams, conscious choices, and so-called voluntary behavior can be analyzed and understood as representing a compromise formation that the ego must form between its three harsh masters—the id, the superego, and reality. Kohut (1977) also speaks of "self-state dreams." When the patient is asked for associations to these dreams, the associations lead nowhere and such dreams, Kohut believes, can be best understood as representations of the state of the patient's self at the given time. Perhaps later we may discuss in clinical detail how one practices dream interpretation in psychoanalytic work.

*Donald:* I'm getting impatient, especially about everything being analyzed as representing a compromise formation and about the importance of unconscious fantasies in the subsequent behavior of people. Do you really believe all that stuff?

*Richard:* Donald, I have heard this question before. It was asked by a student at a school of psychology that confers the Psy.D. degree, unfortunately a student who was close to finishing her education toward that degree. It shows a confusion because the basic assumptions behind psychoanalytic practice are not matters of faith, they are matters of experience. The only way to be convinced of these basic assumptions is to have a thorough personal psychoanalysis of one's own. We discussed this yesterday. This is *not* the same as once a week counseling for six months or a year! I told you that as a general rule of thumb therapists should not attempt to perform psychodynamic practice with patients seen at a frequency of more than once less per week than the therapist's own personal treatment took place, and for a shorter total of sessions than the therapist's personal treatment. So, for example, if a therapist was seen twice a week for a year, it would be prudent and ethical to work only with patients seen once a week for less than a year, and so forth. As Freud (1915) pointed out, it is not possible to attain a deep conviction about the basic assumptions of psychoanalytic practice without undergoing a thorough personal psychoanalysis.

*Donald:* What happens if an individual who has never had any treatment of his or her own attempts to do psychotherapy?

*Richard:* It is necessary to emphasize again and again that the dangers of countertransference acting out are very serious when one has not had proper personal psychoanalysis or when one attempts to see patients intensively without having first undergone a completed intensive psychotherapy of one's own. (Students still in psychoanalysis can of course practice intensive psychotherapy under careful supervision.) We are not simply dealing with an ethical issue here, but an issue that actually may involve the very lives of the patients and their families. Chessick (1977, 1983a, b, 1989, 1991) has stressed this issue again and again in his books.

*Maria:* Let's get down to the focus of today's discussion: What is psychoanalytic practice?

*Richard:* Psychoanalytic practice is predicated on the provision of a certain ambience or "holding environment" (Winnicott 1965) in which the therapist practices in an office that is pleasant, comfortable for both the patient and the therapist, reasonably well lighted but not with a blinding light, quiet, and without interruptions by telephones, secretaries, postal deliveries, and so forth. In this reliable ambience, in which the patient is seen on a regular basis at regular times as much as possible, and in which if the therapist has to be away the patient is given ample notice, psychoanalytic practice encourages the patient to utilize free association. The properly trained therapist carefully listens as the patient speaks freely about anything that comes to mind. The interventions of the psychoanalyst are primarily those involving clarification, questions, confrontations, and interpretations. As the treatment proceeds, interpretations are the most frequent interventions; at the beginning of the treatment more is done in the way of the other interventions. Psychoanalytic practice forbids physical contact with a patient except in emergency situations where one has to drop the mantle of being a psychoanalyst and take up the mantle of being an emergency physician or paramedic. It mandates the use of suggestion, education, and persuasion only at times where these are judged necessary for psychodynamic reasons and are later dealt with in a psychoanalytic interpretive fashion. It recognizes that psychopharmacologic agents are sometimes necessary and provides them, but concentrates also on the psychodynamic meaning of this provision by the therapist.

*Maria:* Okay. Then how does psychoanalysis differ from psychotherapy?

*Richard:* In a well-conducted psychoanalytic practice there should be a gradual deepening of the material in which more and more "total interpretations" (Alexander 1956) can be made. These total interpretations connect the current situation and the transference with early childhood situations of the patient. Kohut (1984) makes a similar recommendation, although from a different theoretical standpoint, in distinguishing between psychoanalysis and intensive psychotherapy. To whatever extent education, persuasion, suggestion, authority, and so forth are actively or deliberately used in the therapy it is not psychoanalytic but rather may be labeled supportive. There are situations even during psychoanalysis in which supportive psychotherapy is required and necessary, but the hallmark of psychoanalysis is the predominance of interpretations, especially of the transference.

There is a difference in degree between psychoanalysis proper and intensive psychotherapy. Psychoanalysis proper of course utilizes the couch and requires the patient to come at least three times a week and much more preferably four or five times a week. Uncovering psychotherapy is a derivative procedure from psychoanalysis and attempts to provide a more limited amount of exploration with a larger amount of support. It's more difficult to practice intensive psychotherapy than it is to practice psychoanalysis, because the therapist doing intensive psychotherapy often must shift techniques from session to session depending on the state of the patient at the time, whereas psychoanalysis assumes a relatively high level of ego functioning and more stability on the part of the patient.

At the beginning of today's discussion I pointed out that the more disturbed the patient the less the treatment may be called psychoanalysis and the more it involves influencing, suggestion, correction of expectations, stabilization, superego modification, and model provision for identification or introjection, as well as holding and support, with a focus on solving specific problems.

*Donald:* How do you decide who gets psychoanalysis and who gets psychotherapy?

*Richard:* In our culture this decision is usually made, very unfortunately, by the state of the patient's finances. It is becoming more and more apparent that patients wanting either long-term psychotherapy or psychoanalysis will have to have a large source of personal income, because insurance companies have seized upon the fact that there are not good hard data demonstrating the efficacy of psychoanalysis, using this as an excuse to refuse to pay for it. I regard this as a scandal in our society, part of the entire unfortunate and inequitable health-care situation in our country. Other developed countries are substantially ahead of us on these matters. It follows from what I'm saying that those therapists who wish to practice intensive psychotherapy or psychoanalysis will make a smaller income because they will have to lower their fees in many instances to meet their patients' pocketbooks.

*Donald:* Why are there so many conflicting schools and theories of psychoanalysis?

*Richard:* Every theory projects the personality of the theorist; it is a sort of Rorschach card in reverse. We embrace the theory that makes us the least anxious and that represents the best compromise formation formed by our ego in response to the id, the superego, and reality. Whatever circumstances have placed us in getting our education from a given "school" of psychotherapy or psychoanalysis also has a great influence on our ultimate choice of theory. This is especially true if the narcissistic aspects of candidate psychotherapists are not thoroughly analyzed. If not, the tendency is either to overidealize the theorists of that school or to form an opposition school that is overtly hostile and derogatory toward the original school of the therapist.

*Maria:* Can you give an example of what you mean?

*Richard:* The most famous example of this is manifest in the adventures of Lacan, who was psychoanalyzed by Loewenstein, one of the founders of the ego psychology school of psychoanalysis in the United States. Lacan's influential school was formed in direct opposition to Loewenstein and colleagues' (1966) emphasis on the ego and indeed, it delineated the ego as a false concept that alienated the individual from his or her true self, a radically different notion of the ego than that put forth by Freud or the ego psychologists. Coupling this to a vigorous anti-Americanism, Lacan achieved great popularity in France (Chessick 1992a, Turkle 1978).

What I am suggesting here is that the formation of conflicting schools in the field represented for the most part the inadequacies of early training analyses, especially in the area of narcissism. This inadequacy has been somewhat more recognized especially since the work of Kohut (1971, 1977, 1984) in founding so-called self psychology (Chessick 1985). The result of this better understanding of narcissism has been that conflicting theories no longer tend as much to produce schisms and separate schools, but there is an increasing capacity of conflicting theorists to get along with each other in an uneasy relationship within the same analytic training group. The most famous example of this is the situation in England where the London Institute for Psychoanalysis is divided into Kleinians, traditional psychoanalysts, and those in between, all uneasily contained under one roof. For the exciting details of some of these splits and schisms in the United States, see the fascinating article by Frosch (1991).

*Maria:* But how do you decide which views to choose?

*Richard:* The decision about which views are useful and which views to choose is a very personal one. Consistent with the basic assumptions behind all psychoanalytic practice we have to assume that the ultimate choice of which views to choose and which to reject also represents a compromise formation by our ego in order to deal with its three harsh masters. It also represents in many instances an identification either with an idealized teacher or psychoanalyst, or an identification with the aggressor—if one's psychoanalyst has been sadistic or sarcastic, hostile or destructive, this can lead to a massive identification with his or her views and schools.

*Donald:* I'm having trouble with this. Each time I read a theory it seems like the right theory and I'm influenced by that author. Then I read about *another* theory and want to change views right away. Can you give us some more practical advice?

*Richard:* Only after prolonged introspection and careful thought should one decide which views and theories will be used and which will be rejected in one's own practice. This decision should be reviewed periodically just as Freud (1937) suggested that analysts return to personal analysis every five years. Freud's suggestion did not turn out to be very practical, but there is no reason why a continuing self-analysis cannot go on (Chessick 1990), which, along with clinical experience, leads to changes from time to time in one's choices of views. It is the mark of the psychoanalyst's intregrity that a continual self-analysis and a continual review of theoretical choices are going on *pari passu* with one's clinical practice. This is in contrast to forming rigid stereotyped views early in training that are impervious to change by either self-analysis or practice; individuals of this sort need to be in a personal psychoanalysis or reanalysis.

*Maria:* Which views did you pick and why?

*Richard:* Chessick (1989) devoted a book to describing what he called the five-channel theory of psychoanalytic listening. These are the channels he recommends:

First, Freud's drive/conflict/defense orientation—the classical psychoanalytic approach as delineated and illustrated, for example, by Arlow (1985b). This is always the primary and preferred mode of listening and is the initial stance for any form of psychoanalytically oriented investigation and treatment.

Second, the object relations approach. Especially useful is the work of two of its originators, Melanie Klein and Wilfred Bion, Klein's analysand. This approach constitutes what Greenberg and Mitchell (1983) call the "relational/structure model" and focuses on the formation of psychic structure as a consequence of the earliest object relations, rather than as a consequence of the nonspecific need for drive discharge.

*Donald:* I've always had a great deal of difficulty with the theories of Klein and Bion because they read almost like science fiction to me. Are they really valuable?

*Richard:* Yes, they are quite valuable, and as we shall see, they offer a useful way of characterizing very primitive material that arises especially in the treatment of seriously disturbed patients. Although the earlier formulations of such theories by Klein and Bion are quite fanciful, they have the advantage of offering a more sharply delineated alternative to the drive/conflict/defense channel of psychoanalytic listening, which focuses more on ego functioning. Kernberg (1976) is the best-known proponent of the more-modernized version of object relations theory based on the earlier work of Klein and of Jacobson (1964), and we will discuss object relations theories in detail later (Chapter 10).

*Maria:* You have named only two of the channels. What are the others?

*Richard:* The third channel is the sociocultural approach, initiated by Hegel, Feuerbach, Marx, and Nietzsche in philosophy and carried into the field of psychoanalytic psychotherapy and psychiatry by such authors as Horney, Fromm, Sartre, Lacan, and Foucault. This approach attributes the formation of psychic structure primarily to cultural determinants and denies any universal or permanent human essence or nature. What we "hear," when tuned in to this channel, is a reflection of the kind of relationships and cultural milieu that are implicitly built into the prevailing economic system and ideology. The cultural background practices forming the patient's self are manifested to the therapist either directly in the speech of the patient, or indirectly as they are mediated through the family while it forms the child's personality. Since the method used by psychotherapists such as Jaspers (1972) who are advocates of this approach is often called *phenomenology*, it is usually referred to as the phenomenological channel.

The phenomenological stance is to examine one's reaction to what is simply there in a felt experience; the therapist does not disconnect, isolate, or interpret aspects of this experience. It demands refrainment from judgment about morals, values, causes, background, and even from separating the subject (patient) and objective observer (therapist). One pays special attention to one's experience or state of consciousness in the presence of a patient. The therapist must continue to observe and listen, staying with the patient's material and directly experiencing the patient rather than searching for hidden processes.

*Donald:* My head is starting to spin! And you have named only three channels. What else does one have to know?

*Richard:* The fourth channel tunes in to the realm of the self, developed into a precise technical investigational procedure with a theoretical base by Kohut (1971, 1977, 1984). An interesting alternative to Kohut's way of focus on the self, with controversial emendations and "improvements," has been presented by Gedo (1979, 1981, 1984, 1986). In considering this channel, it is also important to review an excellent early attempt by Gedo and Goldberg (1973) to connect this realm of the self with Freud's changing viewpoints. The psychology of the self, whether one follows Kohut, Gedo, or others, is very important in psychoanalytic listening; it is a most exciting though still incomplete field of exploration with vast potential (for a complete exposition see Chessick 1985).

The final channel, the interactive approach, focuses on countertransference or more generally on the here-and-now factors in the treatment, emphasizing the role of the analyst's participation. For example, Thomä and Kächele (1987, 1992), whose work we discussed on the first day, contend that the analyst must always ask, "What am I doing that causes the patient to have this anxiety and provokes this resistance?" and "What do I do to contribute to overcoming this resistance?" Such authors stress the interactional aspects of the psychoanalytic or psychotherapeutic process throughout the therapy.

*Donald:* What about some of the other famous pioneers? You haven't mentioned a number of them.

*Richard:* You will notice as we go along that other views have peripherally influenced me, such as those of Fromm and Horney. I consider Adler's views to be very narrow but in a sense the precursor of the work of Kohut; I have found nothing of value in the work of Jung or Rank for the contemporary practice of psychoanalytic therapy.

The literature is replete with arguments and counterarguments about which stance or which channel is best; these arguments vary from intense insistence that one and only one channel is the proper one—often with the implication that therapists tuned to other channels are in need of further analysis!—to Kohut's (1984) rhetorical argument that it makes no fundamental difference which stance the therapist uses, so long as the patient recognizes an empathic response.

*Maria:* How important is it for us to know these various theoretical disagreements in order to do psychoanalytic practice?

*Richard:* As Greenberg and Mitchell (1983) portray it, the central contrast is between the drive/structure orientations and the relational/structure models; there are also so-called mixed-model strategies. Understanding these concepts is fundamental to the study of our subject and will naturally lead us to examine the strategy of appropriate validation of our interventions and to consider how to listen to patients in such a way as to convince ourselves that we have heard them properly.

*Donald:* I'm anxious about practicing psychoanalytic treatment. That is why I worry a great deal about the role of the therapist. I know we have touched on this before. What does the therapist have to bring to the treatment to avoid making a mess?

*Richard:* Bion's (1963, 1976) work, written in his unique rhetorical style and stressing the need to listen to the patient without memory, desire, or understanding, becomes especially significant in situations that confuse or stump us. Our only other recourse—and one that should be used more often than it is—is to seek consultation or supervision, or even to return to our own personal psychoanalysis. It will be repeatedly stressed that, regardless of orientation, *only the thoroughly psychoanalyzed therapist can listen properly and appropriately to the patient's material.* Any attempt to listen by an unanalyzed "therapist" will result in a collusion to disguise the basic problems and often results in a mutually destructive acting out.

The therapist's basic maturity and human qualities, along with his or her thorough personal psychoanalysis, are the fundamental requirements for accurate judgments, successful psychoanalytic practice, and valid, in-tune interventions. It is primarily these interventions that demonstrate the therapist has indeed heard the patient properly, and that, along with providing the proper ambience, can build a trusting relationship and propel the treatment forward. Papers by Greenson (1974), Lipton (1977, 1979, 1983), and Stone (1981) should be consulted as illustrations of these fundamental human qualities.

*Maria:* I find myself confused because the various theories seem to contradict each other in so many ways. Is this the state of the art at this time?

*Richard:* It is indeed important to note that the various views are diametrically opposed to each other in many ways, both in terms of their epistemological assumptions, their conception of how psychoanalytic practice heals, and their notions of the essence of humans. For example, the contrast between the philosophers Merleau-Ponty and Sartre has a parallel in psychoanalysis in the attitudes of Winnicott and Kohut on the one hand and the Kleinians on the other. The former group of psychoanalysts view life beginning in a mutually enhancing nursing couple, a prereflective unity of mother and infant, whereas the latter group views life beginning with a process in which the infant has to deal with its innate self-destruction by projecting outward and developing the paranoid–schizoid position with its accompanying *terrifying* sense of alienation and fear. Merleau-Ponty, like Kohut, would say that the processes described by Klein are secondary to an archaic failure in the prereflective unity of the nursing couple, and represent an attempt by the infant to deal with the rage and disappointment of such a failure, with its fundamental calamitous effect on the self and body image.

*Donald:* There seems to be a lot of danger in this, and I think that is adding to my anxiety. What efforts can you make to reassure yourself that your psychoanalytic practice is in the best interest of the patient?

*Richard:* I have already told you, Donald. One must always ask one-self if one is utilizing theories and practices and the interpretations based on them defensively, in a collusion to avoid facing the patient's core unique childhood oedipal and preoedipal fantasy activity and the reverberations of it in the analyst's core fantasy activity. Similarly, one must not allow the mutual enactment of these fantasies instead of recognizing and interpreting them. These are common and dangerous mistakes by the unanalyzed, untrained, and unsupervised. Continuing self-analysis is required in each and every treatment process.

*Donald:* My head is spinning. You covered so many topics today! I'm not familiar with many of them. Is there some reading you would advise for me as "homework," while we go along, if I have trouble understanding you?

*Richard:* For unfamiliar concepts and terms you could refer to Chessick's (1993) *Dictionary for Psychotherapists.* Later in our discussion I'll return in detail to some of the basic concepts introduced today, with emphasis on their clinical application. I hope today's dialogue will simply serve as a foundation for our further study of the controversial elements of psychoanalytic practice.

*Maria:* I also found today's dialogue somewhat overwhelming, but I'm glad we have managed to make a start. I hope tomorrow we can begin at the beginning with the details of psychoanalytic practice. For example, how about discussing the thorny issue of what, when, and how to interpret?

*Richard:* An excellent idea! I've enjoyed your hospitality, Maria, and appreciate the questions that both of you have put to me. I look forward to our discussion tomorrow.

# 5

# The Fifth Day:
# Interpretation

*Donald:* I'm delighted to return to your house, Maria; I've been fretting since our meeting yesterday about whether I really understand what to interpret and *how* to interpret when I work with my patients. Richard has made me increasingly nervous over the last few days!

*Maria:* Welcome, Donald; good morning, Richard. The day is beautiful and sunny; what a crisp and clear new morning for us! Why not begin as usual with Freud? He considered psychoanalytic interventions wild unless there'd been adequate preparation consisting of the careful analysis of resistance so that the repressed material was very near to consciousness. He also pointed out that there must be an important attachment to the analyst before one makes an interpretation because otherwise the patient will flee from the analysis in order to avoid bringing repressed material to the light. This attachment will of course have significant transference aspects.

*Donald:* I know there are four categories of legitimate interventions in psychodynamic therapy that are aimed at eventually recovering repressed material. These are clarifications, confrontations, questions, and interpretations. The first three are obvious and easy to understand, although of course any of them can be used as manifestations of countertransference, but it is not so clear what to interpret, and there seems to be great disagreement about it. Not everyone follows what Freud has advised, nor did Freud always practice what he preached, as one can see from his first writings on parapraxes and dreams. Wouldn't the interpretations that abound in Freud's early (1900, 1901) analyses of dreams and parapraxes be the examples of wild analysis?

*Richard:* This issue has become somewhat confused in the literature and I don't blame you for not being clear about it. One person's appropriate interpretation is another's "wild analysis." If one looks at Freud's (1910) paper on wild analysis one finds a gross example of what is not analysis but direct counseling based on a complete misunderstanding of Freud's theories. Such obvious bungling is not what becomes a problem in labeling certain interpretations as wild analysis today. Schafer (1985) reviews the work of Klein, Kohut, and Gill "in order to bring out different conceptions of interpretation that is wild, sound, or too tame" (p. 298). For instance, Gill recommends that in making interpretations of transference we must first pay attention to the reality of the interpersonal transactions within the analytic situation. For Gill the patient's material is filled with various allusions to the conscious and preconscious experiences that the patient has with the therapist, and this becomes the central focus for interpretation. Schafer claims that, "Gill has replaced the inferred, reconstructed, and progressively recalled and experienced drama of infantile passion, terror, and misunderstanding with the lesser drama of an actively confrontational, often highly conjectural, and limited dialogue in the consulting room" (p. 286). At least this is what traditional Freudians would say.

*Maria:* Does this mean that Gill has broken with traditional Freudian psychoanalysis?

*Richard:* Not really. Gill was a psychoanalytic pioneer. He was trying to make a correction within the psychoanalytic tradition in order to bring attention to the important role of the analyst's input and the many signals, both direct and indirect, both verbal and nonverbal, given by the analysand about the analyst's participation in the interpersonal transactions. This participation always has some countertransference aspects to it. One does not have to follow Gill's approach entirely in order to benefit from his work in this area, because all of us need to pay close attention to the analyst's input and to the various allusions in the patient's material to what the patient is experiencing. This is the essence of the interpersonal channel of listening and tends to be ignored because of Freud's early warning that the analyst should be a neutral nonparticipating observer who merely reflects back to the patient what the patient has said. This of course cannot possibly happen, and the understanding of the importance of the analyst's input is one of the most important advances in the psychoanalytic field in recent years.

*Donald:* What about Kohut? Are his interpretations "wild"?

*Richard:* Kohut has been criticized for his notion of "self-state dreams." In such dreams associations seem to lead nowhere and from that fact Kohut (1977) directly interprets the dream as representing the state of the self at the time of the dream. This is a fundamental departure from Freud's views. The question is not only whether or not self states can be directly represented in dreams. Kohut's interpretations of the state of the self are clearly not traditional psychoanalytic interpretations. The latter focus on derivatives of repressed primitive sexual and aggressive drives, defenses against the emergence of such drives in the psychic economy, and the conflicts that result. Kohut believes that interpretations of self-state dreams as expressing drives, defenses, and conflicts will be experienced by the patient as unempathic and in that sense as wild analysis. Traditional psychoanalysts, on the other hand, would regard Kohut's direct interpretation of self-state dreams as wild analysis. There is no agreement!

*Donald:* It seems to me that in the systems of both Gill and Kohut there is the implication that the patient is a sort of victim of the vicissitudes or theoretical preoccupations of the analyst! Do you have this impression?

*Richard:* Since Gill emphasizes always first ascertaining the input of the analyst as a central contribution to the transference, there definitely is a certain exoneration of the patient in this method as compared with the traditional approach. Furthermore, Schafer (1985) writes that according to traditional Freudians, in Kohut's system the analysand is also seen as a victim: "The system seems to discourage adequate scrutiny of the analysand's unconscious, highly ambivalent, powerful, active, and early part in experiencing and even arranging a life of inhibition, suffering, and mistreatment" (p. 292).

*Maria:* I suppose the traditional Freudians would also argue that Kohut is fostering rather than analyzing and removing repression, because he emphasizes the real traumatization and deprivation that the patient has received at the hands of the parental figures, ignoring the influence of imagined traumatization and deprivation. As I understand it, his idea of the basic etiology of psychopathology stems from the significant actual failures of parental empathy. So in this sense the patient begins as a victim and reexperiences victimization in the office of the analyst. This view seems somewhat oversimplified to me, but do I understand it correctly?

*Richard:* It's a common misunderstanding of Kohut's theories that the patient is seen as a victim in the analytic situation. What we're interested in, when we use Kohut's system, is when the patient *perceives* himself or herself to be a victim—that is to say, when the patient experiences what he or she considers a lack of empathy from the analyst. The task of the analyst is to carefully listen for evidence that such a lack of empathy has been experienced; this evidence is usually manifested by narcissistic rage, a haughty withdrawal, or, in more extreme instances, grandiose self-isolation and even significant acting out in sexual and aggressive spheres outside of the analytic situation. Then, having listened on the self psychology channel, the first task of the analyst according to Kohut is to acknowledge that the patient has experienced such a lack of empathy. This by itself has an important meliorative effect in allowing a reintegration or increased cohesion of the self of the patient. Along with this improved self-cohesion there naturally comes better ego functioning, which enables the patient along with the analyst to study what has happened.

The therapy becomes a psychoanalysis, says Kohut (1984), when the analyst can demonstrate to the patient the connection between currently perceived empathic failures in the analytic situation and the patient's experiences of parental empathic failure in the past, along with all the defenses and compensations that the patient as a child had to develop in order to deal with the pain of the disappointment and the concomitant rage. This is still an extremely important and valuable channel of psychoanalytic listening and if properly carried out such interpretations cannot be labeled wild, regardless of the controversy over self-state dreams.

*Donald:* They would be wild, would they not, if the analyst actually had failed the patient empathically and refused to admit it! Here there would be a clash in reality testing. What about that?

*Richard:* One of the values of Kohut's system is that it calls the analyst's careful attention to his or her input and requires continual self-analysis. In situations where the patient is raging, or an impasse or failure has occurred, or the patient is being labeled borderline, it is extremely valuable to see if the analyst has actually failed the patient empathically. Such situations can be salvaged if the empathic failure can be recognized and discussed, but if the analyst for various reasons refuses to recognize that he or she has actually failed the patient, then what is typical is a raging withdrawal or acting out and the patient is labeled borderline. This indeed would be wild analysis.

*Maria:* Can you give us a clinical example?

*Richard:* I was once called for a consultation on a patient who had been hospitalized and diagnosed as a borderline personality disorder. Since hospitalization the patient had become very difficult to handle and had begun to cut herself with shards of glass in various places on her skin. The hospital staff was becoming quite alarmed. The staff was sophisticated and was aware of the various problems borderline patients cause on the ward as a result of their tendency to splitting, dividing up members of the staff on one side or the other, and so forth. This had been discussed and none of it was significantly going on at the time. Nobody could explain why this patient was becoming increasingly difficult and self-mutilating.

I spoke at length with the patient, who also could give no direct explanation of why she had become subjected to increased impulses to cut herself. Finally I began asking her about the psychotherapy she was receiving. It turned out that she was being seen four times a week by a social worker on the hospital staff who was attempting to do intensive psychotherapy with her. It was his opinion, based on a misunderstanding of Kohut's writing, that what the patient needed was a warm, loving, empathic parent in order to make up for the deprivations of her childhood. So he was trying to act warm and loving, and in attempting to be empathic with what he regarded to be her needs, he began having her sit on his lap during the sessions. There was no sexual fondling and the therapist was not attempting to have sexual relations with the patient; the therapist was deliberately attempting to play the role of a loving mother with a small child and ignoring the seductive connotations of what he was doing. Ferenczi (1988) tried this years ago to no avail, but I don't think the therapist was aware of Ferenczi's work.

As the therapist introduced these ministrations, the patient became increasingly self-mutilating. Now what was the reason for this? Clearly it was a failure of empathy and understanding on the part of the therapist. His efforts to be warm and loving made the patient feel too guilty to rage at him directly and she probably got some gratification out of being held, as many borderline patients have a great need for holding and touching and will even trade sexual relations for it. But the patient intuitively realized that the kind of "therapy" she was being offered was not what she needed, nor would it do her the slightest bit of good. It is never possible to replace in adult life what one has missed as an infant, and that is not at all what Kohut was talking about or suggesting. Neglect of the obvious erotic aspects of the situation represented what Ferenczi (1933) called a "confusion of tongues between adults and the child," and constituted another emphatic failure and countertransference acting out.

*Donald:* What would a correct reading of Kohut be in this case? How should the patient have been treated?

*Richard:* Assuming she was a reasonable candidate for intensive psychotherapy, the therapist would urge her to talk about whatever she had in mind. Eventually a selfobject transference would form, assuming no countertransference interference by the therapist. Then failures in empathy as perceived by the patient, such as therapist vacations, cancellations, and so forth, would produce a narcissistic withdrawal. This constitutes the appropriate moment for interpretation and for eventually connecting up the present with the past. No role playing or deliberate nurturing or loving behavior is necessary, and any attempt to somehow make up for the mothering the patient missed is simply counter-transference acting out.

*Maria:* This is clear. Perhaps we should go in another direction away from Freud's recommendations about when to make an interpretation. Do you think Melanie Klein's system involves wild interpretations? Klein believed that interpretations should be directed at the deepest and earliest layers of conflict, not because it is assumed that there is no resistance—obviously there is—but the theory claims the best way to reduce anxiety and resistance is to attack it at its deepest sources through interpretations (Segal 1967).

*Donald:* This certainly does swing to the opposite extreme!

*Richard:* Yes it does, and as you know there was a substantial quarrel between the followers of Melanie Klein and the followers of Anna Freud, who appropriately considered herself the representative of Freud's traditional structural theory. The greatest danger of these immediate deep interpretations is that they may be experienced by the patient as an assault, an intrusion, an aggression. Then the patient, through identification with the aggressor, might accept these interpretations and accept the theoretical position of the analyst not out of conviction but out of the defensive need to deal with the assault. Regressive transferences in this situation would be fostered through fear.

*Maria:* There's a great temptation to use the Kleinian system in its original form because it completely ignores the input of the analyst and makes no reference to the intersubjective, here-and-now aspects of the analytic relationship. It places the analyst in a position of authority and as the expert on what is or is not "reality." Why bother with it?

*Richard:* I think the Kleinian system is very important and everyone who does uncovering psychotherapy, psychodynamic therapy, and psychoanalysis should be quite familiar with it. In the first place, the work of Klein and Lacan has become increasingly influential in South American psychoanalysis. In dramatic contrast to psychoanalysis in the United States, the situation for South American psychoanalysis is one of growth, flowering, and expansion. The work of Klein and Lacan have had an important role in this expansion because these pioneers are so stimulating and controversial, calling attention to very important aspects of the human psyche. One does not need to be a Kleinian or Lacanian to learn from a study of their works.

As Spillius (1994) points out, there are many differences between Freud's approach and Klein's approach. For example, Freud thinks of drives as biological forces that almost fortuitously become attached to objects through postnatal experiences, whereas for Klein drives are inherently attached to objects. Spillius explains that there is a significant difference in the use of fantasy in Freud and Klein: "In [Freud's] central usage phantasy is resorted to when an instinct is frustrated (Freud 1911). For Klein unconscious phantasy accompanies gratification as well as frustration, but, further, it is the basic stuff of all mental processes; it is the mental representation of instincts" (p. 327). It is not necessary here to review Klein's various theories about the infant's knowledge of objects like the breast, mother, penis, womb, sexual intercourse, birth, babies, the Oedipus complex, envy, and so on. Klein's emphasis on this early knowledge as well as her emphasis on early very direct interpretations is what causes her form of analysis to be labeled as wild by those who disagree with her. However, even if one cannot accept her extreme views on these matters, a study of her work has much value in understanding what is amenable to interpretation in the psychoanalytic process. Furthermore, at least some of the Kleinians have tended less and less to make these deep direct interpretations (Spillius 1990, 1992) and in their actual practice have apparently become more cognizant of the importance of resistance and the interpretation of defenses before content in the traditional manner. So I think there's a very gradual convergence taking place between the actual practice of the Kleinians and the traditional Freudians, although their theoretical differences remain extreme and irreconcilable.

*Maria:* Well then, what is important about Klein's views regarding material to be interpreted that can be useful to us in our clinical work?

*Richard:* Probably her most important useful clinical concept is that of projective identification. This concept has been widely accepted and used by many psychoanalytic schools, although it is defined and used in various ways. The point of it is to understand how the patient attempts to control the object, to acquire its attributes, to evacuate a bad quality, to protect a good quality, to avoid separation . . .

*Donald:* Could you please explain how you use the concept of projective identification in your actual clinical work?

*Richard:* Klein (1946) developed the concept of projective identification, which for her has two aspects, one intrapsychic and the other interpersonal. First, projective identification is characterized by a forceful, aggressive evacuation in fantasy, consisting of either a penetration into the object and a reinternalization of the object that was injured, which may lead to depression, or a reinternalization of the object that was rendered hostile, which may lead to persecutory hypochondria, or both. It also represents a very primitive means of communication, and leads to what we might call "beyond the countertransference distress" in the therapist and to interpersonal interaction. So Klein inconsistently conceived of projective identification both as a fantasy and as an inter-personal relationship, an interactional process.

*Donald:* "Beyond the countertransference distress"—I don't under-stand.

*Maria:* Perhaps we should use Kernberg's (1975, 1976, 1980) view of projective identification as a solely intrapsychic phenomenon repre-senting an incomplete projection, which then may lead to apparently unreasonable behavior on the part of the patient. I like his (1987) case illustrations. In *projection* there is first the repressing of the intolerable, then the projecting of it onto the object, and finally the "separating or distancing (of) oneself from the object to fortify the defensive effort" (p. 796). In *projective identification*, which Kernberg views as more primi-tive, there is a similar projection of the intolerable onto the object, but the patient maintains a relationship with the object. The "object" or ana-lyst is now experienced as what has been projected, and the patient "tries to control the object in a continuing effort to defend against the intol-erable experience, and, unconsciously, in an actual interaction with the object, leads the object to experience what has been projected onto him" (p. 796).

*Richard:* So at the basis of projective identification, patients are thought to first place into the analyst whatever unacceptable internal self or object representations they wish to place there. Then the patient not only experiences the analyst as the projected object but exerts severe interpersonal pressure on the analyst to behave like that object. This pressure produces what I called, rather loosely, "beyond the counter-transference distress." I called it that in order to distinguish it from countertransference distress arising primarily from sources within the analyst's own unconscious. And all this leads to more therapeutic focus on preoedipal fantasies and processes. Attention to projective identifi-cation operating in the therapeutic process emphasizes the patient's ear-liest internalized object relations and yields data on how the patient as an infant organized these relations into self and object representations and then projected and reintrojected various aspects of these images. Understanding these processes clarifies the patient's relationships in the present because all such relationships are perceived and reacted to through the spectacles of these early organized self and object representations.

*Donald:* I'm not convinced. The assumption here is that the infan-tile ego is capable of such organization—but recent research on infants (Stern 1985) suggests that this is unlikely! Empirical investigation of infants carries the hope that as we come to understand the capacities and limitations of the mind of the infant and child, we will have better criteria on which to choose or reject such conceptions. Furthermore, it seems to me there are some major points of disagreement between Kleinian and Freudian theory about all this. What are we to think about that?

*Richard:* You are correct. Klein connected "phantasy" with part object relations developed by introjection and projection starting from birth, whereas Anna Freud believed in a narcissistic and autoerotic phase for the first few months of life in which the frustration or gratification of instincts rather than object relations are overwhelmingly important. On the whole, Anna Freud's view seems to have moved into eclipse, for the whole thrust of modern psychoanalytic thinking is that a nursing couple, an intense object relationship, exists from the beginning of life. It is hard to maintain anymore that the infant is autistic for some period of time.

*Maria:* On the other hand, it is extremely difficult to accept the complex nature of "phantasies" that are attributed to the infant in the first few months of life by Kleinian theory, as Donald pointed out. For example, Hayman (1994) explains that "the Klein-Isaacs view was that the toddler who was loving after being naughty is trying to make reparation, because of inner conflict and guilt . . . but to Anna Freud, the toddler who is naughty and loving by turns is experiencing these different feelings successively without either influencing the other, in the way contradictory feelings were thought to exist side by side in the unconscious" (p. 352). How does one resolve this sort of disagreement? Observing infants doesn't really seem to help, because everyone brings a certain mental set to what they observe.

*Richard:* In watching my grandchildren and their fluctuation of moods, I'm inclined to agree with Anna Freud, but how could I prove that complex "phantasies" and internal conflict are not generating the behavior in my 2½-year-old granddaughter who one moment is angry and the next moment is loving? She does seem to be uneasy about it and says, "I not angry at you now, Grandma," as if to reassure both herself and her grandma who takes care of her. But how complex and elaborate a fantasy life is behind it, I cannot tell.

The weakest aspect of Kleinian theory is in her use of the death instinct as a clinical concept. I believe this was a fundamental confusion and concretization about what Freud had in mind by the death instinct and a misapplication of it in Kleinian theory (Chessick 1992b, 1993). Arguing that there is a conflict between the death instinct and the life instinct in an infant is a misappropriation of Freud's (1933) instinct mythology, as he called it. On the other hand, from my point of view the most important clinical contribution of Klein was to emphasize the power of aggression as it quickly and universally appears already in the human infant and the child. One does not have to agree with Klein's extreme speculations about what goes on in the mind of an infant in the first six months of life in order to accept the idea that aggressive as well as libidinal frustrations lead to various kinds of fantasy gratification, and that florid fantasies as well as early intense object relations occur very early in life. It is even not unreasonable to argue that object relations begin at birth, but the timing of the occurrence of fantasy is still quite debatable and I don't know how this debate can be resolved. Experiments with infant observations always require inferences, and these inferences by necessity are based on the orientation of the experimenter. Certainly by the age of 2½ all children like my granddaughter and those described in the Kleinian literature have a fantasy life and can communicate about it in play. But interpretation of the fantasies behind the play also always requires inferences.

*Donald:*  Are you saying that the main value of Kleinian theory as far as interpretation and clinical work is concerned is that it makes us extremely sensitive to the manifestations of aggression, just as Freud's theories made us extremely sensitive to the manifestations of the libidinal drives?

*Richard:*  It certainly makes us much more sensitive to aspects of splitting and projective identification, all of which rest on a powerful aggressive component. Whether this aggression represents a "drive" or not is of less clinical importance. When we listen on the Kleinian channel we carefully observe our countertransference and attend to how we feel in our relationship with the patient in order to pick up such aspects as they manifest themselves in the therapeutic process. Furthermore, from Klein's point of view what is important is that everything the analyst is or says is likely to be responded to according to the patient's own intrapsychic makeup rather than the analyst's intentions and the meaning the analyst gives to his or her interpretations.

*Maria:*  But Richard, if we listen along the channel of self psychology, could we not say that the patient showing either intense transference love, usually called the eroticized transference, or intense transference aggression is attempting to ward off a catastrophic fragmentation and is responding to something coming from the analyst that is perceived as a threat to his or her psychic autonomy, or as Kohut might put it, the patient's sense of self?

*Richard:*  Yes, that's true. Intense yearnings experienced consciously as a desperate seeking for a love object, whether it be for objects in one's own real or fantasied past or for the analyst as in the development of an eroticized transference, can have many deep preoedipal roots. They can, for the Kleinians, represent an attempt to construct a defense against a deeper fear of catastrophe—nothingness and annihilation. This is typical, for example, in an individual who is borderline or is suffering from a sealed-over psychosis, and may be acted out as compulsive promiscuity by such individuals. For the self psychologists, the flooding with libidinal or aggressive strivings already represents some dissolution of the sense of self due to narcissistic wounding. This also helps us to understand how countertransference in the analyst could produce his or her unconscious inclination either to offer some form of love or to become hostile to the patient. If the analyst is narcissistically wounded, either by the patient or some concurrent life event, the appearance of libidinal or aggressive countertransference manifestations could represent the incipient weakening of the analyst's self-cohesion and/or the analyst's narcissistic rage. This is a common clinical situation.

This situation can be described in at least three alternative languages: traditional Freudian, Kleinian, or the language of self psychology. The problem we face is that these various descriptions are incompatible with each other and the differences between them are unresolvable. What we lack is a generally accepted method of demonstrating the validity or invalidity of the contentions at the basis of each of these competing theories. So the only recourse that seems to make rational sense today is to remain uncommitted to any of them and instead become familiar with all of them, and perhaps to develop the capacity to describe the same phenomena in several different languages.

*Donald:* My head is spinning! I need some more practical help in how to actually make interpretations of patients' material. Must my brain flit from theory to theory? How shall I go about a relatively organized way of making interpretations and minimize the chances of wild analysis?

*Richard:* I don't blame you for being confused, Donald, since the theoretical situation today in psychoanalysis *is* confusing. I think we must agree with the Kleinians that, as Spillius (1994) says, "The internal world itself is regarded as the result of an ongoing process of development, the product of continuing interaction between unconscious phantasy, defenses, and experiences with external reality, both in the past and in the present" (p. 348). Of course it is part of the analyst's job "to tease out how much his or her own behavior may exacerbate the patient's negative tendencies" (p. 350), but there is the danger that if one concentrates too exclusively on the here and now one will lose sight of the infantile levels of experience and fantasy. So I agree with Spillius that "both levels of expression need to be listened for together and linked with experience" (p. 351).

Of course there's much more involved in transference and countertransference than explicit verbal communication, for there is a continuing nonverbal interaction that goes on and exerts a pressure in both directions. The patient continuously nudges the analyst to engage in a reenactment of certain crucial early fantasies and the analyst of course always has his or her unconscious agenda for the patient. It is, however, the responsibility of the analyst to become aware of both of these agendas and, when appropriate, interpret them to the patient or engage in self-analysis as the need may occur. I believe that Kohut was not correct when he said that data of infant observation could not be pertinent to his theory of self psychology. It isn't permissible for any psychoanalytic theories to be in direct contradiction to empirical data obtained from infant studies. When I say "empirical data" here, however, I must caution you again that every so-called empirical experiment contains hidden behind it a theoretical orientation and there is no such thing as pure empiricism. Philosophers have overcome that naive nineteenth-century concept long ago.

*Donald:* This doesn't help me, Richard. Can you please give me some direct assistance? It doesn't do me very much good to be told that there is a lot of theoretical disagreement about unconscious processes, which of course is reflected in the disagreement about what to interpret. I need some practical clinical help. Can you give me some rules?

*Richard:* I understand your difficulty and I think it is quite appropriate. In order to at least minimize the chances of error you should first of all familiarize yourself thoroughly with at least the five theoretical channels that we have discussed on previous days (see also Chessick 1989). I would suggest that you keep close to the patient's material and do not introduce your own associations. Do not swing wide and far away from the material that the patient presents in your ideas about it. Look for the major themes first rather than the subsidiary themes and details, and keep to the level of the consciousness of the material. Do not, as the early Kleinians did, make deep interpretations of pregenital unconscious material early in the treatment but wait until the material, as Freud advised, is very close to the surface before making interpretations. Otherwise I think that the patient tends to experience deep interpretations as an assault and simply mobilizes defenses and destroys the therapeutic alliance. No matter how unintelligible the associations and dreams may be, at least the main topics and tendencies, the emotional forces, are usually discernible. If you feel completely lost in a session, this may be a problem with a lack of training or a countertransference or both and the only solution is self-analysis and consultation.

*Maria:* I believe that for a therapist of any integrity this will come as a command, self-instigated. In general there are far too few consultations and many disasters could have been avoided by this simple device.

*Donald:* Wait, Maria, Richard is at last giving some practical advice. Please go on, Richard.

*Richard:* Try to keep separate in your head what is current in the patient's present life situation from the transference and from the past or childhood, but at the same time try to find patterns and similarities and reenactments. This is the material for interpretation. Keep a sharp eye on what is going on in the reality situation of the patient at any given time. Ignoring the reality situation soon makes the therapy a sterile intellectual process and is a terrible empathic failure on the part of the therapist. It causes the patient to feel rejected and misunderstood. Be very sensitive to derivatives in the material of libidinal and aggressive drives and try to understand why these derivatives are appearing at the time they appear and what they represent. All five channels of listening will be needed for that.

The beginning of the hour often expresses the theme of the session. The end of a dream represents solutions, or lack of them, to conflicts. In dealing with dreams watch for associations connected with the greatest emotional response . . .

*Maria:* One way I avoid getting bogged down in a great deal of apparently incomprehensible clinical or dream material is to concentrate on those areas that seem to be associated with the most feeling and those that seem to be associated with the least. I look for positive progressive forces in the patient as well as the regressive ones and try not to forget that the patient may be changing and improving as well as regressing at any given time. I'm very cautious about interpreting symbols, slips, errors, and so forth, on an *ex cathedra* basis. Do you agree, Richard?

*Richard:* I do, since one of the most common beginner's errors is to attempt to impress the patient with wild analysis, a countertransference problem. Keep in mind that the patient must be ready to receive an interpretation and that the interpretation should be as total as possible, that is to say, it should attempt to connect actual life situations with past experiences and with the transference. I don't agree with those psychoanalysts who maintain that only transference interpretations are meliorative, but I do feel that any interpretations that can be connected with the transference have a more powerful effect. Interpretation should be realistic and in the clear, simple, and everyday language of the patient. It should be presented in a matter-of-fact way, in a friendly and practical manner, and should be brought out in such a way that the patient can accept and think about it without feeling put upon or forced to accept it. Here we are dealing with tact.

*Donald:* Are there any rules about what goes into a correct interpretation?

*Richard:* A correct interpretation is based on a great deal of evidence, focuses on main issues and not side issues, is presented in a nontechnical fashion, and is narrowed down to the presenting material. Wait until you have enough material and information so that the patient is almost making the interpretation by himself or herself. If you have made a correct interpretation it should be demonstrated by an improvement in the therapeutic alliance or some sharp reaction, which of course can be negative in certain instances. If material continues on in a boring static manner, the interpretation was probably incorrect. If the interpretation was correct, the therapist has demonstrated an ability to understand accurately the patient's unconscious and the central emotional forces in the material at hand. This may by itself increase the cohesion of the patient's sense of self. So we cannot say that the recovery of repressed material is the only function of interpretation; one might argue that feeling understood has just as important a meliorative effect as an increase in self-knowledge. I think that both are active.

*Donald:* Are there ever certain clinical situations where deep interpretation is necessary, interpretations of a Kleinian nature that go to the very roots of the patient's earliest infantile fantasies and fears?

*Richard:* I believe there *are* such situations. For example, if the therapist feels that the whole therapy is in danger unless some form of resistance or acting out is stopped, the therapist may then have to interpret widely and deeply in an attempt to put a stop to therapy-threatening or even life-threatening behavior.

*Donald:* Can you give us a clinical example of this?

*Maria:* I can! Recently I saw a patient who posed a definitive suicidal danger. It was clear in the material that whenever the patient became aware of any kind of dependent needs she took the attitude toward herself that was characteristic of her mother's attitude toward her as a child, namely, that this made her a worthless nothing that should never have been born. She was the fifth of five girls; her parents were desperately trying for a boy. The patient had made an association between dependent needs and punishment, and her way of dealing with her dependent needs was self-mutilation in an attempt to punish herself for them and to repress the needs. This conflict was so intense that the patient was in danger of killing herself when she could not adequately repress her infantile longings. Although she hadn't been in treatment for a very long time I felt it necessary to interpret this directly, presenting it to her more or less as a Pavlovian conditioning, in which dependent needs had become associated in her childhood with mother's hatred and punishment. This did not remove the association, which continued for several more years into the treatment, but it did attenuate the suicidal danger. The information given to her ego made it possible for the patient to interpose a sort of pause between the sense of the dependent need and the instant wish to inflict pain on herself during which time she heard my voice. This served as a kind of break or inhibitor.

*Donald:* But, Maria, couldn't we say that the patient experienced your deep interpretation as an assault and thereby identified with the aggressor? And since this interpretation, coming early in the treatment, violated some of Richard's rules above, how do you know that it was not an inexact interpretation? Or a wrong interpretation?

*Maria:* I agree with the first part of what you said, Donald. It is probably correct that deep early interpretations produce a kind of identification with the aggressor. I think that is why the early Kleinians sometimes emerged from their training analyses with Kleinian analysts as fanatic Kleinians, and showed severe aggression toward those who disagreed with them. The clinical example I just gave was an emergency, not something I do every day, but a technique for the use of interpretation in situations where the entire treatment is threatened. Above all, it is the analyst's responsibility to try to preserve the treatment. This means of course above all preserving the patient's physical health and life and also not abandoning the patient if the patient suffers unexpected financial reverses that did not represent acting out!

*Richard:* Even an inexact interpretation can be useful in such a situation. The purpose of it is to deliberately offer an interpretation in order to provide a definitive meaning to a certain arrangement of material, a meaning that in the unstated opinion of the therapist actually probably falls short of the truth. The therapist either does not know the truth yet or has judged that the complete truth would be dangerous or intolerable to the patient. The patient seizes the inexact interpretation eagerly, because it helps to continue to repress the truth. The process at work here is effectively one of displacement and is fostered by the therapist to bolster the patient's defenses.

*Maria:* Isn't it true that a traditional psychoanalyst would say that giving such an emergency interpretation is a parameter (Eissler 1953) that must be later analyzed?

*Richard:* It is indeed a parameter, but it may not be possible to analyze it. The need for such interpretations, whether inexact or Kleinian ("depth") in nature, may represent the horizon or limits beyond which the patient cannot go. A patient who needs many such interpretations is probably borderline or psychotic and the treatment then becomes more a psychotherapy and aimed at directly shoring up the wobbly ego's defenses.

Tarachow (1963) points out that the therapist must realize the difference between an inexact interpretation and a wrong interpretation. An inexact interpretation is deliberately handed to a patient to enable the patient to shore up ego structure and to maintain stability of defenses. A wrong interpretation is simply a mistake by the therapist that the patient eagerly seizes to shore up the forces of resistance. This will cause difficulties in the progress of the therapy unless the therapist is always alert to the patient's responses to any of his or her interpretations and realizes that a mistake has been made. The best test of an interpretation is the response that it receives from a patient.

*Donald:* That helps, Richard; I'm getting at least some kind of outline of how to proceed. I'm also getting tired and I wonder if we haven't had enough on this topic for today.

*Richard:* Unfortunately we're still not finished, Donald. There is an argument even among traditional psychoanalysts about what to interpret. Should one interpret drive derivatives or should one interpret resistances? Or should one first interpret resistances and then interpret drive derivatives? The old rule of interpreting resistances before content is still a good one, it seems to me, but Gray (1994) has a different approach. He argues that if we follow the trend of traditional psychoanalysis as it moved from the work of Freud to the work of Anna Freud, we must shift from analysis of the id to analysis of the ego, and he discusses why there is a resistance to such a shift. Of course it is best to aim interpretation at what can be drawn to the patient's attention; otherwise the patient must take the interpretation on faith, which is useless. If you find yourself behaving like a benign authority, making pontifical interpretations that the patient must accept because you are so wise, you are doing work with a patient who cannot tolerate analysis of his or her ego defenses or for countertransference reasons you need to make such interpretations. Gray argues that it is a mistake to deal with a patient's material as realities rather than as items in the behavioral or associational stream, for this leads to discussions that are aimed at controlling the patient's behavior or thinking. For example, he seems more interested in understanding why a dream is told at a given point in the therapeutic situation, how it functions as a defense, rather than in an interpretation of the hidden wishes or impulses that are manifesting themselves in the dream through a compromise formation between drives and defenses.

*Maria:* If I understand you correctly, Gray is saying that the problem with deep interpretations, or interpretations of drive derivatives defended against, is that such interpretations must be taken on faith and therefore the patient's ego is not a partner. He stresses that we must invite the patient's ego to participate with us in understanding how the patient's ego defends itself against drive derivatives. Is this correct?

*Richard:* Yes, it is. The goal is to help the analysand gain access to his or her habitual unconscious and outmoded ego activities that serve resistance. This means that the therapist will have to have two mental sets at the same time or rapidly fluctuating when working with a patient. The first of these is, as Freud (1912) put it, the basic mental set for the technique of psychoanalytic listening using evenly suspended attention: "It consists simply in not directing one's notice to anything in particular and in maintaining the same 'evenly suspended attention' in the face of all that one hears" (pp. 111–112). Freud continues:

> To put it in a formula: he must turn his own unconscious like a receptive organ towards the transmitting unconscious of the patient. He must adjust himself to the patient as a telephone receiver is adjusted to the transmitting microphone. Just as the receiver converts back into sound-waves the electric oscillations in the telephone line which were set up by the sound waves, so the doctor's unconscious is able, from the derivatives of the unconscious which are communicated to him, to reconstruct that unconscious, which has determined the patient's free associations. [pp. 115–116]

*Maria:* What a superb writer! No wonder Kohut said, when asked what one should read after studying Freud, "Read Freud again!" Every time I go back to reading Freud I learn more.

*Donald:* You've interrupted again, Maria. Please go on, Richard, with what you were trying to explain.

*Richard:* Compare Freud's approach for picking up unconscious and preconscious derivatives of the unconscious drives to the second mental set as it is described by Gray (1994):

> Recognition of the *defense against* drive derivatives—that is, ego analysis— usually involves a different kind of perceptual attention and intelligence from that required strictly for awareness of the drive derivatives themselves. The difference is that observation of the ego's defensive ways (usually potentially distinguishable from the drive derivatives) involves not only a greater degree of purposefully directed thinking, but also a different aspect of the analyst's perceptual apparatus. [p. 6]

This is fairly obvious and focuses on the question of what to interpret. Gray adds that even the superego should be interpreted primarily when it is used for the purpose of the ego's defensive work. He assumes that when drive derivatives cause resistance, the interpretation of the defenses that are used in this resistance will allow the drives to emerge automatically. He even wishes to divide psychoanalysis into "essential psychoanalysis," which consists of uncompromised resistance analysis, and "wider scope psychoanalysis," in which one must preserve the defense transference, the transference of authority, in order to achieve therapeutic goals. Gray of course is solidly on the side of drive theory and structural theory rather than an object relations theorist, but we will discuss this on a later day (Chapter 10).

*Donald:* Can you give a clinical example of what all this is about, to clarify it in my mind?

*Richard:* There is an excellent example in Gray's book. From Gray's point of view, "the emphasis is on learning about the infantile context in which perceptions of danger opposing these impulses were so frightening that, for safety, the child cathected inhibiting, not gratifying objects" (p. 125). Thus we move away from asking the question of how and why the infant expressed powerful aggressive drives to, "What was it, as a child, that made you need to stop knowing that you could hate some individuals enough to want to destroy them, and how did you manage to stop knowing?" (pp. 125–126). For Gray, one interprets superego activities as chronically maintained or repetitively activated ego processes primarily mobilized for defensive purposes, especially concentrating on the extent to which this process inhibits derivatives of aggression. This has direct clinical importance because we often see patients who have dealt with aggression early in childhood by attempting to stop knowing that they are capable of such hatred. I have seen patients who had to stop knowing everything and were therefore labeled as mentally retarded as the result of a kind of generalization of this core need to stop knowing about their own hatred. The way in which the patient manages to stop knowing will have a profound influence on his or her interpersonal relations.

*Maria:* Do you agree with Gray's point of view?

*Richard:* I don't agree with Gray's contention that once resistances are properly interpreted drives will emerge by themselves. Just as on a previous day I told you that I do *not* believe that once the proper selfobject transferences have been interpreted and worked through—as recommended by self psychologists—there is an inherent developmental process in the patient that will take care of the rest of the treatment. I believe that it is important both to use mental sets in working with the patient and to follow the old rule of interpreting defenses before drive derivatives.

I also agree with Freud's (1912) instruction to leave transference alone until it becomes an interference with the treatment, at which point the transference is becoming used as a defense. Today we're aware that the so-called defense transference is often in operation from the beginning of the treatment, and we're more sensitive to the aggressive derivatives that underlie idealization as well as the so-called therapeutic alliance or even compliance with the treatment process. Of course there are other reasons for idealization as the self psychologists have pointed out, and each case must be understood individually. We will discuss this another day (Chapter 8).

Gray himself recognizes that there's a danger in his approach of the therapy becoming too intellectual, but he is certainly right that the patient's ego must be enlisted as an ally in the psychoanalysis. In fact, I feel that in a successful treatment the patient's ego gradually takes over the treatment to the point where the therapist is no longer necessary, and I feel that the treatment goes on indefinitely through the patient's self-analysis if we have done our job properly. Kohut (1984) disagrees with this and argues that if self-analysis goes on after the treatment, the treatment has been incomplete, but I don't think so. So just as Melanie Klein goes too far in one direction, it's my impression that Paul Gray goes too far in the other direction. I still think that it is our task, given the current state of the art, to keep all of these orientations in mind and to arrange some sort of orderly approach to the patient's material that utilizes them all, as seems to be necessary.

It is very much human nature to want a basic, consistent, all-encompassing theory. For example, today's psychiatrists are trying to find a consistent neurophysiologic theory that will explain all manifestations of mental illness on the basis of neurotransmitters and electrical systems. Freud (1950) attempted this, but of course he failed because he ran into the mystery of human consciousness. Experts on artificial intelligence are stumbling today on the same problem. I believe we are better off accepting the limitations of our knowledge and understanding as these limits are at this time, and working with partial theories rather than attempting to develop a unified theory that makes us more comfortable but overlooks significant aspects of the patient's psychodynamics and psychopathology.

*Maria:* The sun is setting, gentlemen. Let us have dinner together, a fine bottle of wine, and enjoy some light conversation, something entertaining and easy, before we resume the struggle to learn and understand tomorrow. Richard has already hinted in today's material that we will have to look at the most serious sources of difficulty in the psychoanalytic process, issues involving intense aggression, erotization, countertransference, and fragmentation of either the therapist or the patient.

*Richard:* Dinner now, by all means, and as my guests please!

*Maria and Donald:* Agreed! Thank you.

# 6

## The Sixth Day: Countertransference

*Maria:* I am certainly glad to be back in my own house and in my own parlor this morning. After working with so many patients yesterday, I had trouble sleeping last night! Erotic dreams! It is most disconcerting.

*Richard:* You may wish to have a look at Gabbard's (1989) collection of essays on every conceivable aspect of sexual relations between the therapist and patient. Gabbard describes the therapist who has fallen in love with his (or her) patient as the "lovesick therapist." Typically, a male middle aged therapist gets sexually involved with a female patient an average of 16.5 years younger than he is. They have a great need for each other's presence, and intrusive thoughts of the loved one force their way into the therapist's dream and waking life. The same is true for the patient who is involved. The therapist tells himself that this is something so special that it transcends all ordinary ethical and professional rules.

*Donald:* Is there any particular type of patient that seems to call forth this type of boundary violation?

*Richard:* Gutheil (1989) points out that patients with borderline personality disorder are particularly likely to evoke boundary violations in the therapist including sexual acting out. He notes, "These patients apparently constitute the majority of patients who falsely accuse therapists of sexual involvement" (p. 597). This makes sense because psychotic patients are not perceived as attractive and neurotic patients are usually healthy enough to know better than to become sexually involved with their doctors. Gutheil adds that the most relevant features of patients with borderline personality disorder in evoking these boundary violations are "borderline rage, neediness and/or dependency, boundary confusion, and manipulativeness and entitlement" (p. 598). Therapists often feel trapped or pressured by the potential rage of such patients into unusual and inappropriate degrees of social interaction with the patient or into considerable self-disclosure, including disclosure of their most intimate personal problems. It is remarkable how patients with borderline personality disorder possess this ability to seduce, provoke, or invite therapists into boundary violations.

The therapist is sometimes in a "drugged" or dreamlike state when with the patient who is his loved one, and so takes extraordinary risks with her that may irrevocably damage his career, incur legal penalties, and so forth. He may claim that he is trying to heal the torment in the patient's psyche, perhaps in the experimental manner tried by Ferenczi (1988)—although he soon admitted it did not work—or on the basis of numerous other rationalizations. The dynamics involve regression to blurred ego boundaries with a consequent blurring of the therapeutic boundaries, often only with this one patient. The therapist is usually a well functioning narcissist who may work satisfactorily with other patients, but in his personal life he has typically entered into some sort of mid-life crisis. His susceptibility to using the patient to resolve this crisis often shows itself first by such maneuvers as inappropriate self-disclosure to the patient, which can sometimes result in an actual reversal of roles.

*Donald:* Can some sort of psychopathology diagnosis be placed on this situation?

*Richard:* According to Gabbard this all represents a perversion in which the core is the sadistic wish to destroy the female. This forms the distinguishing feature of the "lovesick" therapist that separates it from so-called "normal" states of falling in love that we have all experienced at one time or another. The patient being similarly exploited is defending against her great rage and hostility to men, often generated by an abusing or sadistic father. The mid-life "crisis" of course is usually generated by dissatisfactions in the therapist's personal life and marriage, if any, and by a sense of loss of purpose and direction in life.

*Maria:* From my experience with these situations another factor is present. The patient wants to be "special" in the most desperate way, out of an intense archaic need for mirroring that is often generated by regression in the transference, or that is present to some extent even in all her relationships as well. The therapist, on the other hand, because of the narcissistic disequilibrium from which he suffers, wants sadistically enforced control of an archaic selfobject to restore that equilibrium. For example, the situation may represent a reversal of roles in which the therapist as a helpless child was sadistically controlled in every aspect of his mental and bodily functions by a narcissistic mother who used him as a selfobject for the purpose of maintaining her own narcissistic equilibrium, or, even worse, to prevent a total fragmentation of herself. Here we have a restitutive drama acted out by the therapist at a time when his own self is threatened.

*Donald:* Perhaps we could look at it from a neurophysiological point of view. The sexual pleasure involved, like the use of drugs, can set up a self-reinforcing feedback loop, an artificial drive, both out of the pleasure from the experience and perhaps from the tension reduction that takes place as a consequence of both the orgasm and the reassurance of his control over the archaic selfobject that is acted out in the sexual encounter. One way of checking this is that such therapists themselves notice an increasing frequency of sexual acting out or drug taking or alcoholism just at times when for various reasons they are immersed in some tense activity, such as giving a paper, culminating a risky business deal, having trouble with their children, being investigated by the Internal Revenue Service, and so forth.

*Richard:* The greatest harm done to the patient, I believe, appears when the acting out is stopped for one reason or another. The patient experiences this as a profound loss of an important mirroring selfobject function, and often the risk of suicide appears, as Gabbard's book documents. The patient is left with an unbearable rage that must be dealt with in some manner.

I know of some cases where the therapist actually divorced his wife and married the patient, and the marriage worked out apparently satisfactorily. But it is clear that involvement with a patient sexually carries risks that are unacceptable to both the patient and the therapist, both psychologically as well as legally. No rationalization should be allowed to justify such behavior because it is simply unethical, and that is the bottom line. It is an immoral violation of trust and the healing vocation. But considerable further research is needed into this subject. We especially need reports on the details of the psychoanalysis of acting out therapists or professionals who have used patients or clients in this manner, and more information as to whether this always results in harm to the patient.

*Donald:* But you seem to be describing far more than simply sexual acting out by a therapist!

*Richard:* Yes, because I believe it has not been sufficiently recognized just how pathological therapists are who act out in this fashion with patients. Labeling the therapist "lovesick" tends to emphasize the oedipal aspects of the therapist's pathology, but in my experience there are many archaic, preoedipal, and narcissistic aspects there also. The "lovesick" therapist is in a great deal of difficulty, at least at the time he or she behaves in such a manner.

*Maria:* He or she behaves in such a manner?

*Richard:* Yes. I have treated cases where the therapist was a woman and the patient was a younger man.

*Donald:* It would help, Richard, if you would go over this in some clinical or practical detail and enlighten us on some of your dynamic concepts as they unfold in these situations.

*Richard:* One way I attempt to understand the character of therapists who act out sexually with patients is in a phenomenologic fashion. Phenomenology comes to understand the truth of something not simply by reference to scientific study and terminology but by moving around it, experiencing it from different perspectives, and letting the manifestations of each perspective communicate the truth of the subject directly. I look for signs of gradual fragmentation in stages throughout their life cycle, sometimes even capable of resulting in final homicide and suicide. They often also have a strange conscience, but one not so unusual in physicians. Parts of it seem hypertrophied and very concerned with the suffering of this world, and other parts seem blind to the implications, devastation, and self-destructiveness of some of their behavior.

The classical "lovesick" therapist is attempting to somehow regain his shattered narcissistic equilibrium by a pathetic kind of sexual boundary crossing with a patient.

*Maria:* In this day and age of sexual acting out, why do you not make it more extreme and explicit?

*Richard:* Because I think a modified kind of sexual acting out goes on in these situations more than is generally recognized. Where actual sexual liaison outside of the office has occurred, we usually have the most blatant instances of personal disaster, but there are many relatively minor bits of acting out confined to the office. Even the therapist who does nothing more than allow a female patient to sit with part of her body or underclothing exposed is engaging in that sort of acting out. One must maintain a continual self-analysis! It is the mental set the therapist brings to the patient that I regard as the central issue in these boundary violations. The entire responsibility rests on the therapist.

*Maria:* Langs (1982) has written a great deal about the attempt of the patient to cure the therapist so that the therapist may subsequently function as the therapist that the patient needs.

*Donald:* Of course for both patient and therapist dreams often portray pathological trends which later, when ego functioning collapses, become part of conscious life; typically depression or eventual paranoia and hallucinations. The material moves in a downward spiral toward more and more archaic metaphors and allusions until it spills over in misbehavior.

*Richard:* The point is that the lovesick therapist who engages in boundary violations with patients may well be in a stage of incipient disintegration or fragmentation. My experience in the psychoanalytic treatment of such therapists has invariably demonstrated that these individuals are sicker than they appear to be on the surface. There is often what might be labeled a psychotic core around which a semblance of normality has been constructed. Punishment and a proscribing of their acting out with patients may satisfy society and protect the patients, but it leaves the so-called "lovesick therapist" with serious unresolved conflicts and pathology, and renders him or her liable to even more self-destructive disintegration.

*Maria:* A further implication is that if any psychotherapist finds himself or herself engaging in boundary violations with patients, the greatest protection is a consultation. This will only happen if we can convince therapists that boundary violations, no matter how small, must be treated as neurotic symptomatology on the part of the therapist and as warnings that the therapist is in psychological difficulty. No rationalizations should be allowed, and the patient's provocation, borderline or not, should not be blamed for the situation or allowed to take the focus off of the therapist's pathology. As an eroticized transference may be a last-ditch defense against the danger of melancholia or against an impending breakdown of the self (Bak 1973) of the patient, so falling in love with a patient may also be a last-ditch defense against the danger of melancholia or against an impending breakdown of the self of the therapist. This breakdown may well have begun before the therapist started treatment with the patient, and whatever provocations the patient offers become a precipitating factor in the disintegration of the therapist. The roots of both the eroticized transference and falling in love with a patient may be hidden by the language of love and tenderness, but they are firmly planted in infantile psychopathology and should not be confused with a mature love relationship.

*Donald:* You have used the term *fragmentation* repeatedly today. Can you explain more precisely what you mean by this concept?

*Richard:* Kohut's self psychology has been criticized (Schwartz 1978) because it lacks a clear definition of the term *fragmentation*. The fragmenting self occurs when the patient reacts to narcissistic disappointments, such as a perception of the therapist's lack of empathy, by the loss of a sense of cohesive self. Signs of this impending fragmentation are disheveled dress, posture and gait disturbances, vague anxiety, time and space disorientation, and hypochondriacal concerns. The concept of the fragmentation of the self seems to be equated with psychotic-like phenomena, at which time reality contact is in danger of being lost. It is characterized as a regressive phenomenon, predominantly autoerotic, a state of fragmented self-nuclei, in contrast to the state of the cohesive self (Kohut 1971).

*Maria:* In his early work Kohut (1971) calls fragmentation of the self "dissolution of the narcissistic unity of the self" (pp. 120–121), and explains how it is often accompanied by frantic activities of various kinds in the work and sexual areas of the person's life, especially in an effort to "counteract the subjectively painful feeling of self-fragmentation by a variety of forced actions, ranging from physical stimulation and athletic activities to excessive work in their profession and business" (p. 119).

*Donald:* We have been discussing an extreme form of malignant countertransference. Before we go today, could you say more about countertransference in general?

*Richard:* The immediate consequences of countertransference are that it may distort or hinder the perception of unconscious processes in the patient by the therapist, or it may not interfere with the therapist's perception of what is going on but it may impair the interpretative capacity of the therapist. So, for example, the manner, behavior, tone of voice, the form of the interpretations, and even the attitude toward the patient consciously or unconsciously may be vastly influenced by the countertransference. When a patient complains of the tone, manner, or voice of the therapist, it is not always a manifestation of transference to the therapist! It may instead represent the patient's perception of a countertransference problem in the therapist. Arlow (1985) reminds us that, "much as we observe and study the patients, the patients do the same to us. They observe our reactions, often in order to ascertain what they can do to provoke gratification of their infantile strivings" (p. 172).

*Maria:* There seems to be more than one definition of countertransference. The most limited definition of countertransference is that it consists of a set of therapist transference reactions in the form of fantasies, feelings, thoughts, and behavior, to the transference manifestations of the patient.

*Richard:* The formal psychoanalytic definition in use today usually amends this to include therapist's transference reactions, involving the significant persons in the therapist's childhood, to any aspect of the patient's personality, including the patient's transference (Reich 1973).

*Donald:* Then what is a totalistic countertransference?

*Richard:* This encompasses the total reaction of the therapist, both transference and realistic reaction, to all aspects of the patient's transference and general personality. Kernberg (1975) pointed out that the early appearance of such totalistic countertransference, usually in an intense and uncomfortable form, is typical in the treatment of borderline patients. An extreme example of this is the countertransference hatred described by Maltsberger and Buie (1974), which can develop in the treatment of borderline, psychotic, and suicidal patients. Nadelson (1977) also discussed the profound effect on the therapist of being exposed to "borderline rage." Totalistic countertransferences tend more to develop as a response to intense archaic transferences.

*Maria:* It seems to me that the crucial issue is to be aware that countertransference is taking place. Unanalyzed countertransference is most likely to be acted out and to present a barrier to understanding and interpreting.

*Richard:* Conversely, to identify what aspects of the patient are producing countertransference gives us further valuable understanding of the patient. The difference between the novice and the experienced psychotherapist is that the experienced psychotherapist is constantly on the look-out for the countertransference, becomes aware of it when it occurs, engages in continuous self-analysis, keeps countertransference in check in terms of not permitting the acting out of countertransference feelings, and holds it in abeyance or even utilizes it for the purposes of the psychotherapy.

*Donald:* As usual I am not quite satisfied because this discussion is a little vague. Can you suggest more specifically what to look for in order to become alert to the appearance of countertransference?

*Richard:* There are a number of signals and indicators that you can use. If you cannot understand certain kinds of patient material at all or you have depressed and uneasy feelings during or after the sessions with the patient, countertransference may be the problem. Similarly if you find yourself careless with regard to arrangements for the patient's appointments, forgetting the appointments, being late for them, letting the session run overtime for no special reason, falling asleep during the sessions or even persistently feeling drowsy, these are signals of countertransference. In situations where you are not behaving appropriately in either your financial arrangements with the patient or regarding time arrangements and changes in appointments, or you feel strange or unreasonable affectionate or hateful feelings towards the patient, countertransference is at work. If you find yourself trying to impress the patient or a colleague with the importance of the patient, or have an overwhelming urge to publish or give a lecture about the patient, or cultivate the patient's dependency, praise or affection, these are signs of countertransference. Sadistic or unnecessary sharpness toward the patient in your behavior or the reverse of this, or arguing with the patient or becoming too disturbed by the patient's reproaches or arguments represent countertransference. If you feel that the patient must get well for your sake or you are afraid of losing the patient, or find yourself trying to help the patient in matters outside the session, countertransference is present.

If you cannot gauge the point of optimum anxiety level for smooth operation of the therapeutic process so that the therapy alternates from one extreme of great patient anxiety to the other extreme where the patient is bored, uninterested, and shows no motivation, or you experience sudden feelings of increased or decreased interest in the patient, countertransference is manifest. Certainly severe countertransference motivates getting involved in financial deals and arrangements with the patient on a personal or social level, or experiencing recurring impulses to ask favors of the patient with all kinds of rationalizations as to why one is asking the favor from that particular patient. Dreaming about the patient and much daytime preoccupation with the patient or the patient's problems during leisure time means that countertransference is also highly developed and at a danger level.

*Maria:* Langs (1979) points out that after the therapist has established a particular structure and routine of procedure with each patient, the therapist should carefully examine any departures from the structure and routine that he or she subsequently introduces because they may be well related to countertransference. This includes the decision to offer ancillary psychopharmacologic agents and other modalities. I have found this suggestion very helpful.

*Donald:* In general I have tried to follow the famous maxim of Benjamin Franklin's *Poor Richard's Almanac*: "Do not do that which you would not have known." I try not to behave with the patient in psychotherapy in such a way that I would be unwilling to have it generally broadcast and known to my colleagues. But what do I do if I find a countertransference problem becoming severe or growing in spite of my best efforts to contain it?

*Richard:* There are at least three alternatives. The first of these, and the simplest, is to keep one's therapeutic interventions and activity at a minimum for a short period of time, while busily working through countertransference problems in self-analysis. A general rule of thumb is that if one feels anxious with a patient, that is a good time not to make interpretations or therapeutic interventions, because they will almost invariably be meant to allay one's own anxiety. If you feel chronically anxious with a patient, you need to seek help from a colleague.

Assuming that the therapist has already had a thorough personal psychoanalysis, he or she must deliberately and meticulously self-

investigate and see where the problem is coming from. If this is not successful, the therapist ought to consult a colleague. My experience has been that a consultation is extremely helpful and important in dealing with countertransference. Many cases of personal disaster, suicide, sexual acting out, stalemate, and failure in psychotherapy or psychoanalysis could have been prevented if the therapist had had the courage to get a consultation from a respected colleague at the point he or she became aware of the countertransference manifestations that were appearing.

*Maria:* That is more difficult than it sounds. It takes a lot of courage and a certain amount of residual health to expose one's self to the narcissistic injury inevitably involved in admitting to a colleague in consultation that one is floundering with a patient.

*Donald:* It certainly does! What about checking countertransference acting out by following these rules: Never be either exploitative or retaliative towards your patients. Always behave as you would toward a guest in your home with your spouse present.

*Richard:* These rules are fine, but courage is necessary if one is going to get involved in tampering with the psychic structure of other people in a therapeutic endeavor. We cannot demand from our patients absolute honesty and self-disclosure if we are not willing to do the same things ourselves when we are in difficulties. I have found this unwillingness to be the main obstacle in seeking consultations, even a greater obstacle than the cost of the consultation. This is true even though the cost of consultation is a common excuse to avoid it.

*Donald:* Is countertransference therefore always a bad thing?

*Richard:* It only becomes bad and negative and interferes in psychotherapy when it is not correctly recognized and handled. The aim of the therapy of the therapist is not to remove the possibility of all countertransference reactions but to make the therapist capable of being aware of these reactions and of dealing appropriately and maturely with them. Sometimes these reactions, if studied objectively, can lead to further vital information and data about the patient. If the therapist notices a countertransference reaction and analyzes this, it may lead to awareness that something the patient is doing or something the patient is saying is producing countertransference. I have found this to be a powerful tool in enhancing my understanding of patients. Often I have not been aware previously of the message or communication the patient was trying to send. Instead of listening I was suffering from a countertransference reaction. Analyzing this reaction often opens the door to new aspects of the patient's psychodynamics and provides a better understanding of projective identification as we have discussed it on previous days.

*Donald:* Kohut (1971) has offered some excellent rules for picking up typical countertransference responses to the mirror and idealizing transferences encountered in narcissistic personality disorders . . .

*Maria:* And also in other oedipal or preoedipal disorders, where patients have defensively regressed to such transferences.

*Donald:* He explains that the typical countertransference to the idealizing selfobject transferences occurs through the mobilization of the therapist's archaic, grandiose self, leading to an embarrassed "straight-arming" of the patient by denial of the idealization in various ways. Typical countertransference reactions to mirror transferences are boredom, lack of involvement with the patient, inattention, annoyance, sarcasm, and a tendency to lecture the patient out of counter-exhibitionism, or attempts to gain control of the therapy by exhortation, persuasion, and so on.

*Richard:* Gunther (1976), utilizing self psychology, has also offered an excellent explanation of certain countertransference phenomena as aimed at restoring narcissistic equilibrium in the therapist. The psychiatrist may be suffering from an increasing imbalance of narcissistic equilibrium and is using a variety of techniques including acting out with a patient or former patient, in a desperate attempt to restore this equilibrium. But the therapist's narcissistic equilibrium is especially endangered in the treatment of preoedipal cases by intense archaic demands from the patient. In my supervisory experience, narcissistic disequilibrium problems are the most common generators of countertransference, although of course it is not possible to judge from supervision whether these problems defend against deeper unresolved infantile sexual conflicts.

*Donald:* Thank you very much, Richard, for expanding on countertransference. Now I think I am ready to relax and have dinner. May I invite you both to be my guests for this evening?

*Maria and Richard:* With pleasure!

# 7

## The Seventh Day:
## Impasse and Failure

*Donald:* What a gloomy day! I don't think the sun will come out at all and the wind chill factor must be below zero.

*Maria:* There won't be much here to cheer you up either, Donald, as today we're planning to discuss impasse and failure in psychoanalytic treatment. An impasse in psychoanalytic treatment is an insidious arrest of the psychoanalytic process that often results in failure or, worse, transference and countertransference acting out. As Etchegoyen (1991) writes, "It tends to perpetuate itself: the setting is preserved in its basic constants; its existence is not obvious as incoercible resistance or technical error; it is rooted in the patient's psychopathology; and it involves the analyst's countertransference" (p. 786).

*Richard:* An impasse occurring even in one single case is very serious for the conscientious psychoanalyst or psychotherapist. It forces one to review his or her choice of profession and theoretical orientation, and it questions the discipline of psychoanalytic psychotherapy itself. It is not the same as blatant failure or interruption of treatment, which usually can be traced to relatively obvious personal and recognizable faults in either or both the patient and the analyst. The impasse, on the other hand, involves a very subtle interaction between the analyst and the patient so that it may go on for months or even years before the analyst realizes what has happened. In some cases, the patient who is suffering the impasse not only often does not mention it, but will resolutely deny it if it is suggested by the analyst. Of course that isn't always true, since some patients complain of experiencing an impasse from the very beginning of the treatment and never budge from that position.

*Donald:* I understand that an impasse is complex and multidetermined and countertransference is often deeply and subtly involved. In my own experience, when I realize that an impasse has occurred, it has been shocking and humiliating. I wonder if all patients who drop out of therapy could be said to have first been at an impasse.

*Richard:* Chessick (1983b) reviewed the patients encountered in the first fifteen years of his private practice. One category included all patients who dropped out of therapy some time after at least three initial interviews but without mutual agreement to terminate. However, these patients were not all failures. They included teenage patients who were taken out of treatment after a year or so of twice weekly psychotherapy by their parents. Even though they had made substantial obvious progress, their parents did not approve of their growing health and independence. In the same category also were patients with schizophrenic episodes and some with depressive episodes who had gained symptomatic remission and good return of previous functioning capacity, but who refused to go further into uncovering psychotherapy. In my experience, there also are some patients who had to leave me before I gave any signs of leaving them; such patients tend to have a very rigid and brittle ego structure.

*Maria:* There are also patients with massive chronic fixed paranoid delusions, secretly held for many years and clearly inaccessible to psychoanalytic treatment. Patients like this terminated treatment with me after about five to fifteen visits, and one or two patients with a previous history of hospitalization became psychotic again during treatment and had to return to the hospital.

*Donald:* Sometimes I see patients who drop out after one to four months because, in spite of repeated explanations, they expected fast results and therefore were easily disappointed. Most prominent in this group are oral characters, alcoholics, drug addicts, and patients with hypochondriacal complaints. A few of my patients realized they could not really afford psychotherapy and admitted they had lied about their financial capacity because they secretly hoped to have an unusually quick treatment. The husbands of several of my women patients stopped paying for treatment despite having initially agreed to do so, because they had hoped for a quick change in their wives that did not materialize. I suppose it couldn't be said that any of these represent an impasse leading to failure.

*Richard:* Some patients are simply outright failures and there has been no impasse first. In spite of all my efforts occasional patients either made no improvement or gradually went downhill over a period of 50 to 200 sessions. In order to understand what happened in such cases a patient-by-patient analysis is required; generally they were severe borderline patients, often with alcoholism or drug addiction and a history of repeated failures in various therapies. A few were homosexuals who had an increasing paranoid development that I could not check. Of those whom I could follow up, a small number reported definite improvement after leaving therapy. A few went on to see another therapist with variable results, and two "improved" with subsequent group therapy.

*Maria:* Not all dropouts are failures in treatment and not all successes are terminable! It can be quite difficult to determine success or failure in psychotherapy or to recognize the clinical danger periods for failure, impasse, or dropping out. Patients who refuse treatment or unexpectedly fail to return after a diagnostic workup represent an immediate and obvious failure at the outset. Some have a need to inflict a narcissistic wound on the therapist. Some are simply too frightened to continue. This failure is at times attributable to the flawed skill of the therapist—and/or conscious as well as unconscious factors in both the therapist and patient that reject either an alliance or psychotherapy. Regardless of the humiliation involved, therapists should try to follow up these patients as much as possible in order to learn more about themselves and the patient and the reason for the failure.

*Richard:* That's correct. Outright failures after treatment begins, due to a basic defect in the therapist or the patient (or both), represent a tricky and stubborn problem as well as an unfortunate waste of time and money. The best hope for preventing these failures is to train psychotherapists adequately and encourage them to gain insight into themselves. Outright failures usually occur when there is no solid therapeutic alliance or when the therapist does not sufficiently recognize, interpret, and work through resistances before dealing with psychic content. It goes without saying that in order to develop a reasonable working alliance the therapist must first present himself or herself in a reasonable and realistic fashion. This will automatically rule out a whole variety of bizarre procedures that are presently being foisted upon the public in the name of therapy.

*Donald:* Can you give some clinical rules for the therapist to follow in dealing with resistance? After all, resistance is what can develop into an impasse and failure if not properly handled. It's almost a circular definition, because we traditionally define resistance as anything that interferes with the work of the treatment!

*Richard:* Greenson (1967) presents the technical aspects of dealing with resistance, beginning of course with the importance of recognizing the resistance. The resistance is to be demonstrated to the patient by allowing it to become manifest through waiting for several instances; at times it is necessary to intervene in such a way as to increase the resistance in order to help it become demonstrable. Next the motives and modes of resistance must be clarified. What specific painful affect is making the patient resistant? What particular instinctual impulse is causing the painful affect at this time? What precise mode and method does the patient use to express his or her resistance? The interpretation of the resistance should explore what fantasies or memories are producing the affects and impulses behind it and pursue the history and unconscious purposes of these affects, impulses, or events in and outside the analysis, including the past. The mode of resistance is to be interpreted, including similar modes of activity that represent resistance and acting out in and outside the psychoanalysis or psychotherapy. Finally, the history and unconscious purposes of this activity in the patient's past and present need to be traced and worked through and one hopes the resistance is to be dissipated by repetitions and elaborations of these procedures.

*Donald:* Can you offer a clinical example of an outright failure in intensive psychotherapy?

*Richard:* Chessick (1984) described a dramatic failure in the psychoanalytic psychotherapy of a remarkable schizophrenic patient. I believe that the primary failure in his case occurred because his effort to reverse the patient's psychotic so-called new self formation failed, due to the fact that the patient was unable to form a stable idealizing transference. The patient's psyche consolidated into a form of chronic paranoid schizophrenia in spite of the therapist's best efforts. The most distressing experience of the treatment for him was to witness this consolidation under his very eyes while being unable to effectively do anything about it.

*Maria:* I am familiar with that case. The extreme ambivalence of the patient made it impossible for her to form a sufficiently long-lasting relationship with the therapist in order to make therapeutic intervention possible. The crucial conflict of wishing to be simultaneously close and distant from other people was manifest both in this patient's history and her relationship with the therapist, and resulted in a life of chronic frustration. Pao (1979) calls this "a desperate struggle against the symbiotic pull" (p. 183). The distancing that the patient used seemed very much "the best possible solution" that she could find to prevent further fragmentation experiences. These fragmentation experiences or "organismic panics" were rendered inevitable by her narcissistic demand for the absolute perfection of the selfobject, which could not be either modified or interpreted, because the rage was so great whenever these imperfections were experienced that the patient in essence broke off the relationship and dismissed anything that the therapist had to say.

*Richard:* What was missing in this patient was the capacity to stay in the relationship in spite of minor disappointments in the wished-for perfection of the therapist. Instead, a regressive process occurred in which the therapist became utterly devalued and the patient retreated into a delusional core fantasy for the purpose of autistic soothing. It is this vital step that made the patient essentially untreatable by the method of intensive psychotherapy. It is not the amount of raging that the patient does that represents the limit to the possibility of the treatment, but the patient's refusal to stay in the relationship and insistence on falling permanently and irreversibly back on an inner world of his or her own making, which in this case she did very suddenly, quickly discarding the therapist. The patient was aware that by staying in a long-term treatment she would have to experience inevitably from time to time frustrations and perceived failure in the therapist's empathy. These experiences were so painful for her that she could not allow them to happen; thus, the best possible solution for her was to withdraw from all interpersonal relationships.

*Donald:* How do you know this patient was not simply reacting to some idiosyncratic problem of the therapist?

*Richard:* All the therapists who had previously worked with this patient ended up with a sense of being trapped and frustrated because their best efforts toward her somehow were extremely devalued. She refused to cooperate with even psychopharmacological psychiatrists. The patient was inflicting on the therapists what her mother had inflicted on her—that is to say, no matter how hard the therapists reached out to her and how many ways they attempted to empathize and interact with her, she somehow saw to it that the situation ended not only in disappointment but a disappointment in which the therapist somehow felt devalued, guilty, and frustrated.

*Maria:* It is common for schizophrenic or borderline patients to painfully inflict on the therapist the experience they received at the hands of the mother or father and to enact their consequent fantasies of revenge. Chessick (1982) described how inflicting painful revenge on the deep unconscious of the therapist was a crucial step for a borderline patient of his, enabling the resumption of development and attainment of mental health. The schizophrenic patient we've just talked about was also compelled to act out her revenge, destroying her treatment—a not uncommon behavior in such patients.

*Donald:* What about the impasse? This is obviously a more subtle kind of failure, a stalemate. Does stalemate invariably reduce itself to issues of self-analysis or reanalysis, or does it involve the need for better conceptual and technical tools? Must the analyst invariably assume the burden for the analysand's intransigence, and should priority be given to countertransference issues?

*Richard:* In at least one category of therapeutic stalemate the answer to this question is *no*. Maguire (1990) points out that there are stalemates or impasses that occur "as an inescapable fate of those analyses in which the analysand's intuitive perception of the analytic task ahead generates such incalculable tensions, and consequently such intractable resistances, as to preclude the regressive mobilization of the transference neurosis" (p. 64).

*Maria:* I think it is *very* important to distinguish, as Maguire does, between negative reactions in therapy that are founded on resistance, those that represent the negative therapeutic reaction, and therapeutic stalemate. Impasse or stalemate is insidious and often recognized only retrospectively. It may begin, as Maguire writes, with "the analysand's initial failure to engage the therapeutic process affectively," or be indicated "by the analysand's gradual and insidious withdrawal of affective investment from the process once engaged" (p. 66), leading to a loss of vitality in the entire process.

*Donald:* Now we're getting to some real clinical pearls! Are there other indicators the therapist should look for as warnings that an impasse is evolving?

*Richard:* There are certain additional presumptive signs of a developing impasse. For example, be warned when the frame of the treatment becomes a problem, involving such behavior as persistent tardiness or absences that remain inaccessible to interpretation—or when, on the contrary, an excessive compliance with the frame appears. Ogden (1995) uses the sense of aliveness or deadness in the transference–countertransference as a measure of the status of the analytic process at any given time. Impasse is a concern if the patient lapses into progressively longer periods of silence or engages in a highly intellectualized process with an endless recycling of old issues. As Maguire (1990) says, the patient may regress "to a fixed state of hostile dependency, challenging the analyst's competence and good will by evincing a defensive demandingness that preempts further engagement. . . . the analysand oscillates between unremitting recriminations about the process and a general state of lethargy" (p. 67).

*Donald:* Is this a hopeless situation? Can the situation be reversed or salvaged?

*Maria:* Maguire believes that if there is an early recognition by the analyst of the development of an impasse before the whole credibility of the procedure becomes irreparably damaged, and if the analyst can accept the patient's negative perception of the treatment as real and meaningful, and if there is some minimal good feeling left in the patient that could be mobilized, there is *still* the possibility of a favorable outcome to the impasse. He presents a patient who was unable to enter regressively into a transference neurosis because she intuitively anticipated an experience in it from which she would not be able to recover.

*Richard:* Kohut (1977) mentions this type of danger. Some patients do intuitively recognize that if certain aspects of the mirror transference are activated, such an activation would expose the patient to the danger of permanent psychological disruption through the reexperiencing of uncontrollable primordial rage and greed. In such patients, for example as in Kohut's case of Mr. U., behind the more apparent layers of frustration "there hovered always a nameless preverbal depression, apathy, sense of deadness, and diffuse rage that related to the primordial trauma of his life. Such primal states, however, can neither be recalled through verbalized memories, as can traumata occurring after speech has developed, nor expressed through psychosomatic symptoms" (p. 25).

*Maria:* Clearly those patients intuitively sense that psychoanalysis, if leading them to become engaged in a transference neurosis, would be what Kohut calls "a regressive voyage from which there is no return" (p. 25). Chessick (1996a) tried to depict this situation of nameless underlying dread, and Grotstein (1990, 1990a,b, 1991) has written at length to call attention to these very early unendurable archaic states, which patients must avoid at all costs. As in the case of Maguire's patient, such patients still may be able to make use of the analyst in a circumspect and distancing manner.

*Donald:* I'm getting uncomfortable because the phrase *transference neurosis* keeps coming up. As I understand it, this is a controversial concept these days. Am I correct? Can you explain just what it refers to?

*Richard:* It *is* controversial, but I would like to discuss it along with the general notion of *transference* in both the classical and self-psychological sense, and the related concept of idealization, when we meet tomorrow. Returning to today's discussion, Etchegoyen (1991) throws additional light on the problem of impasse by utilizing Bion's (1963) idea of "reversible perspective." Bion introduced this concept to denote a drastic attempt on the part of the patient to destabilize the analytic situation through a remarkable reversal of the processes of thought. The patient silently, either consciously or unconsciously, experiences the entire psychoanalysis from a different set of premises than those held by the therapist. The analytic contract is actually violated, although the patient appears on the surface to be cooperating with the treatment. Etchegoyen explains that in this situation the patient "is continuously reinterpreting the analyst's interpretations so that they can blend with his own premises, which is also a way of saying that the analyst's premises have to be silently rejected—silently, because between analyst and analysand there is manifest accord and latent discord, of which the analyst usually becomes aware only when he realizes that the process is completely stagnant" (p. 759).

*Donald:* I need a clinical example to clarify this. Can you supply one?

*Richard:* The clinical example Etchegoyen offers is that of a homeopathic physician who ostensibly came seeking psychoanalytic treatment for anxiety and crises of depersonalization as well as hoping for a modification of the psychological factors to his bronchial asthma. Actually, the patient was guided by professional rivalry and simply wanted to reassure himself that the method of homeopathic medicine was superior to the method of psychoanalysis.

Reversible perspective is often operative in patients who are chronically late. In those situations, as Etchegoyen explains, "To interpret at the level of defense mechanisms is not enough. Because as one interprets lateness or silence in terms of fear, frustration, revenge, envy, Oedipus complex, castration anxiety, omnipotent control or whatever, one has not reached a level at which the conflict is rooted" (p. 766).

*Donald:* Again, are there other clinical signs or signals that reversible perspective is taking place?

*Richard:* The reversion of perspective needs to be suspected when everything seems to be going well in the treatment but no change is taking place in the analysand. This is not an infrequent occurrence in training analyses, where the analyst thinks he or she is helping the patient to resolve neurotic difficulties, but the patient—a candidate analyst—is simply intending to use the training analysis as a source of borrowed knowledge and accreditation. This is an example of reversible perspective that also often appears in narcissistic personality disorders; a common and extreme type of such patient enters analysis secretly not in order to be cured of neurotic difficulties but to demonstrate to the analyst that he or she does not need analysis at all. The very premise that the patient is the patient and the analyst is the analyst constitutes a painful narcissistic blow for some people; this is especially difficult in the analysis of mental health professionals and in patients with narcissistic or borderline personality disorders.

*Maria:* I have encountered a similar situation when treating colleagues in the mental health profession who attempt to use the analysis to "teach" the analyst that the analyst's theoretical orientation is incorrect and to persuade the analyst to adopt the analysand's theoretical orientation. Other variations of this from my own clinical practice are, for example, the patient who spent many hours trying to convince me that her difficulties were caused by various chemicals in the air that she breathed, or mental health professionals who enter psychoanalysis because they've been involved in unethical behavior and wish to strengthen their case when it comes up in front of the licensure committee by being able to state that they are seeking treatment for their difficulty.

*Richard:* In certain of these latter cases the patient's sole aim is to impress the licensure committee; they secretly believe that they have no mental health problem. The patient who was convinced her difficulties were due to the chemicals in the air, as you told me when I was supervising this case, Maria, was a brilliant woman who actually accumulated a large library of volumes purchased in local bookstores and written by so-called experts and even physicians practicing outside the mainstream of American medicine. She did this so effectively that she convinced her whole family that she was correct and sent them all off seeking a bizarre variety of antidotes to the supposed chemical dangers, utterly obsessing and preoccupying them with finding a completely chemical-free environment in which to live and work—a task that of course never succeeded.

*Donald:* I found the suggestions of Gedo and Gehrie (1993) very helpful in my clinical work. They present several common pitfalls that often lead to an unsatisfactory course of many psychoanalyses. These involve errors in the diagnosis, nosology and strategy of treatment, commitment to a favored clinical theory, failure to agree on rational goals for the treatment, the problem of a cultural gap, countertransference issues, an unfortunate neglect of careful scrutiny and analysis of superego contents, and uncertainty about whether to concentrate on the transference in the here and now, versus emphasizing reconstruction of the past. We have already talked about this latter problem, and I suspect that it also plagues supervisors.

*Richard:* You are correct! They explain that a common difficulty occurs when there is confusion in the mind of the therapist about the way in which vital unresolved issues are relived within the psychoanalytic situation: "Instead of relating the relevant vicissitudes of the patient–analyst relationship, [the candidates] tended to summarize a series of reconstructions about the childhood past. What is worse, often they did not specify whether those conclusions were reached on the basis of the unrolling of a sequence of transference reactions or whether they were the kinds of 'dynamic formulations' demanded of participants in psychoanalytic training programs, that is essentially speculative" (p. 8). It has also been my supervisory experience that this is a common confusion displayed by students in the mental health professions.

*Donald:* I like Gedo's suggestion to meet adaptive distortions that have occurred in the patient which interfere with our attempts to provide ordinary developmental assistance in a confronting fashion, with an effort to correct them. He also warns that conversely the envy of a patient's superior abilities and creativity may lead to a depreciating attitude on the part of the analyst that in turn leads to an impasse.

*Richard:* The crucial test in evaluating such interventions or, for that matter, any of our interventions, is to carefully observe the effect of each intervention. The correct interpretation of a defense leads to psychic or behavioral alteration; interpretations based on an overestimation of the patient's resources leads to rage and/or disappointment in analysis and carries the danger of an impasse. Gedo (Gedo and Gehrie 1993) emphasizes the necessity for the analyst to transform enactments into verbal statements, in a sense teaching the patient a new language, and he insists that we must not impose a technique on the patient but instead devise a technique that the patient can use. He explains, "Correct interpretations are experienced as assaultive if they put the analysand in the position of unacceptable passivity—in terms, for example, of causing excessive anxiety or even pleasurable overstimulation" (p. 212). This is a very important point.

*Donald:* Earlier you mentioned that not all patients share the analyst's sense of impasse. Can you give a clinical example?

*Maria:* Renik (cited in Coen 1994) describes a patient who was quite content with her relation to the analyst and considered him as supplying a missing vital part, in an almost quasi-delusion. In psychoanalyses where the patient in this fashion is using the analyst as a fetish, claims Renick, "such analyses must lead to impasse" (p. 1227).

*Richard:* More generally, the pressure on the analyst to abandon his or her ordinary role, either coming from certain new psychotherapy theories or from the patient, has become more intense recently as the literature pays more attention to developmental processes and deficits. According to Spence (cited in Coen 1994), analysts these days are especially tempted to take the role of a nurturant mother and to imagine that psychoanalysis is a process for correcting development. In discussing the various cases of impasse reported by members of a panel on impasses at the American Psychoanalytic Association, Spence pointed out that each analyst was forced by his patient into playing some role other than that of the interpreting analyst: "Once the analyst could recognize and interpret this false role, the impasse was interrupted . . . For the impasse to be resolved, the analyst must indeed get out of such false roles and return to the position of interpreting analyst" (p. 1231).

*Donald:* I don't understand. Does this mean we should never change our technique with any patient?

*Richard:* Chusid (Rosenblum 1994) points out that there are some resistances that simply do not yield to interpretations: "As a result, we change our technique with different patients. Whatever the deviation each of us adopts, to the extent it deviates from what we consider our standard analytic technique, it reflects an internal decision that the patient needed something different in order to do the work of analysis" (p. 1259). This leads to an unresolved issue in the study of impasse. Many rather traditional psychoanalysts claim that deviations in technique are often the *cause* of impasses in psychoanalysis, while a more adventurous group of psychoanalysts maintain that impasses can be avoided or resolved by the willingness on the part of the analyst to consider the point of view of other theories, and to provide interventions that are not called for by the particular theory to which the analyst usually is committed.

*Donald:* It seems to me then that this discussion has reached an impasse!

*Maria:* That usually calls for adjournment for the day and retreat to the cocktail hour. What do you say, Richard?

*Richard:* I don't really think our discussion has reached an impasse. What it has reached is the fact that psychodynamic therapy is as much an art as it is a science. The intuitive capacity of the analyst, or the empathic capacity of the analyst, often helps us in deciding whether to make deviations in technique. Our scientific dedication helps us in evaluating the effect of deviations in technique or of any other interventions. If we are very careful and observe the results of what we are doing in a meticulous fashion, it is possible to be empathic with a patient's needs and function as a decent human being without producing an impasse. Conversely, an excessively rigid adherence to the psychoanalytic frame or set of rules can produce an iatrogenic narcissistic withdrawal on the part of the patient that could easily lead to a countertransference retaliation on the part of the therapies and the production of an impasse. Every case must be evaluated on its own merits, and the argument over whether an impasse is caused by deviations from the frame or leads to deviations from the frame can only be decided by a study of each individual case. The therapist should be studying each of his or her own individual cases on a day-to-day basis to assess the effect of countertransference and of all interventions as they occur. Patients will not let us rest on these matters because they are always springing surprises. That is what makes the art and science of psychodynamic therapy so interesting and exciting, and poses a challenge to the flexibility, self-analytic capacity, skill, and dedication of the therapist.

*Donald:* Are you making the point that studies of the psychoanalytic process tend to be insufficiently detailed, inevitably producing some confusion about the evolution of an impasse?

*Richard:* One should always be skeptical about metapsychological and even psychodynamic formulations, especially if they are not backed up by ample clinical data. It's important to realize that the treatment does indeed involve two people in the same room who continuously interact with one another. Descriptions of the psychoanalytic process in the literature need to be made much more precise by giving specific details of the verbal and nonverbal interaction between the analyst and the patient. Widlöcher (1994), a well-known Parisian psychoanalyst, discusses the entire matter of reporting on cases and so-called clinical vignettes in the psychoanalytic literature. He points out that the question of whether such material constitutes scientific data is moot, and that "the issue of the scientific status of psychoanalysis therefore remains unresolved" (p. 1242).

*Maria:* What about Freud's "case histories" in this instance?

*Richard:* Widlöcher explains that although clinical monographs—that is, long surveys of one case that include "biographical events, clinical symptoms, overt behaviour and latent data discovered in the course of the treatment" (p. 1236)—carry on a tradition that began with Freud's four major clinical presentations; "such monographs prove nothing, but rather offer any willing person the opportunity to share an experience" (p. 1237). This is because of the necessary selection of data and the unavoidable decisions involved in the way the data is presented. But sharing an experience is very important indeed, and it offers a chance for the reader to get an idea of what the two persons continuously interacting in the same room went through together. Surely this sets the stage for our discussion of idealization and transference tomorrow.

*Donald:* Now can we join Maria for the happy hour of the day?

*Richard: Bien entendu!*

# 8

## The Eighth Day:
## Idealization and
## Transference

*Richard:* Yesterday we focused on the complicated problem of impasse in psychoanalytic treatment. There are chronic and enduring impasses, for example an analysis caught up in a persisting sadomasochistic, predominantly negative, and predominantly maternal transference that cannot be overcome by interpretive intervention. In such situations one wonders whether deviations in technique would worsen or ameliorate the situation. So, for example, a particular intervention designed to accommodate an appropriate request of the patient could backfire and intensify rather than soften the patient's transference perceptions. There are of course also micro-impasses in our everyday work that need to be discovered by careful attention to the effects of our interventions, and impasses of a longer or shorter duration in which the patients may have to blur the distinction between fantasy and reality in order to safeguard and sequester certain tenacious fantasies about their relationships with their analyst.

*Donald:* I suppose an example of this type of fantasy would be idealization. Yet I understand that there is a considerable disagreement about the psychodynamic function of idealization when it appears in the therapeutic process.

*Richard:* That's correct. For example, idealization occurs in both of Klein's basic positions, the paranoid-schizoid and the depressive, as a defense against sadism and destruction in fantasy (Segal 1974, 1980). For the Kleinians, internalized bad objects are no longer projected in the depressive position, nor are they reintrojected; instead, the total object is experienced and the bad objects remain inside, forming the basis of the primitive superego, which attacks the ego or self with guilt feelings. Idealized good internal objects attenuate this attack.

*Maria:* Obviously this idealization of good internal objects leads to problems because the standards set by or the demands coming from the idealized good internal objects become, when combined with sadistic superego precursors, cruel demands for perfection leading to an unremitting harshness of the superego. This is complicated, in cases where there is much sadism, by the need to protect the good objects in the superego by excessive idealization.

*Donald:* Wait a minute! Wouldn't it be wise to begin with some kind of definition of idealization? This Kleinian jargon makes my head spin!

*Richard:* Students often have a great deal of trouble understanding or accepting Kleinian theory, but I can assure you it is well worth studying and absorbing into your channels of psychoanalytic listening as we have discussed these channels. In general, idealization represents an unrealistic exaggeration of a subject's personal attributes. It may occur in both the transference and narcissistic neuroses. It is related to the state of being in love, but it can be much more eerie and unrealistic even than that. In the transference neuroses, which we will discuss today as I promised to do, idealization does not lose touch entirely with the realistic features and limitations of the object. In typical neurotic situations, idealization can represent a projection of the analysand's idealized superego onto the analyst and can form a part of the positive transference, or defensive idealizations can form against transference hostility.

*Maria:* But in Kohut's (1977) theory of self psychology, which deals primarily with the narcissistic disorders, the unconscious is fixated on an idealized selfobject for which it continues to yearn. According to self psychologists, persons with such disorders are forever searching for external omnipotent powers from whose support and approval they attempt to derive strength.

*Richard:* In the narcissistic idealizing transferences, there is a sense of a vague idealization that becomes central to the material. This can lead to the extreme belief that the therapist is divine. The therapist, then, is not able to relate to the patient as one human being to another, but rather must deal with an eerie quality of unreasonable exaltation coming from the patient.

*Donald:* I can certainly see how the therapist would react with embarrassment and negativism if he or she does not understand such material. It also seems logical that the intensity of the distortion gives the therapist an idea of how desperate the patient is. The greater the desperation, the greater the requirement for soothing from the therapist. But I know that not all psychoanalysts are self psychologists, and here we have an important unresolved debate.

*Richard:* Yes, one will have to make some choices. The collision between the followers of Klein—or the modified Kleinians such as Kernberg—and the followers of Kohut involves the question of whether idealization as it appears in the transference is defensive or whether it represents the breaking through of archaic unresolved narcissistic needs for an idealized parent imago. Idealization of the parents is important in the formation of the superego and can continue throughout life, becoming an especially important growth-promoting feature during adolescence.

*Maria:* Freud originally discussed idealization as part of the sexual overestimation of the love object, but apparently the term has been used in a more general sense to deal with narcissistic needs in which some of the self-love of the child is transferred or displaced onto a substitute that becomes the ego-ideal or superego and is looked upon as the possessor of all perfections.

*Donald:* This is all somewhat confusing. Can you clarify the difference between idealization and the "idealizing transference"?

*Richard:* I have already offered a general definition of idealization. According to the self psychologists, as a consequence of developmental arrest and failure to integrate the archaic structures of the grandiose self and the idealized parent imago, characteristic selfobject transferences (Kohut 1977) occur in the treatment of narcissistic personality disorders. These transferences, or transference-like situations, are the result of the amalgamation of the unconscious archaic narcissistic structures with the psychic representation of the analyst under the pressure of the need to relieve the unfulfilled narcissistic needs of childhood.

*Maria:* It remains questionable whether these should be called transferences in the strict sense. They are *not* motivated by the need to discharge instinctual tensions, nor are they produced by cathecting the analyst with object libido. I like to think of them as transference-like phenomena, although self psychologists usually refer to them as selfobject transferences.

*Richard:* According to the self psychologists, the goal of the idealizing selfobject transference is to share, via a merger, in the power and omnipotence of the therapist. Occurring as the result of therapeutic mobilization of the idealized parent imago are two basic types of such transferences, with a variety of gradations in between. The most obvious type is a later formation, usually based on a failure of idealization of the father, that stresses the search for an idealized parent to which the patient must be attached in order to feel approved and protected. A more archaic type of selfobject transference may appear or be hidden under the other types; this transference is usually related to a failure with the mother, in which the stress is on an ecstatic merger and mystical union with a godlike idealized parent.

*Donald:* This makes a lot of sense to me, and helps to explain some of the experiences I've had with patients manifesting narcissistic personality disorders. These experiences have been very unpleasant for me, especially when such a transference, having been formed, is disturbed!

*Maria:* Yes! As Kohut explains, clinical signs of the disturbance of a narcissistic idealizing selfobject transference are a cold, aloof, angry, raging withdrawal that Kohut believes represents a swing to the grandiose self; also feelings of fragmentation and hypochondria due to the separation consequent to the withdrawal, and the creation of eroticized replacements by frantic activities and fantasies, especially those involving voyeurism, with many variations.

*Richard:* The typical countertransference to the idealizing selfobject transferences, Kohut (1971) wrote, occurs through the mobilization of the archaic grandiose self in whatever unanalyzed residue is present in the therapist. This leads to an embarrassed and defensive straight-arming of the patient by denying the patient's idealizing, joking about it, or trying vigorously to interpret it away. Such countertransference produces in the patient the typical signs of disturbance and retreat to the grandiose self that Maria just mentioned.

*Donald:* You have spoken of transferences and transference-like phenomena. The customary definition of transference that I learned in training was given by Fenichel (1945): "In the transference the patient misunderstands the present in terms of the past; and then instead of remembering the past, he strives, without recognizing the nature of his action, to relive the past and to live it more satisfactorily than he did in his childhood. He 'transfers' the past attitude to the present" (p. 29). As I understand it, then, transference is a form of resistance in which patients defend themselves against remembering and discussing their infantile conflicts by reliving them. It also offers us a vital and unique clinical opportunity to observe and experience derivatives of the past directly and thereby to better understand the development of the nuclear childhood conflicts in the patient.

*Richard:* Very good, Donald; that's correct. The importance of the concept of transference in any form of psychoanalytic psychotherapy should be clear. Many authors argue that the basic difference between intensive uncovering psychotherapy and supportive psychotherapy or conditioning therapies lies in the way that the transference is recognized and dealt with. It is the observable and often generally predictable orderly unfolding of the transference during a well-conducted psychoanalytic treatment that firmly anchors this discipline in the realm of science, regardless of the hermeneutic and other aspects involved.

*Donald:* I would appreciate some clinical discussion of the appearance and handling of transference in general.

*Richard:* The outstanding trait that overrides all others in the transference is that of inappropriateness. As Greenson (1967) puts it, "It is inappropriateness, in terms of intensity, ambivalence, capriciousness, or tenacity which signals that transference is at work" (p. 162). Of course transference doesn't arise just in psychotherapy but can appear in many kinds of interpersonal situations and play a very important role.

*Maria:* Positive transference, as it manifests itself in love, fondness, trust, liking, concern, devotion, and so forth, is not as much a problem in treatment as the appearance of negative transference. This latter involves a series of reactions based on various forms or degrees of hate and destructiveness. According to Greenson, these include "hatred, anger, hostility, mistrust, abhorrence, aversion, loathing, resentment, bitterness, envy, dislike, contempt or annoyance, etc." (p. 233). It is *always* present, although perhaps much more difficult to uncover than the manifestations of positive transference at least in some instances.

*Richard:* There are many possible reasons for this clinical fact. The two most obvious are that patients do not like to become aware of transference hate or to express it, and that therapists do not particularly enjoy being the object of transference hate and having to deal with it or be exposed to it. Negative transference can be very uncomfortable for the therapist and can wear the therapist down over weeks and weeks of expressions of ferocious hostility and sadism from the patient. So it's extremely important for the therapist to be aware of subtle manifestations of negative transference at all times and to directly interpret and deal with them.

*Donald:* Why is this true?

*Richard:* Therapists tend to overlook or disavow the subtle manifestations of negative transference; it is much more pleasant to bask in the sunshine of a positive transference than to have on one's hands an irritated, disgruntled, or extremely hostile and sadistic patient. If these early manifestations of negative transference are not detected and interpreted, a number of unfortunate results may take place. For example, there may be a sudden explosion of previously ignored and accumulated negative transference with an intensity that wrecks the treatment. In some cases the negative transference may not surface in full impact until after the treatment is over, and then an apparently grateful patient suddenly becomes a bitter inimical ex-patient who may even join various antipsychiatry movements or institute a malpractice suit against the psychiatrist! Clearly if a person wishes to do psychoanalytic psychotherapy, he or she must be prepared to be exposed to powerful negative and positive emotional feelings coming from patients, often on a highly irrational basis.

*Maria:* This exposure to such powerful feelings can lead to many mistakes, retreats, and confusions in psychotherapy if therapists are either not expecting them to appear, not prepared to deal with them, or are so primarily preoccupied with their own needs and problems that they cannot perceive clearly what is going on. There is a strong all-too-human tendency in psychotherapy to deflect emerging manifestations of powerful erotic or negative transferences by various forms of interventions, such as making a joke, extra kindnesses, and so forth, resulting in a collusion to avoid these uncomfortable emotions.

*Richard:* It is solely the responsibility of the therapist not to allow this to occur. The patient needs to experience negative transference and to have a therapist who can "contain" the hostility and sadism without retaliating, being destroyed, or abandoning the patient.

*Donald:* That much is clear. What is not clear, of course, is the concept of transference neurosis that you promised to discuss today!

*Maria:* Freud's original designation of the transference neurosis was from a clinical psychoanalytic situation in which the patient developed such intense transference feelings to the therapist that everything else in his or her life became of lesser importance. The classical conception of the transference neurosis has it that the infantile feelings and conflicts of the patient are focused almost exclusively onto the analyst. The transference neurosis was thought of as an object relationship, extremely important or even temporarily the most important one, of the patient's life.

*Richard:* Unfortunately the concept of transference neurosis has run into difficulty because often, even in a properly conducted formal psychoanalysis, the classical transference neurosis simply does not appear. One sees a great many varieties of transference phenomena, but a focal, sharply defined transference neurosis cannot always be expected to take place. The reasons for this failure of transference neurosis formation are a matter of considerable debate, but it's not always just the result of poor technique. Because of this, many contemporary authorities would like to eliminate the concept, and also they wish to eliminate it because it's so difficult to define with precision.

*Donald:* Where is the best place I can read about the transference neurosis?

*Maria:* An issue of the *Journal of the American Psychoanalytic Association* (Calef 1971) is devoted almost entirely to the subject. Generally speaking, the transference neurosis revives the infantile neurosis—it is created out of frustrated demands for love arising from the abstinence in the therapeutic situation, and manifests symptoms that are dynamic, shifting, and changing. The mechanisms of regression and repetition are important in the development of the transference neurosis and, if the transference neurosis appears as it is supposed to do, the previous symptoms of the adult neurosis that the patient complained about when he or she came to therapy seem to be much improved. The patient becomes preoccupied with the transference.

*Richard:* Notice that the transference neurosis is *not* identical to and does *not* describe in a one-on-one manner the nature of the infantile relationships that have been transferred. There is a process of layering of subsequent meanings onto infantile relationships, as we discussed on the first day of our meetings, and these layers coalesce into meaningful transference patterns. This is very important to understand.

*Donald:* I take it to be correct then, as I said, that the transference and now the transference neurosis become involved in a resistance to treatment. A resistance to the resolution of the transference could appear clinically by refusal to see the determinants in it from the past or by a demand for gratification of the transference wishes. I run into this problem frequently. How do we manage that situation?

*Richard:* Of course if the therapist breaks Freud's "rule of abstinence" and provides significant deliberate gratification, further insight becomes impossible and a stalemate usually results, with an interminable therapy. The management of the transference neurosis, according to classical psychoanalysis, permits the undoing of repression and is the central issue of the treatment. The emphasis on interpretation as resolving the transference neurosis differentiates so-called classical psychoanalysis from other forms of treatment. Such interpretation permits an undoing of the transference neurosis, which, in turn, frees the patient from the nuclear infantile conflicts by allowing the adult ego to resolve them in new ways. It is the preoccupation with the transference neurosis that differentiates psychoanalysis from other forms of treatment. I think it is largely a semantic issue of whether one wishes to speak of a transference neurosis or simply an intense transference. Perhaps the transference neurosis was seen more regularly in the treatment of Freud's classical patients, whose neuroses tended to be based on an Oedipus complex; today the patients we see tend to suffer from preoedipal or borderline disorders.

*Donald:* I certainly know that a transference neurosis or intense transference may also surface in psychotherapy. It isn't necessary for a patient to come in four or five times a week and lie on the couch for this to happen, although if it's going to appear it is more likely to under the conditions of formal psychoanalysis. The actual occurrence of an intense transference can be very dramatic, and when it happens in my clinical work it's a remarkable experience for both the patient and myself. I should add that sometimes it makes me very uncomfortable indeed!

*Maria:* Actually the sharp focusing of infantile demands and powerful emotions on the therapist in a totally inappropriate manner, when both the patient and therapist are actually aware of the irrationality of this phenomenon and have observed it develop *de novo* out of the psychotherapy situation, can be the most crucial experience of psychoanalytic treatment.

*Richard:* It is also an experience that lends the greatest conviction to the power, validity, and efficacy of the psychoanalytic method. Unless one has experienced in one's own treatment the appearance of an intense transference, one's convictions about psychodynamic therapy tend to be more theoretical. Conversely, if one has received what has purported to be a thorough psychoanalytic treatment and never had the experience of an intense transference, something has gone terribly wrong in the treatment process. Often what has gone wrong is "reversible perspective," as we discussed it yesterday, for example in the training analysis or other "treatment" of mental health professionals.

On the other hand, the appearance of intense transference or a transference neurosis is not always a reason to be jubilant. It can arise in situations where the patient has a very weak ego state and poor defenses. In such situations the patient cannot actually utilize the intense transference toward the working through of intrapsychic problems. If a profound transference neurosis seems to be developing in psychotherapy, the therapist must be careful to ascertain the ego state of the patient and to determine by the use of interpretation whether the patient is actually capable of utilizing the developing intense transference. If the patient cannot utilize it, efforts should be made to break it up by decreasing the frequency of the treatment, by active interpretation and support, and so on.

*Maria:* Of course borderline patients especially can develop a highly negative or strongly eroticized transferences very early, even in once-a-week psychotherapy. If one is following Kernberg's (1975) modified Kleinian concepts of projected split-off all-bad or all-good self and object representations, early interpretation is necessary. Or, if self psychology is utilized, transferences powerfully infused with lust and aggression appearing early and suddenly in the therapy are analyzed as manifestations of the patient's profoundly disappointed expectations of empathy from the subjectively perceived analyst. Failure to resolve such disruptive transferences typically destroys the therapy.

*Donald:* Even worse than that, a transference psychosis sometimes appears in which the patient has absolutely no insight into the intense transference and denies completely that the phenomena he or she is experiencing are transference at all! Such situations as falling desperately in love with the therapist can be understood in this manner. Such falling in love refuses to yield to any kind of interpretation; the patient insists that the love is genuine and based on the marvelous qualities of the therapist, and definitely refuses to see any transference phenomena involved in it. I think this can be differentiated from the idealizing transference of self psychology, because it is an object-instinctual transference that has exploded without insight. The idealizing transference of self psychology contains a more eerie and vague form of idealizing of the therapist, and interpretations are met with rage because the patient needs such a transference and experiences the therapist's attempts to break it up by interpretation as a severely disappointing failure of empathy and understanding.

*Maria:* This leads us to the problem of the patient's wish for gratification in the transference. Quite frequently patients develop a strong wish for some kind of gratification at some point in the therapy. The patients may concentrate on that, refuse to cooperate with the treatment, and rage for many hours because they are not getting the gratification they want. The kind of gratification demanded can be of all varieties. Sometimes it's a very minor matter, such as raging by a female patient because a male therapist won't help her on with her coat. In other instances it can be major, such as demanding that the therapist go to bed with or marry the patient, give the patient advice or drugs, and so on.

*Richard:* The problem of how much gratification to give a patient in psychotherapy is a very thorny one indeed. One general principle that can be kept in mind is that the more gratification the patient is given in the transference the less uncovering will be possible, and the more difficult it will be to resolve the nuclear conflict. On the other hand, there are some situations in which the transference demands become so overwhelming that the therapy cannot go on unless something is done. When this happens repeatedly, it's often an indication that the patient cannot tolerate uncovering psychotherapy, and the therapy should be shifted to a more supportive and less frequent approach. But some therapists are so concerned about gratification of the patient that they create a cold and sterile ambiance in the treatment, which leads the patient to withdraw into an iatrogenic narcissistic neurosis.

*Maria:* There are also defensive transference reactions, a situation in which—just as the patient would be expected to arrive at a certain insight out of the material being presented—there suddenly appears instead a powerful transference reaction, most typically a negative transference.

*Donald:* Can either of you give a clinical example of this?

*Richard:* A patient who has been through an absolutely dreadful and frustrating childhood is beginning to arrive at the point where he's becoming aware of his tremendous yearnings for love and affection from one of the parents. This has come about only after a long working through of many defenses and resistances against anyone meaning anything to him, against needing anyone, even against forming a therapeutic alliance itself. At the point where one might expect the patient to show the first signs of some transference yearnings for the therapist, there appears suddenly, without any previous warning, the explosive feeling that everything the therapist says is a form of hostile criticism. If it isn't in his actual words, it is in his tone of voice. The patient absolutely cannot shake off the feeling that everything the therapist is saying is hostile and critical.

An investigation of this reaction brings the patient to the realization that his mother was a very hostile and critical person who was constantly making the patient an object of her criticism. The working through of this maternal transference defense, which came up suddenly in the middle of a session when the patient was on the verge of experiencing some positive feelings for the therapist, enabled the patient later on to begin experiencing those yearnings and permitted the future development of deeper and more powerful transference phenomena. So the sudden and sometimes dramatic appearance of strong transference manifestations at a sharp point in a psychotherapy session gives rise to the possibility that the patient is using the transference to defend against feelings, memories, or emerging insight that must be denied at the time.

*Donald:* Clearly the therapist must be vigilant and constantly aware of the appearance of transference manifestations whether they show themselves in dramatic explosions or in small subliminal ways. But can you differentiate clearly between "defensive transference reactions" and "defense transference"?

*Maria:* Some authors (Schlessinger and Robbins 1974) use the term *defense transference* as a transference that forms to defend against awareness of a deeper more important transference. They write, "It is the characterological defensive organization, evident at the onset of an analysis, which serves as a shield against a transference neurosis, and as a major coping mechanism of the ego in the face of conflict" (pp. 547–548). For example, according to Kernberg a highly idealized transference commonly develops as a defense against the awareness of a hidden negative transference. Here one form of transference is used habitually to defend the patient from the emergence of another more intense and upsetting transference into awareness, and so the defense transference serves the function of tension regulation. I suppose one might call all this *character transference* phenomena. This term as it is used in the literature is somewhat misleading and confusing, but what distinguishes this form of transference from others is that the reaction to the therapist is part of the patient's habitual, representative, and typical responses to people at large, and the transference behavior is characteristic of the patient's relationships in general.

*Richard:* It's this quality of nonspecific behavior that has led to the term *character transference*. The important point from the clinical point of view is that the patient may be reacting to the therapist with his or her habitual reactions to a *different* kind of person than the therapist actually is! This is what the therapist has to be aware of in watching for character transference phenomena. However, one should be aware that patients have some very confused notions of what the transference is supposed to be or not supposed to be in psychodynamic treatment. For example, some patients begin the treatment by asking the therapist whether they are expected to fall in love. This kind of question—"Am I supposed to fall in love with you?"—hides behind it a number of anxieties and concerns that should be dealt with in a very straightforward manner. The patient is told that he or she is expected to report whatever thoughts and feelings come to mind, but there is nothing that is *supposed* to happen. It is impossible to predict exactly what kind of transference phenomena will occur, how intense they will be, or what their focus will be. We deal with whatever arises in the therapy in a nonanxious interpretive manner. However, it *is* possible to have a general set of predictions as to the nature of the transference phenomena that will occur in any given case, and even in what sequence. This is quite helpful, for when our predictions do not come true it is an indicator that either our initial evaluation or our current clinical process is not going properly.

*Donald:* What about the so-called archaic transferences? I know these include the transference-like phenomena described in self psychology that do not involve instinctual wishes that cross the repression barrier and are rather a demand for a selfobject to fill intrapsychic deficits. I know that archaic transferences are marked in preoedipal disorders by an intense and overt demand for gratification, making me feel almost like a prisoner and forced away from an analytic analyzing attitude. If I refuse to comply, seriously disruptive rage and chaos is likely to occur. Also I suppose that the affectual instability of the transference is an important hallmark of an archaic transference and it poses extremely difficult problems for the therapist. In certain situations some gratification is clearly necessary, but always followed by interpretation.

*Maria:* Kleinian therapists characterize these archaic transferences as projective identification in the transference, marked by pressure placed on the therapist to do something, which of course represents an obstruction to understanding. Chessick (1977) warns of the danger of externalization in the archaic transference, in which therapists are subtly made to feel and even to behave like the person or introject projected onto them. The identification and handling of archaic transferences is a very specialized aspect of psychodynamic treatment and requires a willingness to work with very primitive and disruptive patients. Especially in such cases the therapist must be carefully aware of the serious danger of acting out the transference outside of the therapist's office. So all reports by the patient of interactions outside of the therapy, even dreams containing such interactions, must be closely examined for veiled allusions to the transference.

*Donald:* Early in our discussions we reviewed the work of Gill, who was especially concerned with the therapist's here-and-now behavior as profoundly influencing the transference that develops. He argued that the therapist must continuously look for the transference as manifested by allusions to it in dreams and associations, to interpret the patient's resistances to awareness of it, and finally to translate the disguised and displaced expressions of it into direct experience and discussion. The most controversial premise of Gill's (1982, 1984) view is his assumption of the centrality of the transference in all the patient's material, and his emphasis on the role of the therapist in determining the development and nature of the transference.

*Richard:* The greatest problem in the development of transference in psychoanalytic treatment occurs if the therapist misses what is going on. One of the most common causes of stalemate or failure in treatment is when psychotherapists are unable to be aware of important manifestations of transference appearing in their patients. Blum (1973) and others have tried to draw a distinction between the erotic transference described by Freud as expectable, and the extraordinary explosion of love in the transference you mentioned before, Donald, now characterized as the eroticized transference. This transference-love or eroticized transference superficially resembles in every respect the dramatic situation of falling in love. It's usually described in the literature as a female analysand falling in love with a male analyst, and presents the same intense erotic and sexual preoccupation with the analyst that one finds in ordinary states of passionately falling in love. But I have also been consulted in the opposite situation, that of the male patient falling intensely in love with a female analyst, and in situations where both patient and analyst were of the same gender.

*Maria:* Freud (1915a) was stimulated to write his classic 1915 paper by reports of the misunderstandings of psychoanalytic technique manifested in the work of analysts of his time who suggested to patients that they were *supposed* to fall in love with them, or who warned them that

they might, and also by such unfortunate situations as Jung's actual con-
summation of a love affair with his analysand Sabina Spielrein, as well
as the ongoing debate with Ferenczi about the latter's innovations with
his patients. The self psychologists argue that such eroticized transference or intense transference love really represents a disintegration product in the analysis when the patient has experienced repeated empathic
failure by the therapist. It doesn't matter whether the therapist actually
failed the patient empathically, or did something as simple as announce
a forthcoming vacation, or actually disrupted and canceled sessions; what
counts is whether the patient was chronically narcissistically wounded
in his or her perception of the analyst's lack of empathy. Transference-
love and transference-hate can in some ways be thought of as two sides
of the same coin of counterdisruption of the treatment.

*Donald:* I remember that in his 1915 paper Freud thought transference-
love was a resistance that occurred when the patient faced the lifting
of a repressed memory and he advocated explaining this to the patient.
He left unresolved the question of how one differentiates real love from
transference-love.

*Richard:* One should not forget about the countertransference contribution of the analyst to the development of intense transference-love.
The kind of countertransference I'm referring to is subtle, and should be
distinguished from the behavior of the naive untrained analyst who
pushes the patient or tries to persuade the patient to fall in love, which
is simply narcissistic acting out on the part of an insufficiently analyzed
therapist. Here I speak of the minimal signals and cues that are given to
the patient suggesting a collaborative falling in love, or even the failure
to interpret the incipient development of transference-love early enough,
as important factors in the development of this unfortunate situation.

*Donald:* Have you any suggestions on the clinical management of
intense transference-love?

*Richard:* The handling of intense transference-love or the eroticized
transference today is perhaps less restricted by the rule of abstinence on
the part of the analyst than was recommended by Freud in 1915. But
this leads to a technical question as to what constitutes an acceptable
use of countertransference and what represents pathological acting out
on the part of the therapist. Self psychologists would perhaps be more
relaxed about accepting the expressions of intense transference-love
without necessarily attempting to remove this form of idealization
by aggressive interpretation. However, intense transference-love and
especially the eroticized transference can be disruptive and destructive
to the analytic situation and it isn't really possible to let it continue for
long in its full-blown form. In fact, the destructiveness of the eroticized

transference is now clearly recognized and thought by some to hide envy and aggression.

*Maria:* On the other hand, as Schafer (1993) cleverly points out, a subtle countertransference "fanning the flames of the female analysand's desires" (p. 86) might be present from the male analyst who wishes to avoid overt manifestations of hostility and aggression, or for narcissistic reasons, or to avoid recognition of the analysand's maternal transference by heating up the heterosexual transference, or to avoid recognition that one is "dealing with an analysand who at that time is emotionally 'dead'" (p. 86).

*Richard:* The patient's intense transference-love could be viewed as blocking access to negative transference, as a desperate effort to feel something other than deadness, or as a bargain in which sexual favors are offered in exchange for the wish to be held and soothed. This latter situation is often characteristic of borderline patients (Chessick 1977).

*Donald:* Could it be that the eroticized transference or intense transference-love is an attempt on the part of the patient to ward off a catastrophic fragmentation, and a response to something coming from the analyst that is perceived by the patient as a threat to his or her psychic autonomy or, as Kohut might put it, to the sense of self? . . . Of course I know that the Kleinians view narcissism quite differently than does Kohut. For example, Kleinian analysts regard all but the most temporary states of narcissism as basically destructive. But the Kleinians also help us to understand how countertransference could produce in the analyst an unconscious inclination either to offer some form of love or to become hostile to the patient. The patient facilitates this process by trying to provoke affects in the analyst, and the analyst is the more likely to respond to the patient's provocations at those points where he or she has lost empathy with the patient.

*Maria:* Well said, Donald! You are becoming more comfortable with the Kleinian channel.

*Richard:* Intense yearnings experienced consciously as a desperate seeking for a love object, whether it be for objects in one's own real or fantasied past, or in the development of an eroticized transference, can have many deep preoedipal roots. For example, in the individual who has recently been subjected to some near-death procedure like open-heart surgery, it can represent an attempt to construct a defense against a deeper fear of catastrophe—fragmentation and annihilation. In an individual who is borderline or suffering from a sealed-over psychosis, the same kind of eroticized transference or yearning for idealized love objects or acting out of compulsive promiscuity can have a similar function. This situation can be described in at least three alternatives languages: traditional Freudian language, Kleinian language, or the language of self psychology. The problem we face is that these various descriptions are incompatible with each other and the differences between them are unresolvable. What we lack is a generally accepted method of demonstrating the validity or invalidity of the contentions at the basis of each of these competing theories. The only recourse that seems appropriate at this time is to remain uncommitted to any of them, become familiar with all of them, and develop the capacity to describe the phenomena in several different languages. I believe that a narcissistic investment in any one of these theoretical positions to the exclusion of all others is an additional form of countertransference and actually serves to restrict and impair our understanding of our patients and ourselves.

*Maria:* Clearly the eroticized transference may appear in the language of love and tenderness but because it's rooted in infantile psychopathology it should *not* be confused with mature love relationships. Blum (1994) writes, "What is unique about psychoanalytic treatment, and what differentiates the psychoanalytic relationship from all other relationships, is that the relationship itself is analyzed and the patient's childhood is reconstructed." Blum continues, "the unconscious infantile transference fantasies and the disguised traumatic experiences that the patient attempts to repeat in the transference are uncovered and interpreted . . . It is interpretation and insight, particularly into the oedipal and preoedipal roots of erotized transference and their relation to regression and resistance, that demystify the patient's experience" (p. 634).

*Donald:* What about the clinical management of patients who are suffering from an eroticized transference? Or of patients who come cooperatively and regularly to the treatment for years but nothing really happens. In either of these situations there has to be a developing frustration on the part of both the patient and the therapist.

*Maria:* From the point of self psychology Basch (1992) suggests that the patient's developmental selfobject needs are not being accurately identified or properly met. The patient stays in therapy in the hope of the required experience taking place because the therapist potentially represents a needed selfobject experience. Or, as Basch puts it, "The patient, in spite of his or her lack of improvement, will keep coming to the sessions, because to some extent the amorphous relationship with the therapist is satisfying an unidentified selfobject need" (p. 94). So what keeps the patient coming in during these long periods of frustrating lack of progress is either the patient's hope of having a need met or some amorphous selfobject need that is *being* met, or both.

*Donald:* Can you be more specific about such situations?

*Maria:* Basch, in contrast to Kohut, claims there is hierarchy of self-object needs. He states that *kinship* (a term he prefers to Kohut's *twinship* or *alter ego*) needs must be met first, which then allows idealization of the therapist. This in turn can permit the satisfaction of mirroring selfobject needs. He prefers the term *validation* to Kohut's term *mirroring*. Appreciation and acceptance meets kinship needs and allows the person to feel less alienated. Idealization strengthens the person through reassurance that he or she can draw on the wisdom and power of others. Affect attunement or even recognizing a person's needs and giving help meets validating needs.

He emphasizes the clinical evaluation of the patient's capacity to meet kinship (twinship), idealization, and validation (mirroring) selfobject needs. He cleverly suggests that it is the mark of borderline patients to be unable to meet the selfobject needs for kinship. So they thrash about, trying vainly to establish a soothing selfobject transference but always ending up by projective identification with disappointment, fear, rage and impulsivity. Basch insists that developmental problems must be resolved before patients can relinquish their symptoms, and he rests his entire approach on Stern's (1985) research establishing a developmental line for the formation of the sense of self. This developmental line involves the emergent, core, subjective, verbal, and narrative sense of self.

*Donald:* I'm beginning to get a headache. How does one evaluate all these in clinical work?

*Richard:* In evaluating the patient's emergent sense of self, Basch suggests that we observe their orientation to their situation or see how dilapidated or disorganized they are at the time. The strength of the core sense of self is made manifest by investigating the patient's coping strategies and decision making. The subjective sense of self, which Stern says requires affect attunement, can be evaluated on the basis of the patient's complaints of feeling alone and not understood, or their sense of lack of attachment and having no insertion into an empathic matrix. The verbal or symbolic or private sense of self is demonstrated by the capacity to think clearly and objectify events. The narrative sense of self is evaluated by whether or not the patient can articulately describe his or her difficulties to the therapist. Basch then aims his therapeutic strategy at the level of the first developmental area of weakness in the sense of self. This is very important.

*Donald:* I get it! For example, a patient who has a weakness in the core sense self who needs help in coping strategies will *not* feel an empathic response from the therapist when the therapist attempts to convey affect attunement. To respond to affect attunement such a patient is in need of the subjective sense of self, which cannot develop until the core sense of self begins to be established. It's the task of the therapist to focus the treatment on which aspect of the sense of self requires reparative selfobject experiences and to provide these for the patient. Therefore a great deal of actual teaching and affectual interaction with the patient goes on in this form of psychotherapy.

*Richard:* The greatest value of Basch's approach is when it is applied to stalemated situations, which often are the result of the patient's selfobject needs not being met at the level where the patient's sense of self has become developmentally arrested. This gives us a strategy to evaluate stalemated psychotherapies and impasses in psychoanalysis in an efficient and effective manner. Thus, for example, our interpretations may be correct in a given treatment, but they may be beside the point because the treatment is not aimed at the developmental level where the patient is at. Basch maintains that if this is corrected, and the patient receives an appropriate selfobject experience at the level where the sense of self has become developmentally arrested, dramatic changes will occur in the treatment and the inherent capacity for the growth of the sense of self will take over. Furthermore, in adult patients all the aspects of the sense of self will be strengthened if the proper level of developmental weakness is addressed in the treatment. This enables us to understand why certain short-term strategies can bring about surprising improvement. Validation that the selfobject needs are being properly met is provided by the patient making better decisions and manifesting improved behavior, higher competence, and increased self-esteem.

*Maria:* This is helpful, but it brings us back to the work of Gill, mentioned earlier today. In his final work, Gill (1994) insists that the patient and therapist continuously shape each other. We have discussed this before. He objects to self psychology because he claims it goes to an extreme in which the archaic selfobject is given no independent existence, "being only what the subject makes of it to realize its own purposes" (p. 16). So the archaic selfobject is given no attributes of its own. Gill would argue that even the archaic selfobject can shape the subject. Can you clarify once more Gill's differentiation between psychoanalysis and psychotherapy?

*Richard:* For Gill the decisive criterion of psychoanalysis is that the transference—which he defines as "the patient's experience of the interaction"—is "analyzed as much as is possible" (p. 62). In psychotherapy the transference is more or less deliberately unanalyzed, writes Gill. He quickly adds that the transference is not based solely on the immediate interaction but of course is also determined by what both participants bring to the interaction. So, "If the intent is to analyze the interaction as much as possible, the situation is a psychoanalytic one; if it is not, the situation is a psychotherapeutic one" (p. 63).

*Donald:* It follows from this that the frequency of the sessions, the use of the couch, and so forth, are not decisive factors in defining what is or is not psychoanalysis. The psychoanalyst as well as the psychotherapist is allowed a greater degree of spontaneity providing the interaction is continuously analyzed if the situation is to be called a psychoanalysis.

*Richard:* As Gill describes it, the so-called analytic conversation begins when the patient associates freely and is then interrupted by the analyst's interventions. To quote Gill:

> His principal concern in listening to the associations following an interpretation should thus be to evaluate them, that is, to see whether the content of his interpretation seems confirmed or disconfirmed by, or even irrelevant to, the patient's concerns; he must likewise be attentive to the interpersonal impact of the interpretation. It is this close attention to the patient's response to his interventions that makes a genuine conversation or dialogue out of the analytic situation rather than a series of alternating monologues, quite apart from who talks how much. [1994, p. 96]

*Donald:* Are there any clinical rules that answer the obvious and crucial question that arises from Gill's view, regarding how the analyst should behave?

*Richard:* Gill writes, and I agree, that one cannot prescribe the same attitude for everyone because of differences in temperament and personalities among analysts, and clearly analysts will behave differently with different patients. Neither Gill nor I advocate Ferenczi-style mutual analysis, but he suggests (and I agree) that the analyst should "permit a degree of spontaneity, with the idea that he will regularly, from time to time, stand back and assess the transference-countertransference interaction" (p. 116). There is a certain danger to this "spontaneity" on the part of the analyst because it is advocated on the assumption that the psychoanalytic readers of Gill's book have achieved substantial self-analysis and a thorough personal psychoanalysis.

*Donald:* Well, my head is spinning. On this day we seem to have brought up more unresolvable issues than on any previous day of our discussions. Also, I would like to see some applications of these various concepts to our clinical work.

*Maria:* Yes, Richard, what do you actually do when confronted with these archaic transferences, eroticized transferences, stalemated situations, and intense transference reactions?

*Richard:* Perhaps the best demonstration of these in an extreme form comes from the study of the borderline patient—unfortunately, Donald, another highly controversial area. Let's concentrate on the borderline patient tomorrow. Since I've introduced so many controversial and un-resolved issues today resulting in some confusion in your minds, please let me absolve my guilt by inviting you both to be my guests for dinner tonight.

*Maria and Donald:* With pleasure!

# 9

## The Ninth Day: Borderline States

*Donald:* I feel so angry this morning! On my way here some impulsive fool changed lanes without warning and dented my new Porsche. When we pulled over to look at the damage she jumped out of the car and started screaming at me as if it were my fault; surely a nasty borderline personality disorder!

*Richard:* Not every person who is hot-tempered and angry is a borderline patient. Not every patient who annoys the therapist by a variety of techniques including gross raging and even damage to his furniture by "accident" is a borderline patient. Not every patient we dislike is a borderline patient. This label has tended to be used in a pejorative sense in the literature because at least one category of borderline patients, those usually who require hospitalization, produce tremendous problems on the ward for the personnel and for other patients. The literature is filled with description of how they cause "splitting" among the staff and all sorts of dissension and difficulties. However, there is a spectrum of borderline patients, and at the other end are those who can be successfully treated as outpatients. Although borderline patients are always very difficult treatment cases, and often must have preliminary psychotherapy before they're ready for psychoanalysis, they are treatable if the therapist is willing to put up with disruptive chaos, confusion, and rage. At the same time they can be quite loyal and work very hard in their psychoanalytic treatment.

*Donald:* Still, the profound volatility and anger of these patients probably have a constitutional and genetic basis as well as a genesis in environmental and developmental factors. There are even studies (Akiskal 1981, Gunderson and Elliott 1985, McGlashan 1983, Stone 1990) in which an attempt is made to link the so-called borderline personality disorder to other disorders such as alcoholism or the affective disorders that have a more generally accepted genetic basis. Of course I didn't mean what I said about the woman driver seriously, but how would you make the diagnosis?

*Maria:* Either the tremendous rage of these patients or their extraordinary capacity for seductiveness produces what Kernberg (1975) has labeled a global countertransference that he considers a diagnostic indicator of the condition. Such patients frequently insist there should be no limits to their entitlement and behavior, often leading to a number of self-defeating characteristics that get the patient in trouble. There is an obvious overlap with the narcissistic personality disorders, but reality testing is more impaired.

*Richard:* Borderline patients provoke hatred and exhaust the endurance of the therapist in order to substantiate their projections, assaulting especially the narcissism and self-esteem of the therapist. Typical therapist defenses against such global countertransferences are (1) repression, in which the therapist becomes bored, restless, or inattentive; (2) a turning against the self in which the therapist feels low self-esteem and even "sick"; (3) a reaction formation of overconcern, or "love" and fantasies of rescuing the patient; (4) projection, which manifests itself by a dread that the patients will commit suicide, act out, or leave treatment; and (5) distortion of the therapist's reality-testing to validate countertransference hatred, in which the patient is devalued as hopeless or dangerous. In extreme cases therapists may even fear loss of control of their aggression toward the patient. All of this may result in the development and acting out of a sadomasochistic relationship with the patient or, alternatively, getting involved in erotic interchanges or gross sexual acting out with the patient as we have seen on previous days. The result is the destruction of the treatment and serious consequences for both parties. It happens all too often, especially when the therapist is not properly trained.

*Maria:* As I understand it, Brenner (1982) conceptualizes all symptoms and behavior as a compromise formed by the ego among the demands of the id, the superego, and reality. So change of symptoms, change of behavior, so-called structural improvement, would all represent a change in the compromise formations produced by the ego. The problem with borderline patients is that narcissistic rage can be so overwhelming that a critical value is crossed: previous compromise formations such as their obsessional rituals or masochism are suddenly overshadowed by massive projection and projective identification. This produces an emergency and can break up the treatment if the ego's capacity to respond to interpretations is lost. I am sure we would all agree that this poses a common serious problem with borderline outpatients and constitutes an ever-present danger in their psychotherapy, no matter how long the treatment has been going on and how confident the therapist might be that he or she has formed a good working alliance with the patient.

*Donald:* What is a borderline patient? What are the clinical signs and symptoms that you look for in labeling a patient with that diagnosis?

*Richard:* Signals to watch for at the start of the therapy are a sense of entitlement, magical expectations or thinking, an impaired differentiation between fantasy and reality, episodes of anger and suspicion with no sense of humor, and fears of rejection or hints of paranoia. There are no pathognomonic symptoms of borderline patients, and there's no consensus on their characteristic metapsychology, dynamics, or precise stage of failure in development. It is the quality of the therapist's ongoing experiences with the patient that is key to the diagnosis, which introduces an unavoidable controversy about establishing the diagnosis in cases where *DSM-IV* criteria are not immediately apparent.

*Maria:* Do you feel that borderline patients are arrested at a specific point or stage in their development?

*Richard:* No, it isn't necessary to insist on that. The borderline condition arises as a consequence of the first three years of a disastrous and disappointing ambiance in the mother–child interaction perhaps combined with genetic or constitutional factors, which is then complicated by the inevitable failure of an appropriate solution to the Oedipus complex.

*Donald:* What about the role of the father?

*Maria:* This is very important, because many borderline patients I believe have been saved from a more overt psychosis by their interaction with their father in the presence of a cold, unresponsive mother.

*Richard:* I agree. It is not necessary in practical clinical work to have recourse to a highly complex developmental theory of object relations in dealing with the day-to-day treatment of these patients, although the temperament and cognitive functioning of some therapists may require such an elaborate theoretical structure to enhance their own sense of understanding of the patient. I question the value of speculations based on adult patient material as to what kind of psychodynamic processes and images occur in the mind of the 1- or 2-year-old child.

*Maria:* So then you do not agree that there is a specific metapsychological entity described by Kernberg (1975) as a "borderline personality organization"?

*Richard:* I do not agree with Dr. Kernberg. It is a mistake not to take into consideration that adult patients have had to undergo all developmental phases by the time they come into treatment; certainly failures of the later phases because of a faulty foundation or structure are also going to affect the symptomatology and behavior of the patient. I am not convinced there will be much further theoretical understanding of the borderline patient, because I am not convinced that it constitutes an independent autonomous entity; the value of the concept lies in the clinical descriptive diagnosis with the implications of poor ego functioning and consequent special requirements for a proper therapeutic approach.

*Donald:* Well, Richard, then you do agree that this is a clinical diagnosis and describes a confusing patient who is filled with rage!

*Richard:* It is very misleading to label as borderline any patient one does not understand. For example, a patient reacting with rage to a gross empathic failure on the part of the therapist is showing neither a transference nor a borderline personality organization, but rather is responding appropriately to deep disappointment. Borderline patients especially react with angry disruption or suicidal behavior to therapies that they intuitively recognize as inappropriate to their intense personal suffering, such as certain types of paternalistic counseling, or so-called touching-and-feeling treatments; these reactions are not simply manifestations of psychopathology but rather represent an increase in desperation and disappointment in yet another encounter with lack of empathy and a misunderstanding of the patient's basic needs by a parental figure.

*Donald:* Then how do you differentiate the borderline patient from other personality disorders?

*Maria:* I think there is a definitive diagnostic difference between the borderline patient and some character disorders. In the latter, there is one set of well-known characterologic features that consistently dominates the clinical picture in a relatively rigid and all-pervasive way; so we have the obsessive-compulsive personality disorder, the narcissistic personality disorder, the histrionic personality disorder, and so forth. But in the borderline patient any variety of neurotic or quasi-psychotic, psychosomatic, or sociopathic symptoms, in any combination or degree of severity, may be part of the initial presenting complaint. Either a bizarre combination of such symptoms may cut across the standard nosology, or the relative preponderance of any symptom group is frequently changing or shifting. The borderline may present a very chaotic or stormy series of relationships with a variety of people, or a bland and superficial but relatively stable set of relationships. Vagueness of complaint or even an amazingly smooth or occasionally socially successful personality may be encountered, but careful investigation reveals a poverty of genuine emotional relationships sometimes well hidden behind even an attractive and personable social facade.

*Donald:* How do you distinguish between the borderline personality disorder and disorders on the schizoid spectrum such as schizophrenia or the schizotypal personality disorder?

*Maria:* The capacity for reality testing and ability to function in work and social situations are not as catastrophically impaired in borderline patients as in schizophrenics, although the degree of functioning may vary from time to time and may be quite poor. On the whole, borderline patients are able to maintain themselves, sometimes raise families, and otherwise fit more or less into society. Although their functioning is more impaired than narcissistic personalities, they do not present as isolated drifters, chronic hospital or long-term prison cases, totally antisocial personalities, or chronic addicts.

*Richard:* They have, however, often tried everything and may present a variety of sexual deviations, but they are not functionally paralyzed by these or by their various symptoms or anxieties for very long periods of time. Borderline patients suffer from an unpleasant but relatively stable and enduring condition. They may experience what appear to be transient psychotic episodes either for no apparent reason or as a result of stress, alcohol, drugs, improper psychotherapy, and so on, but they do not remain psychotic for long. Usually, they spontaneously snap out of these episodes and often learn what will enable them to do so by administering a self-remedy, which sometimes consists of dangerous acting out.

*Donald:* I'm aware already from my clinical experience that one is usually compelled to be more active in the psychotherapy of borderline patients than in the treatment of many other conditions. I know that one must often actively inquire what is going on in the patient's life outside of therapy hours. I realize that the therapist being interested in the patient's real everyday life can be viewed as a form of gratification, but it also constitutes a form of limit setting. Obviously the therapist must have a great deal of flexibility to work with borderline patients and must learn to suit the treatment to the patient, not the patient to the treatment.

*Richard:* Careful listening often tells us what the patient needs in the way of treatment and what the patient can and cannot tolerate. If we follow this, we will have as smooth and workable a relationship as possible and also demonstrate that we have some empathy with the patient's fears and anxieties. It is extremely important that the structure of the treatment be flexible and reasonable, and above all it has to make sense to the patient. If borderline patients can even vaguely understand the reason for the structure and the limitations, they may still fight against a framework of the treatment but will not be basically impeded by it.

Such patients do very badly if structure is simply imposed on them by fiat without discussion and if the therapist is unwilling to negotiate.

*Maria:* Problems inevitably come up over such issues as fees, frequency of sessions, limits on telephone calls to the therapist, charging for missed hours, changes of appointment time, and so forth, that often result in narcissistic rage explosions and disruption of therapy, creating considerable stress for the therapist. Therapists who are puritanical, anxious about possible malpractice litigation, extremely conventional, or prone to sermonize about ethics and sexuality do poorly with borderline patients.

*Donald:* There are times when it is inhumane not to give a patient medication for various conditions such as extreme anxiety or insomnia, and it seems to me that it can be a manifestation of countertransference to withhold medication in emergency situations as well as to prescribe indiscriminately. If one is reasonable and very careful, there is certainly a place for psychopharmacologic agents in the treatment of borderline patients—although for the majority of such patients it isn't necessary to write prescriptions except on rare occasions. When prescriptions have to be written they should be marked "Not refillable," and only a small number of pills or capsules should be given to the patient at a time, so each time a patient runs out it forces a new discussion of the medication.

*Maria:* We seem to be in agreement on the relatively commonsense measures in the treatment of borderline patients. We hope that dangerous acting out becomes limited as a function of the growing working alliance, in which the patient becomes increasingly interested in working on and understanding his or her own problems rather than in the primary-process gratification of impulses. At times, especially early in treatment, sharp limitations may have to be demanded by the therapist, always presented as being in the best interest of preserving the patient's life and enabling the therapy to proceed.

*Donald:* Of course. A person behaving in a wild or self-destructive fashion cannot work out his or her problems and runs a serious risk of accident, death, or imprisonment, which make the therapy impossible. It's our task as physicians during the entire therapy to demand a limitation on any behavior of the patient that is future-foreclosing for either the patient's career or life or therapy. This limitation comes first and nothing else should be discussed in the therapy until it is observed. If the patient refuses to limit such activities, no therapy can take place. So the ultimate test of whether a patient is really motivated for psychotherapy rests on a willingness to limit self-destructive behavior. If it continues, the patient must be hospitalized and vital limits set by the hospital milieu.

Winnicott (1958) and Chessick (1977, 1990) have emphasized providing an experience or an atmosphere for the borderline patient sometimes depicted as "good-enough holding." What measures are required from the therapist to provide this?

*Richard:* Because these precepts are so often violated, it is perhaps worth reviewing them, although most of them simply require common sense. The therapist should consistently and frequently be at the service of the patient, at a time arranged to suit mutual convenience, and should be there reliably and on time. During the session the therapist must keep awake and be professionally preoccupied with the patient and with nothing else such as telephone calls, note-taking, tape recorders, and so forth. I think it's a bad idea to tape-record sessions and also to take notes during any patient's session, regardless of the diagnosis. If one is being supervised, one should allow time at the end of each session to write up process notes before one starts with the next patient.

There needs to be a sincere and dedicated attempt to get in touch with the patient's psychodynamic processes, to understand the material presented and where the patient is at, and eventually to communicate this understanding by properly timed and formulated interpretations. A nonanxious approach of objective observation and scientific study with a concomitant sense of physicianly vocation is the obvious attitude required from the therapist. Therapeutic work must be done in a room that is quiet and not liable to sudden unpredictable sounds and yet not dead quiet; there must be proper lighting in the room, not a light staring in the face and not a variable light.

*Maria:* The therapist must keep out of the relationship both moral judgment and any introduction of details of the therapist's personal life and ideas. The therapist must avoid temper tantrums, compulsive falling in love, and so on, and in general be neither hostile and retaliatory nor exploitative toward the patient. The therapist must maintain a consistent, clear distinction between fact and fantasy, so that the therapist is not hurt or offended by a patient's aggressive dream or fantasy.

*Donald:* I suppose it is important also that both the therapist and the patient consistently survive their interaction! Assuming that the therapist has performed a "good-enough holding" function, which is certainly difficult with borderline patients and is largely, I suppose, a consequence of the therapist's own successful personal psychoanalysis, what else is there specific to the psychoanalytic psychotherapy of the borderline patient?

*Richard:* From the beginning of the therapy to the end, I focus on the development of the patient's autonomous ego function, starting with the simple, clear tasks of dealing with the reality at hand. Whenever possible I always take an uncovering stance rather than an authoritative counseling or advising stance.

*Maria:* Taking an authoritative or counseling stance invites the patient to trap us and frustrate us by following our advice and yet somehow ending up making a greater mess than ever before.

*Richard:* A substantial period of time is usually required for the patient's ego capacity for adaptation to daily life to improve to the point where there is time in the therapy to begin to look in detail at the patient's past. This length of time varies from case to case and is sometimes hastened by pointing out to the borderline patient that the sooner he or she is able to deal with some of these reality situations, the sooner we'll be able to go deeper in understanding the developmental aspects of what has happened. Sometimes this supplies motivation for better and better ego functioning.

*Donald:* We have said a lot about the transference earlier in our discussions. What about the transference in borderline patients?

*Richard:* During this long time of preparation for in-depth exploration, we often observe the development of certain characteristic archaic transferences in the borderline patient. The first type constitutes the narcissistic transferences depicted by Kohut (1971, 1977) in his description of the narcissistic personality disorder. That is to say, borderline patients who shade over into narcissistic personality disorders at the healthier end of the spectrum often show typical mirror or idealizing transferences. Another characteristic type of transference that develops is the transitional object transference described by Modell (1968, 1975), in which the patient clings to the therapist or therapy as a kind of magical protection and security against the hardships of the external world.

*Maria:* An important aspect of the transference of borderline patients is the intensity of their annihilation anxiety and the primitive defenses of magical thinking, denial, and narcissistic omnipotence used against it. The therapist is experienced as a selfobject perceived somewhat vaguely outside of the self—the therapist's qualities are distorted by fantasies arising from the patient, and he or she is assigned a real role in the life of the patient. Borderline patients will put the therapist in this role no matter what the therapist says or does and whether he or she likes it or not.

*Richard:* A third group of transferences is described by Kernberg (1975); these appear early and are often disruptive. They are marked by extreme affect, usually negative, but sometimes by highly eroticized positions. Kernberg insists, and I agree, that such transferences must be resolved by interpretation and not allowed to continue unabated.

*Donald:* But what kind of interpretation do you choose in these situations?

*Richard:* Kernberg uses interpretations based on his developmental theory of object relations. I use a technique less bound to that theory. It consists at first of helping the patient again and again—as tactfully and calmly as possible—to examine phenomenologically the commonsense reality of the therapeutic situation, pointing out the discrepancy between the kinds of affect or even the kinds of cognitive distortions the patient is experiencing, and the *reality* of the therapy and the relationship. The better the working alliance, the easier this is to do; thus early in the therapy it is most difficult and potentially disruptive.

*Donald:* Gedo (1977) pointed out how difficult it is to decide on an appropriate analytic response to the patient's archaic transferences, and this has been my experience also. The wrong response usually leads to patient humiliation and outrage. And of course the patient, out of the repetition compulsion, needs to re-create the situation of disappointment and to justify complaints and misbehavior. Just how much the obnoxious borderline can affect the therapist is demonstrated from the clinical material of Nadelson (1977).

*Maria:* As I have learned from supervision with Richard, a substantial and important portion of intensive psychotherapy with borderline patients, once a working alliance has been formed, consists of the meticulous exploration of the patient's current ways of relating to people and dealing with problems, and gradually discovering from this exploration how these adaptations formed in response to the disaster of the patient's childhood and the intrapsychic problem of overwhelming rage. Change in adaptive techniques with subsequent improvement in their lives is consequent on borderline patients examining the nature of their initial and presenting adaptive techniques, and how these came to be. Often borderlines try out new adaptive techniques in the psychotherapy first, since it's a protected situation, and then successfully apply them outside the treatment.

*Donald:* What can you predict about the outcome of psychotherapy in borderline patients?

*Richard:* It's usually not possible to predict which borderline patients can get more out of the psychotherapy than simple pacification and unification. I believe that every patient should be given a chance at psychoanalysis if it seems at all feasible, or a modified form of psychoanalysis or intensive psychotherapy if it does not. My experience is that many of these patients, some even seen three or four times a week and using the couch, can—*if* the therapist shows forbearance and does not get sucked into the dramatics or develop a major, interfering counter-transference—eventually form transferences that are analyzable (see Chessick 1971, 1972, 1977).

*Maria:* The limiting factors are how much the patient is acting out and keeping himself or herself involved in immediate current chaos, and whether the patient is willing to come consistently to the sessions and cooperate with the treatment. So the patients really tell us whether or not they are suitable for a psychoanalytic form of treatment, and what modifications will have to be introduced.

*Donald:* Can you tell us from your clinical experience some of the pitfalls in dealing with borderline patients?

*Richard:* The first danger in dealing with the archaic transferences of these patients is the danger of the therapist's panic. Flamboyant acting out often stirs up countertransference anxiety and hatred, manifested by fears of patient suicide or malpractice litigation. It looks as if the patient is exploding and unless the therapist has a dynamic grasp of what is going on, he or she can be stampeded into doing something radical or even getting rid of the patient. I have treated a number of borderline patients referred by the therapist in desperation because this happened.

*Maria:* Another pitfall is therapist impatience. The therapist must be willing to sit sometimes for years with a borderline patient while he or she gradually catalyzes the rebuilding of ego structure. Many therapists simply do not want to do this, as it is stressful, tedious, painstaking work that can be ungratifying for long periods of time. Borderline patients tend to set up in external reality the kinds of situations they need to have occurring. Sometimes they are quite expert at this, and the therapist gets sucked into playing various kinds of roles, depending on the projection assigned to the therapist. This leads to serious chronic counter-transference problems.

*Richard:* When the raging begins it is usually impossible to argue a borderline patient out of his or her accusations. If on careful objective assessment it turns out that the accusations are correct, then the therapist needs to self-correct and sometimes apologize. If the accusations are based on distortions or projection, the proper approach to this is a patient, calm, nonanxious and consistently nonretaliatory stance, with eventual interpretation of what is happening. It is this consistent stance that provides the basic ambience of the treatment. Any disruption of it vitiates the subliminal soothing that is always going on in a well-conducted treatment of a borderline patient. No matter how we may wish to get away from this in our theoretical conceptions, the ambience or subliminal soothing the therapist provides, coming from consistency, reliability, and integrity—the ambience of the therapist's office, the therapist's personality, the deep inner attitude toward patients that cannot be faked—these provide the basic motor that permits the psychotherapy of the borderline to go forward.

*Donald:* But sometimes the rage of borderline patients is stirred up directly by their need for omnipotent control of everything, and sometimes it is a secondary phenomenon to paranoid projection or an intense transference. So in a sense these patients are correct when they predict that all human relationships will end up badly for them, with disappointment and dislike coming from everyone around them. They respond selectively to the negative aspects of significant people and develop a dossier based on selected negative perceptions for expecting attack from all sides, which then justifies for them a preemptive strike.

*Maria:* Their chronic calculated attacks on the therapist's inevitable defects, if not interpreted, can easily lead to countertransference acting out on the part of the therapist, even to the point of directly or indirectly getting rid of the patient. This is quickly taken as proof or confirmation by the patient of his or her expectation of apparently unprovoked betrayal and abandonment.

*Richard:* You are both correct. Psychotherapists of borderline patients painfully experience the intensity of the patient's effort to manipulate them into validating the patient's projections. The therapist feels the inner conflict as he or she struggles against this manipulation. The most benign therapist approaching a borderline patient in a raging archaic transference finds himself or herself transformed into a horrible monster very quickly by the patient's selective perception, and unless the therapist is aware of this danger the tendency is either to retaliate or to irritably and defensively challenge the patient's extremely unflattering portrayal. This sudden transformation of the therapist into a horrible monster can occur at any time in the treatment, even when there seemed to be a good working alliance. It often leads to therapist discouragement and burnout, with a lingering sense of depression and injured self-esteem.

*Donald:* How does one as a consultant assess these situations, where the patient is raging and the therapist is struggling against his or her countertransference?

*Richard:* The clinical phenomena must be studied to see what the therapist is actually doing with the patient regardless of the theoretical model the therapist professes to follow. For example, Kohut's technique in which the idealization of the therapist is permitted over a long period of time so that the full transference involving the search for the idealized parent imago is permitted to develop, may easily be used by an untrained or unanalyzed therapist as an excuse to permit a flattering kind of worship and massage for the therapist's own narcissism. Conversely, the technique of Kernberg, in which more confrontation occurs, can be used by the therapist to act out hostility and aggressiveness, and to produce chaos or even a sort of counterprojective identification.

*Maria:* I have learned from supervision with Richard that meticulous attention to the phenomenological details of the interaction is the best starting point in dealing with patients who are subject to explosions of rage in the treatment. What is important is not the therapist's minor empathic failures per se, but the way in which such failures are experienced by the patient. The patient may use these minor empathic failures to relive a dreadful interpersonal experience in a protective effort to further the need for distancing in interpersonal relationships. What we are listening for in the psychotherapy is how the patient is experiencing the interaction with the therapist and in what context these experiences are being placed within the patient's preexisting patterns. It is only after we have been able to establish this information with the patient that we can begin asking why these experiences are placed in a particular context.

*Donald:* In our discussions on previous days you mentioned certain common central or core fantasies that emerge in the psychoanalytic treatment of various patients. What are the most common fantasies that emerge from the unconscious of the borderline patient?

*Richard:* These are not oedipal fantasies but narcissistic fantasies and fantasies of rage and of world- and self-destruction, which cover a deep fear of penetration and annihilation. The acting out of conscious derivatives of such rage and of world- and self-destruction fantasies endangers the patients' very lives. The acting out of disavowed narcissistic fantasies often renders them poorly adapted and causes great difficulties in their interpersonal relationships.

At the deepest point of the treatment these core narcissistic and destructive fantasies emerge and are worked through, not by giving the patient a metapsychological explanation but by allowing such fantasies to emerge into the light, studying their genesis, and showing the patient how the acting out of such fantasies interferes with aims and goals in life.

*Maria:* The borderline disorder is similar to the narcissistic disorder in that narcissistic transferences and fantasies often appear, but is different from the narcissistic personality disorder in that the intensity of the raging, fear, mistrust, and annihilation fears and fantasies is much greater.

*Donald:* I suppose there is no agreement in the literature about whether we are dealing here with symptomatology based on developmental deficits or conflicts. For example, Arlow (1991b) and his group would argue that theories of pathogenesis related to specific preoedipal phases are quite speculative, cannot be validated, and are essentially doctrinaire. They also object to preoedipal models that emphasize failure of adequate parenting and structural defects rather than conflict.

*Richard:* Borderline patients seem to present a combination of structural defects and conflicts. The conflict areas are of course more amenable to an eventual psychoanalytic approach, but the structural defects sometimes have to be dealt with by techniques "beyond interpretation" that Gedo (1979) advocates. We have mentioned these techniques before, as well as Gedo's argument that failure to help borderline patients with structural defects by deliberate after-education simply represents another failure of parental empathy.

*Donald:* But how do you know you are not making an error in trying to correct a structural defect that is actually due to conflicts and represents a compromise formation by the ego?

*Maria:* Of course the attempt to do deliberate after-education is a parameter in the psychoanalytic treatment of borderline patients and should not be undertaken unless the therapist is convinced that the defect exists and is not an apparent defect as the consequence of a conflict. This is a clinical judgment that is often quite difficult to make.

*Richard:* If one must err, in my experience it is best to err on the side of mistaking a defect for a conflict-related problem, because in due time this error can be corrected. Approaching a conflict-related problem as a defect by direct after-education produces a therapist–patient collusion that tends to drive the conflict out of sight and make it no longer amenable to the uncovering process. A therapist should be very cautious in offering any patient after-education, for this is a common manifestation of countertransference acting out when the therapist's narcissistic equilibrium is wounded because the patient is not responding to analytically based interpretations.

*Donald:* Just what is it that goes on in the day-to-day clinical process of the psychotherapy of a borderline patient?

*Richard:* Stress must be placed on empathic attunement to the patient, staying with the patient through the many vicissitudes of long-term treatment. The patient makes developmental use of the long-term treatment, reliving certain phases of development in the transference. Acquisition of internalized controls may need to occur in this way before the patient is even ready to utilize interpretations. The extreme difficulties in convincing insurance companies and other third parties to support the long-term psychotherapy of the borderline patient remains one of the most serious practical problems in the treatment of such patients. It's a source of tremendous frustration for dedicated psychoanalytic psychotherapists and it has reached scandalous proportions in our society.

*Maria:* As with schizophrenic patients in psychotherapy, Fromm-Reichmann (1950) was correct when she said that the patient needs an experience, not an explanation. Therefore I do *not* think that interpretation in the early phases of treatment of the borderline patient is as important as do those authors who feel an imperative to interpret projections in the transference at once, and to also interpret idealization as a defense against rage. I think most of the early phase of treatment, besides allowing the self-cohering effect of the holding environment to take over, should be devoted to the identification of conflicts and a minute study of the day-to-day production and disappearance of rages, a phenomenological investigation along with the patient's experience that these rages can be tolerated by the therapist and do not bring retaliation or separation. Focus is on the crucial borderline problem, the patient's inability to work fruitfully with another person in a close personal relationship with another individual.

*Richard:* As the patient in a holding environment slowly builds tension-reduction capacities through internalization, the intensive psychotherapy or the psychoanalysis begins more and more to resemble a classical treatment, the transferences become less archaic, and the patient is more ready and more amenable to proper interpretation and genetic reconstruction. I fear that early interpretations and genetic reconstructions strike the highly tense and upset patient, who is struggling desperately with impulse control, as an unempathic lack of understanding of where the patient is at, and generate a rage on that basis alone. Such early interpretations are also sometimes experienced by the patient as an assault and are reacted to very defensively and angrily. The danger is to then subsequently interpret that rage as due to the projection of an "all-bad" object representation.

*Donald:* Am I to assume then that you're in agreement with the approach to the borderline patient of Abend and colleagues (1983)?

*Richard:* Yes, but I disagree with their statement that no special techniques or confrontations "need be recommended for the analysis of borderline patients" (p. 200). These authors admit their cases represent a special group of analyzable borderline patients "although analyzable with difficulty" (p. 200). I think the patient, by his or her presentation in the office, informs us as to whether special techniques and confrontations will be necessary. The fact that they are does not mean per se that the patient is not analyzable, it just means that a preanalytic period of help with tension reduction is required.

*Donald:* Are there any absolute contraindications to analyzability?

*Richard:* If regression in the transference leads to an archaic helplessness or danger of utter fragmentation, especially if there is no family support, the patient cannot be analyzed. If the patient cannot endure the humiliation of facing his or her actual limitations on the basis of a continuing disavowed archaic grandiosity, no psychoanalytic method can succeed.

*Maria:* I take it this ignores the traditional *DSM-IV* diagnosis and the borderline concept. That is, one cannot say on the basis of the severity of the presenting pathology whether the patient is or is not treatable by psychoanalytic psychotherapy or analysis. To make the matter even more complicated, the personality of the therapist is involved. Some patients who are labeled borderline and untreatable by certain therapists do very well in analytic treatment with others.

*Donald:* Where do you stand with respect to the work of various experts in this field such as Kernberg, Masterson, and others?

*Richard:* My approach to the borderline patient and the narcissistic patient, especially in the earlier phases of the treatment, is closer to the work of the self psychologists. The most fundamental meaning of the psychoanalytic arrangement and interpersonal situation lies in the reverberations of them for the damaged preoedipal child within the patient. But after one has worked through the narcissistic transferences and oedipal material begins to appear, the treatment is not over. I mentioned all this to you on previous days. Rather, at this point the stage has been properly set for a traditional analysis. After the archaic transferences have been worked through and a reasonably firm tension-regulation system has been established so the patient can tolerate the development of more traditional transferences, and the frustrations and tensions that the rule of abstinence entails, the treatment becomes more akin to a standard psychoanalytic therapy and may need to go on for some further time.

Some borderline patients develop highly negative or strongly eroticized disruptive transferences very early, even in a once-a-week psychotherapy. These must be resolved by early interpretation, for example, based on Kernberg's (1975) modified Kleinian concepts of projected split-off all-bad or all-good self and object representations. Or, if self psychology is thought best at this point, transferences powerfully infused with lust and aggression appearing early and suddenly in therapy are analyzed as manifestations of profound disappointment in the patient's expectations of empathy from the subjectively perceived selfobject analyst. Failure to resolve such disruptive transferences typically destroys the therapy.

*Donald:* This is not clear. In your clinical work just what do you do when a patient suddenly shows tremendous manifestations of lust or rage?

*Richard:* I first try to get the patient to join me in attempting to identify the point at which these overwhelming affects occurred. If this can
be done, it's a good exercise for the patient in learning self-examination
and improving ego functioning. With borderline patients this is often
not possible because they are so angry or overwhelmed with acting out
rage and sexuality. A second and more interpretive tactic is to try to get
the patient to identify the point at which he or she felt disappointment,
panic, or fragmentation, and to then see how these generated the sense
of rage or sexual acting out. Some borderline patients are able to do this,
especially if the therapist has the patience to wait until they calm down,
and if they are it serves as a template to be used in the appearance later
on of similar surges of uncontrolled affect.

*Donald:* But what do you do if none of this works and disruption
threatens the treatment?

*Richard:* I then attempt to interpret projection or projective identification very much in the style advocated by Kernberg. This technique
carries a certain danger with it if the patient hears the therapist posing
as the arbiter of reality and feels in some sense that the interpretation is
accusatory and demeaning. Because of this the patient may then use
interpretations as confirmatory evidence of the humiliation and attack
coming from the authority-therapist. This problem must be carefully
discussed with the patient.

*Maria:* Clearly at this point a clinical distinction appears between
borderline patients with a fundamentally paranoid core and those who
have a more chaotic or fluid core and so are amenable to discussion and
interpretation. In my experience borderline patients with a fundamentally paranoid core are those patients who have the criteria of unanalyza-
bility previously mentioned. Such patients can only be treated by behavioral therapy methods to teach them to at least limit their explosions
as much as possible. I believe this represents only a relatively small group
of borderlines and one could argue that these are actually paranoid-
schizophrenic patients who've been able to mask their paranoia under a
variety of symptoms that led them to be labeled borderline in the first
place. Careful history-taking sometimes reveals a youthful paranoid psychotic episode forgotten about long ago, or attributed to adolescent
craziness.

*Donald:* Don't we also get help from other views? For example, the
archaic transference is marked in preoedipal disorders by an intense and
overt demand for gratification, making the therapist feel almost like a
prisoner and forced away from the analytic analyzing attitude. Refusal
to comply is often followed by seriously disruptive rage and chaos. In fact,
Adler (1980) points out that the hallmark of the borderline patient's

transference is the rapid disintegration of the selfobject transference as soon as gratification is not forthcoming. He recommends the use of one's best judgment about how much deprivation is tolerable in such situations. Instability seems to me to be the most important hallmark of the archaic transference and poses extremely difficult problems for the therapist.

*Maria:* It's interesting that coming from different theoretical orientations, authors can still agree on the clinical approach to the patient. Perhaps this tells us more about the way in which theoretical orientations are adopted. Often they are simply language used to justify clinical approaches that have been found to be practically useful by the particular author involved. A dramatic example of this is in the book by Kernberg, and colleagues (1989), who present an approach to treatment based on the well-known theoretical views of Kernberg. They treat their patients face to face two or three times a week, and the treatment centers on the perpetual interpretation of the transference. The idea is that each transference dyad contains an object-representation and a self-representation to which is attached a certain affectual charge. In borderline patients the dyads keep changing like scenes in a melodrama. This is an excellent way to conceive of their rapidly fluctuating and often confusing transference manifestations, which produce such chaos and countertransference problems. These authors offer many practical recommendations with which I agree, such as keeping the focus on the here and now as long as the transference remains primitive, and focusing on what is affectively dominant, not on genetic explanations.

*Donald:* But their actual language is different from what we have used here. Their basic concept is that proper interpretation of projected self- and object-representations early in the treatment will enable the coalescence of "part self- and part object-representations" (p. 91) into more realistic images through interpretation. The therapist "labels" (p. 93) these for the patient. They are kept split, the authors hypothesize, due to the anxiety that would be felt if opposing representations with their affectual charges were felt together. Neither of you have advocated anything like this.

*Richard:* This approach perhaps works better with hospitalized borderline patients who are having serious difficulties in reality testing, but it's unnecessary to use it so consistently in the outpatient treatment of such patients. Certainly acting out is highly gratifying and tends to perpetuate itself in patients with a borderline personality disorder—they are heavily invested in sacrificing their lives while ignoring what they are doing to themselves. This is one of the most puzzling and frustrating aspects of working with them and it is a crucial sign of genuine therapeutic progress when it diminishes. Kernberg and his group believe this will occur with the proper interpretation of projective identification. I believe it will occur with the proper establishment of an empathic ambience and directing the adult ego of the patient toward meticulous attention to the phenomenological details of when the patient's reality testing becomes fuzzy and when the patient becomes overwhelmed with disruptive lust or rage.

*Donald:* It sounds as if you function as a sort of an auxiliary ego microscope!

*Richard:* Yes, and I hope the patient's ego will eventually learn to focus on himself or herself as well. At the same time I am providing an ambience or holding environment with structure for the patient to facilitate tension reduction, whereas the Kernberg group primarily uses interpretation of projective identification and splitting.

*Maria:* The techniques are all aimed at the same goals, maturation and better reality testing. But the difference of opinion is over what techniques will best accomplish these goals. The answer may lie in the variety of patients, with certain types responding better to one approach and one type of personality of the analyst, while other patients respond better to a different approach. Along with Meissner (1984), I think we are dealing with a spectrum of disorders, and it would be logical that these would respond to different approaches. This all remains for future clinical investigation.

*Donald:* How often do you have to hospitalize borderline patients?

*Richard:* It is extremely rare that I have had to hospitalize a borderline patient, and when that has occurred, it has often been only for a brief cooling-off period. It is inadvisable to hospitalize borderline patients unless absolutely necessary for the safety of either the patient or those around the patient, because it's all too common for a vicious cycle to be set up in which the patient is going in and out of the hospital every time there is a disruption. Although some must be treated in the hospital, a great many can be successfully treated without recourse to hospitalization at all and usually with very little medication. I do not wish to imply that it is rarely necessary to hospitalize borderline patients, only that those who do primarily outpatient psychoanalytic practice should refer borderline patients who obviously must be hospitalized to other psychiatrists who specialize in hospital work.

*Donald:* So you are not boasting that you're so effective in your outpatient treatment with borderline patients that they never have to be hospitalized?

*Richard:* No, I'm simply saying that if you wish to do predominantly outpatient psychoanalytic psychotherapy you have to be selective in your choice of patients to begin with. A patient who has a long history of repeated chronic hospitalizations is not a very good candidate for outpatient psychotherapy without episodes of hospitalization!

*Maria:* Although the hospital treatment of borderline patients is extremely complicated because it obviously involves the interrelationships of a number of people in a group constituted of patients, ancillary staff, and treating physicians, there are plenty of difficulties in outpatient work with borderline patients also. The majority of lurid stories about therapist–patient disasters and the kinds of situations that become escalated in the popular press or in malpractice suits occur during attempts to treat borderline patients by therapists who have not properly resolved their own personal difficulties. These usually involve patients who have been treated in the office. Borderline patients have an uncanny ability to spot their therapist's personal difficulties and weaknesses, and to utilize them in the service of acting out, just as they do with everybody else in their environment.

*Richard:* I believe that therapists should not take on many of these patients at one time, as they constitute a serious drain on the therapist's psychological resources. Similarly, if the therapist is suffering some current personal problem such as a recent bereavement or illness, this is a very bad time to take on the treatment of a borderline patient.

*Donald:* It's certainly clear that the borderline personality disorder remains a tremendous challenge to our theories of therapy and to our clinical skills. Obviously it is in the fiery crucible of working with such patients that the therapist becomes most painfully acquainted with his or her own weaknesses and deficiencies. Even the definition of borderline is not agreed upon. There seem to be no pathognomonic symptoms, no specific personality constellations, and no compelling evidence for a definitive stage in infant development when this disorder is fixed; all stages are involved, from faulty foundational to oedipal periods. It is a descriptive diagnosis.

Some things I have now learned. Limits must be set first but these must be flexible and reasonable. Medications are used rarely and with care. We attempt to form an alliance by getting the patient to join us in a study of himself or herself, especially a study of when rage and maladaptive behavior emerges and by providing a consistent and reasonable ambience. The ultimate aim is uncovering and interpreting when the patient is ready for it, more and more approximating psychoanalytic treatment as the patient's pathology permits.

*Richard:* While archaic transferences predominate, we serve as an auxiliary microscopic ego and appeal to the rational adult part of the patient's ego in a phenomenological investigation. We interpret early only if we cannot get the patient to examine what has led to the explosions and when distortions or projection without insight continues to predominate. The dangers of early transference interpretation being experienced by the patient as unempathic and assaultive are very important to keep in mind in the production of patient rage. Therapy is long, tedious, and requires the willingness to patiently catalyze the patient's resumed development and endure the periodic disruptions. Countertransference is a serious and ever-present problem.

*Maria:* Today also has been rather long and tedious. Perhaps we should adjourn until tomorrow.

*Donald:* Discussing the borderline patient and his or her therapy inevitably immerses one in various so-called object relations theories. It seems that the treatment orientation chosen by a given therapist depends a great deal on which of these theories is followed by the therapist. And the "results" always seem to prove the theory! You, Richard, use Kleinian object relations theory and self psychology, which might be called a neo–object relations theory, as two of your five channels for psychoanalytic listening. What about Kernberg's theories, which are so popular now, or Fairbairn's theories, or the contributions of Bion, Winnicott, Balint, and others? All of these authors are frequently quoted in treatises on the borderline patient. Can we discuss so-called object relations theories tomorrow?

*Richard:* A good idea. I will present an overview of the subject for you and Maria to consider when we meet tomorrow. Now let's calm down from the inevitable tension that borderline patients generate and relax for the evening at my place—I will provide the entertainment.

*Maria and Donald:* With pleasure! Thank you.

# 10

## The Tenth Day: Object Relations Theories

*Donald:* One of the reasons I was so eager to ask you about object relations theories yesterday, Richard, is that I was reading Celani's (1993) attempt to approach the psychotherapeutic treatment of the borderline patient using the object relations theory of Fairbairn. He claims that using this theory he can get "most" borderline patients to "improve" using once a week psychotherapy for five years! It seems there are several competing object relations theories. They contradict each other in their premises at times. Yet it also seems they are important and useful in the treatment especially of preoedipal disorders, the predominant kind of pathology we see in our clinical work these days.

*Richard:* It is an enormous task to go over all the object relations theories, and I don't think our discussions can do that successfully because one has to study the original sources in some detail. Today I will try to review some of the main concepts of selected object relations theories for you. You are correct that these theories aren't consistent with each other. No way has been found to demonstrate which of these theories most closely approximates what actually goes on in the minds of people.

The basic assumption of all object relations theories is that one can understand the relationship between people only through an examination of the internal images they have of one another. Knowledge of their "drives" is not enough. In the healthiest people, these images correspond rather accurately to the reality of the other person and are continually reshaped and reworked as new information is perceived and integrated. In the less healthy individual, the images are stereotyped, rigid, and relatively unchanged by new information.

*Maria:* This poses an immediate dilemma! There are two psycho-analytic models of treatment. The first model stresses the neutral-interpretive stance of the analyst, as for example in the work of Kernberg. The second stresses nurturing and reconstructive experiences within the analytic interaction, for example in the work of Balint, Kohut, and Winnicott. Here the allowing of regression to traumatic developmental phases is stressed, as well as the resumption of growth through the analytic relationship.

*Richard:* Every clinician must ask himself or herself whether the neutral interpretive stance strictly employed alone does not generate overwhelming resistances due to the inevitable arid interpersonal ambience it produces, and whether the nurturing-reconstructive approach really allows the patient to experience the beneficial aspects of the relationship without first analyzing the rigid stereotyped self and object images. This is a crucial problem in every psychoanalytic treatment of preoedipal disorders, a dilemma that remains unresolved today. A number of object relations theorists have pointed out that it is only when the therapist is differentiated from the internalized archaic images that the patient can introject or identify with the therapist in such a way as to alter internalized structures and form new ones.

*Maria:* I think object relations theories lend themselves too much to medieval scholastics and obsessional disputes, but they are useful to understand the puzzling lack of influence of the benevolent therapist, or why the corrective emotional experience of the relationship with the therapist tends to occur so slowly in many cases.

*Richard:* There are other problems with object relations theories. How does one verify the reconstructions derived from adult psychoanalysis about their assumed early phases of development? Similarly, can one extrapolate from the "analysis" of even a 3- or 4-year-old child to what goes on in the mind of an infant? How does one correlate these reconstructions with the data of direct observation of either infants or adults without the injection of preconceived notions of the observer?

Furthermore, authors vary about so-called primitive internalized object relations. For example, are these a source of motivation and the only such source, or the primary source, or do they constitute an additional explanation for behaviors that have been insufficiently explained by drive theories? These views do not make clear what causes these internalizations to affect behavior; the relationship between "drives" and "internalizations" is not clear. It seems most reasonable to assume these self and object representations distort perception internally, and then the patient's behavior is appropriate to the distorted perception.

*Donald:* You are going too fast, as usual. What *is* an "internalization"?

*Maria:* An internalization can be thought of as all those processes by which a subject transforms real or imagined regulatory interactions with his or her environment into inner regulations and characteristics. Please notice that a perception is not the same as an internalization and that a cognitive creation of object representations is not the same as an internalization! That is to say, internalization is structural, whereas perception and cognitive creation is experiential. The relationship between the structural and the experiential remains unclear in these theories. Also there is a problem in that to go from the experiential to the structural requires already some ego formation, and in some of these theories it is assumed that this ego formation occurs extremely early in life or is even inborn. That seems quite speculative.

*Richard:* Furthermore, authors do not always distinguish, as they really should, between "interpersonal relations," which are real observable interactions between people, and "object relations," which are experiences of either party from within the interaction, their internal experiences of it. This is especially true of the earlier authors and accounts for some of the confusion in the field. So we have to go from "perceptions" to "object representations" to "introjects," which represent an internal foreign presence, to actual "psychic structure." Such transformations are problematical and murky.

*Maria:* Another confusion to watch for is the relationship between "object representation" and "introject." Each author uses these terms in his or her own way. For example, Volkan (1976) differentiates introjects from object representations in that introjects are functional and play a role in the formation and alteration of psychic structure. For him, an introject is experienced as an inner presence because it is beyond an object representation and is not yet absorbed into the psychic structure. So therapy for Volkan leans heavily on getting the introject of the analyst absorbed into the psychic structure, in order to alter or re-form it.

*Donald:* Here we go again. What is "introjection"?

*Maria:* This is Kernberg's (1976) definition:

> Introjection is the earliest, most primitive, and basic level in the organization of internalization processes. It is the reproduction and fixation of an interaction with the environment by means of an organized cluster of memory traces implying at least three components: i) the image of an object, ii) the image of the self in interaction with that object, and iii) the affective coloring of both the object-image and the self-image under the influence of the drive representative present at the time of the interaction. This process is a mechanism of growth of the psychic apparatus, and it is also used for defensive purposes by the ego. Introjection, then, depends on perception and memory . . . but it transcends these not only by a complex and specific organi-

zation of perceptions and memory traces but also by linking "external" perception with the perception of primitive affect states representing early drive
derivatives. [p. 29]

Of course Kernberg later moved entirely away from drive theory!

*Donald:* That is very complicated. Can you distinguish between identification, introjection, and incorporation?

*Richard:* These are all mechanisms of internalization. Identification
is the most mature, less directly dependent on drives, more adaptively
selective, less ambivalent, and a modeling process. It is often automatic
and unconscious, and a mental process whereby an individual becomes
like another person in one or several aspects. It is part of the learning
process, but also of adaptation to a feared or lost object. The crucial clinical point is that identification is growth promoting, and can lead to better adaptation.

*Maria:* I will try again to define introjection. For Freud (1915b, 1917),
introjection was originally used in outlining the psychodynamics of
mourning and melancholia. In that paper he defined it as the lost object
being taken in and retained as part of psychic structure. This was one of
Freud's unwitting first steps toward object relations theory that took place
in his later development. Later Freud used introjection to represent the
taking in of the parents' demands as if they were one's own, in the formation of the superego during the resolution of the Oedipus complex.
Introjection does not simply copy the object as in identification, it is
more encompassing. Freud's definition assumed a solid repression barrier and a cohesive sense of self as well as a functioning ego.

*Richard:* Incorporation is simply a primitive kind of interpersonal relations fantasy. It is a form or model of introjection that involves taking into
the mind the attributes of another person in a fantasy that involves oral
ingestion and swallowing. Identification that is accomplished by incorporation implies change by fantasied cannibalism. For example, a patient said
to me, "I am devouring your book like a hungry wolf." Incorporation is
primary process ideation, and at one time it was thought that this fantasy
accompanies all introjection, but this is no longer believed to be correct.

*Maria:* Schafer (1968) describes an introject as an inner presence with
which one feels in a continuous or intermittent dynamic relationship. It
is often conceived as a person-like thing or creature. It may be unconscious, preconscious, or conscious, and is experienced as exerting a pressure
or influence on the person's psychic state or behavior independently of
conscious efforts to control it. But introjects do not copy external objects,
since they are shaped by fantasies, projections, symbolizations, misunderstandings, idealizations, depreciations, and selective biases originating in

the individual's past history. Once formed, an introject diminishes the influence of the external object, and this is a crucial clinical issue. Introjects are formed due to severe ambivalence or more or less disappointment, in an attempt to modify distressing relations with an external object. Many object relations theorists believe that good introjects are also needed to counteract and protect one from the bad introjects. Once formed, an introject alters the relationship with the external object in a way not correctable by further experiences with the external object, since the influence of the external object is now diminished.

*Richard:* Notice the postulated active role of the psyche in this, even the psyche of the infant! Introject formation represents or expresses a regressive modification of the boundaries and reality-testing functions of the ego. It perpetuates neediness and ambivalence; it just displaces it to the inside. It is not growth-promoting and is a passive mode of mastery, not adaptive in itself. For modern object relations theorists, self and object representations are subjective conceptualizations, the individual's experiential guideposts to behavior. In contrast, an introject is experienced as exerting an influence on a person's thoughts or behavior whether he or she likes it or not.

*Donald:* Is it really necessary to work through all this primitive pre-oedipal stuff in psychoanalytic treatment? It seems very difficult and obscure.

*Richard:* This depends on the patient. One sees such material most clearly in schizophrenic and borderline patients, but according to some authors these patients usually do not have adequate ego strength to work it through until some years of psychotherapy. Other authors disagree and interpret transference and projective identification immediately. It seems to me that deep Kleinian interpretations are useless without a therapeutic alliance, controlled regression, and sufficient ego strength to deal with them. In the psychoanalysis of mental health professionals and their families, often in a second or third analysis, one routinely encounters this material during the regression phases. These individuals usually have more ego strength and can work their primitive and deep issues through. In my opinion they must be worked through for anyone who is a psychoanalytic psychotherapist and dealing with schizophrenic disorders, borderline or other personality disorders, or the psychosomatic or addictive and alcoholic disorders. A classical psychoanalysis centering on the oedipal phase is not sufficient for either the therapist or the patient in these cases, but due to countertransference the therapist may well miss archaic material or reject it. For example Freud thought that schizophrenic patients do not form a transference, and this is patently false. Many failures in traditional psychoanalysis are explained by the lack of working through of this primitive material, and therefore it's crucial to deal with it in a second or third analysis, if this was not done before.

*Donald:* Because of our discussion on previous days, I have been doing some reading about Melanie Klein (Segal 1967, 1974, 1980), who seems to be one of the important founders of object relations theories. As I understand it there are certain crucial concepts that she introduced. In the early infancy stages she says there already exist the Oedipus complex and a primitive superego formation. In these extremely early months there is already the operation of introjection and projection, building up the child's intense fantasy world. This is an attempt to deal with the death instinct, the crucial initial problem of life.

For Klein there are two basic "positions." The paranoid-schizoid position in the first three months of life (can this be?) deals with ambivalence by splitting and projection, and is characterized by persecutory fears. So there is a loved good breast when the infant is satisfied, and this love is projected into the feeling that the good breast loves the infant, which is then internalized again and protects the infant against the death instinct. The death instinct, or oral sadism, and the bad breast, when the infant is frustrated, generate hate. This is projected as the bad breast hating the infant and is internalized to control it. Thus the infant can feel supported or attacked from within itself and the hate can be reprojected and reintrojected, leading to a vicious cycle of an increased sense of persecution. Also the love can be reprojected and reintrojected, leading to a good cycle of increased well-being or trust and gratitude.

In the depressive position, predominant in the second three months of life, anxiety over the loss of good objects without and within prevails. The infant fears its own destructive greedy impulses will destroy the good breast by appropriating it. A state of sadness occurs, and this is a crucial hurdle in ordinary development. If it is too painful, the infant regresses to the paranoid-schizoid position or swings to the manic state and the groundwork is laid for either adult schizophrenic or manic-depressive psychosis. It follows that psychoanalytic treatment must be based on the reintegration of split-off parts that caused the depression through the analysis of the transference, allowing better integration of internal objects and a less harsh and bizarre superego.

*Richard:* Very good, Donald. Although we certainly quarrel with the details of her theories, such as the incredibly early timing of these positions, Melanie Klein in these concepts laid the basis for much of the later object relations theories.

*Maria:* There is more. The good and bad breast in the paranoid-schizoid position are the forerunners of the superego, both in its harsh and benign aspects. For Klein, the oedipal triangle begins in the oral stage and she postulates an inborn knowledge of the genitals of both sexes! The point is, whether one agrees with the details or not, that there is a long and complex prehistory before Freud's oedipal stage, involving a combination of the parents, splitting, projections, and internalizations. There may even be a premature flight into the oedipal phase, not unusual to observe in our clinical work, due to the use of genital love, which is mobilized against pregenital aggression. Klein (1975) also believed in a constitutional variation among individuals of envy and aggression.

*Richard:* To clarify, oral sadism for Klein is the first crucial manifestation of the death instinct. The constitutional strength of aggression or the death instinct varies with individuals and is fundamental to understanding each patient. Chessick (1992b) discussed the death instinct at length; it is an extremely controversial metaphysical concept for which there is little possibility to produce either verification or refutation. In our clinical work it is sufficient to begin with the existence of oral sadism if one follows Klein's formulations. This oral sadism is projected and so experienced as persecutory fears and fear of annihilation by the destructive devouring breast. So the first source of infantile anxiety is from projected oral sadism threatening to destroy and invade the ego or self. It is at the root of envy, greed, and jealousy, and excessive aggression fosters splitting and denial of reality, which leads to serious pathological consequences.

*Donald:* Conversely, the projection of good inner objects leads to trust in later life. Gratitude comes from good experiences, decreases greed, and leads to a healthy generosity.

*Maria:* Reactive generosity, on the other hand, is a defense against envy, and eventually ends in feelings of being robbed. This is a common clinical picture. In the depressive position, the bad objects are internalized and this position leads to a fear of inner persecutors, which constitutes the origin of primitive superego anxiety or hypochondriasis, the sensation that one has bad or destructive internal diseases or parts, another common clinical picture.

*Donald:* In our clinical work we often see paranoid fears. The oral fears involve the danger of being devoured, the anal fears the danger of being controlled or poisoned, and the oedipal fears the danger of castration. For Klein all of these represent aggressive wishes toward and fantasies about the mother, particularly about the contents of her body. Certainly this is crucial in schizophrenic, paranoid, borderline, and schizoid states. As I understand it, in the paranoid-schizoid position all aggression is projected outside in order to preserve the purified pleasure ego. In the depressive position this projection is only partly successful, and there is tolerance and reintrojection of external bad objects, now consequently experienced as internal persecutors. This leads to early harsh superego formation. The crucial fear in the depressive position is not of annihilation from without, but of doing harm to good internal and external objects. Klein talks about depressive anxiety arising from the guilt over the wish to do harm to the internalized bad objects. It requires grief and mourning to work this through.

*Richard:* Besides splitting, idealization also preserves the all-good internal and external objects. When splitting breaks down, we see the fear of destruction from within as well as from without. There is also a secondary splitting that occurs when aggression is strong and there is consequently a predominance of bad objects. These bad objects are further split into fragments. When these fragments are then projected one suffers from multiple persecutors or, as Bion (1963, 1976) called it, "bizarre objects." When these are reintrojected, one gets internal confusion and turmoil. Splitting protects against persecutory anxiety even by disorganizing thought processes, and Bion has emphasized even a splitting of normal cognitive links.

*Donald:* Is splitting the basic defense used in the paranoid-schizoid position? Are there other equally important defenses against the internally directed oral sadism or death instinct?

*Richard:* Besides splitting and secondary splitting, there are other crucial defenses employed in the paranoid-schizoid position. These are idealization, employed here as the denial of inner and external reality in order to deny aggression; the repressive stifling of emotions or an artificiality of emotions; projective identification, which we have discussed on previous days; projection of persecutory bad objects to parts of one's own body, leading to hypochondriacal fears and fear of poisoning from the outside; sexual promiscuity in turning from one idealized object to another in a desperate attempt to escape inner and outer persecutors; and envy as a defense, in which the sadism is turned outward. This envy can be manifested as (1) the projection onto others of one's own envy, (2) the inhibition of the acquisition of all knowledge and learning as a defense against unconscious envy and greed, or conversely (3) the relentless pursuit of knowledge or money as an acting out of this greed, and (4) envy of the therapist, who is thought of as serenely happy, content, and filled with good objects. This latter kind of therapist-envy has an important role in the negative therapeutic reaction and in impasses and failures in psychoanalysis (Chessick 1996b).

*Maria:* The crucial defenses of the depressive position are easier to understand. Idealization in this position protects against aggression toward the internalized good object. The internalized bad objects generate the primitive superego, which attacks the ego or the self with guilt feelings. At the same time, the demands of the good internal objects are contaminated by the bad objects, leading to a superego with cruel demands for perfection; there is an unremitting harshness of the superego when one is entangled in the depressive position. The manic defense, of course, represents triumph over the feared loss of the good object. It involves omnipotence, a claim that one does not need the good object and therefore does not have to attack it; an identification with a sadistic superego, in which external objects are depreciated due to the projection of the bad parts; the expression of object hunger (let's have a feast and who cares if a few people are eaten!); triumph over the dead and dying universe of depression; and exaltation, an extreme of idealization that may even lead to messianic states.

*Donald:* But isn't it clear by now that manic-depressive states or bipolar disorders really have a biological origin? Is it necessary to explain them by the use of such complicated psychodynamics? In my opinion one of the greatest advances psychiatry has made has been in the psychopharmacologic treatment of the bipolar disorders.

*Richard:* This is certainly true, but we can distinguish the mania that Klein is talking about from the bipolar disorders, because the mania that we are concerned with in psychoanalytic treatment appears clinically when the patient slides into the depressive position. Using mania as a defense in the depressive position indicates that the patient has no secure good internal object established. These mechanisms are all used to preserve the shaky good internal object and protect it from destruction by the aggression of bad internal objects. So we are not talking about patients with major bipolar disorders so much here (as Klein was), but rather about the appearance of manic defenses during the regressive phase of psychoanalytic treatment. This already is a shift away from Klein's theories, which were developed at a time when bipolar disorders were thought to be primarily psychogenic in nature. As we already mentioned, all these defenses in the depressive position may be prematurely sexualized or it conversely may lead to severe sexual inhibition as a defense against the wish to use sexualization and genital love for the expression of sadistic impulses. It also helps to explain those patients who can achieve sexual gratification only through the infliction of pain on their partner.

*Donald:* It seems clear that Melanie Klein sees oral drives and conflicts everywhere as fueling and infiltrating development in all further stages. It must follow that psychoanalytic treatment would require the interpretation of primitive fantasies and defenses of the paranoid-schizoid and depressive positions in material from all levels of development. I cannot agree with Klein's pseudobiological notion of an inborn death instinct and its earliest expression as oral sadism, or her claim that the infant has an innate knowledge of the genitals of both sexes and an Oedipus complex. Furthermore, Klein neglects the importance of environmental factors on early development, and she neglects the wide variety differences in clinical psychopathology, tending to attribute all clinical psychopathology to difficulties in her two postulated positions.

*Richard:* Fairbairn and some neo-Kleinians have modified her theories on the basis of some of these objections. This has led to a multiplication of object relations theories, with no agreement on whose theory is best. Each psychotherapist will have to make choices after prolonged self-scrutiny and careful study of his or her clinical material. I believe the choice in each case will represent a compromise formation by the therapist's ego to reduce anxiety by mediating among its three harsh masters (superego, id, external reality). Some psychoanalysts, such as Bion, have moved in a direction even more toward the speculative extreme than Klein, while others, such as Kernberg, have moved away from some of her more extreme views into a theoretical position that is more palatable at least to psychoanalysts in the United States. On the other hand, South American psychoanalysts are inclined to utilize the work of Klein and Bion routinely in their clinical work.

*Donald:* Can you review some of Bion's concepts for us? I find his work so metaphysical and speculative that I have trouble picking out the useful clinical aspects of it.

*Maria:* Bléandonu (1994) reviews his life and some of his ambiguous and obscure theories. Bion was analyzed by Klein. I find his concept of the "alpha function," which converts "beta elements" into "alpha elements," quite useful in my clinical work. Beta elements are essentially a disconnected aggregation of bad objects, terrible experiences, and unacceptable frightening or painful affects. These are projected into the mother as a "container" for them. If she is in a receptive state of "reverie," that is, not filled by beta elements herself and thereby "saturated," and if there is not so much envy and rage at her from the infant that she is not allowed to perform the alpha function, she will then incorporate and integrate these beta elements, exercising what Bion calls her alpha function. In the mother's psyche, the beta elements are converted into alpha elements, which are the appropriate precursors of cognitive thought, dreams, and so forth. Alpha elements are acceptable and constitute a kind of detoxified or "metabolized" beta elements. The infant reintrojects the beta elements in their alpha element form from the mother.

This process in the mother serves as a model of alpha function that the infant can internalize and therefore eventually perform for itself, an internal detoxification of the beta elements. The paranoid-schizoid position characteristically employs the mother for the use of the alpha function; when the infant can develop its own alpha function it has moved into the depressive position. From that point on, frustration, fear, and despair are no longer projected as beta elements but are accepted and dealt with intrapsychically.

*Donald:* How is this useful in our clinical work?

*Richard:* For example, due to frustration and aggression, the future schizophrenic patient immersed in the paranoid-schizoid position attacks his or her own mental apparatus, shatters it, and projects the fragments. From then on the patient's capacity for perception and cognition is impaired and the patient feels surrounded by bizarre objects. Lacking an alpha function, the patient cannot understand his or her predicament or utilize explanations from the therapist. The patient has destroyed his or her own alpha function and this is reflected in the psychoanalytic treatment by the patient's attempt to destroy the therapist's capacity to understand and contain the patient's material. It is an active defense, as anyone who works with schizophrenics soon learns. It stands in contrast to other theories that see the disintegration of cognitive processes as due to regression or ego weakness or basic biological factors. Bion calls it a primitive catastrophe. It is.

*Maria:* Similarly, when the analyst cannot contain and integrate what is placed in the analyst, either due to countertransference or when the patient destroys the relationship and the analyst's capacity to contain this material, the analyst tends to switch from intuitive holding and understanding to omnipotent intellectual understanding and control of the patient by authority, advice, drugs, psychopharmacologic agents, and so forth. Thus the analyst's capacity for creative thinking is destroyed by what Bion characterizes as the patient's attack on linking. This strips meaning from the interaction and communication between the patient and the analyst. In these situations, the unmetabolized beta elements and nameless dread are reintrojected, just as they are in the baby with the mother who is not containing properly. Bion maintains that to allow the self to be used as a container properly, the analyst must approach each session without memory or meaning, so as to be "surprised" by the patient's material, and without desire to influence the patient or move the patient in any special direction. This is dangerous for the legal aspects of the practice of psychiatry, but according to Bion it is necessary to achieve the proper receptiveness. It requires an act of faith that the patient will place in the therapist whatever is needed in order to understand the patient in each session.

*Richard:* Bion's ideas are very impressive and clinically important. He concentrates on the intuitive function of the analyst and tries to clear the way for this function to be exercised as effectively as possible. Many of his formulations are a reformulation of Kleinian psychoanalysis in terms more aimed at emphasizing the nonverbal intuitive aspects of psychoanalysis. Bion's work has a mystical aspect to it, and is endlessly fascinating.

*Donald:* It is my understanding that Fairbairn wrote in opposition to Melanie Klein's pseudo-biology. What I like about his work is that it removes the whole concept of psychoanalytic treatment from any assumed biological roots, and therefore puts an end to the disputes about the biological underpinnings of the so-called drives such as the death instinct and other metaphysical concepts.

*Maria:* That is very true, but I think we should always keep in mind that the crucial issue of all object relations theories is the focus on the complex inner world formed by cycles of projection and reinternalization, which then gets confused with the external world. This is clarified in psychoanalytic treatment through interpretation of the transference projections, so that our emphasis in all our previous discussions on the transference is further justified by the work of the object relations theorists.

*Richard:* Fairbairn in several ways is a forerunner of Kohut. He eliminates the id and begins with a pristine ego, which strives for self-development. The ego itself becomes split in all cases according to Fairbairn, since each splitting of objects into good and bad produces different splits in the experiencing ego; he says the ego cannot be separated from its objects. The ego for Fairbairn is what Kohut later referred to as the psychic self (in my opinion). It is the struggle of this split up psychic self to cope with the outer world that is the problem, not the struggle of the ego with the id. This is a fundamental and crucial difference from Freud, a whole different metapsychology that Fairbairn offers. He rejects Freud's oral-anal-phallic phases and substitutes the following phases of development: (1) immature dependence of infancy, (2) a transitional phase on the way to (3) mature dependence between equal adults.

*Donald:* What do you mean, that according to Fairbairn there is a "split up psychic self"?

*Maria:* Fairbairn offers a threefold pattern of splitting of the ego, with an internal struggle that goes on endlessly. The infantile libidinal ego, perhaps analogous to Freud's "id," in a state of dissatisfaction with the enticing but disappointing mother, is related to an internal bad object called the "exciting object," which excites but never satisfies the child's need. The infantile "anti-libidinal ego," the sadistic part of Freud's superego, identifies with external rejecting objects subsequently internalized, and so turns against the individual's own libidinal needs. Fairbairn sometimes calls this anti-libidinal ego the "internal saboteur." The central ego, or Freud's ego, is the conscious self of everyday living trying to get on and unrealistically idealizing the parents, the idealized objects that constitute the moral aspect of Freud's superego. Here there is a struggle to preserve a good relationship with the parents, the central ego relating to the ideal object, in Fairbairn's terminology.

*Richard:* Guntrip (1974) points out that the ultimate split in schizoid patients is in the "infantile libidinal ego" itself. This splits again, according to Guntrip, into a clamoring orally active hysterical libidinal ego and a deeply withdrawn schizoid libidinal ego. This latter "regressed ego" is experienced by the patient as a compulsive need to sleep, exhaustion, feelings of nonentity, a sense of having lost a part of the self, of being out of touch. It constitutes the phenomena of schizoid states, such as the feeling that a sheet of plate glass exists between the patient and the world. The patient may protect against this sense of annihilation by remaining chronically angry and fighting, so as to keep up his or her energy level. This is similar to Kohut's (1971) concept of pseudodramatization of everything in order to defend against the depleted empty self.

*Donald:* I understand that Fairbairn as well as Balint and Winnicott (and later, Kohut) shift our emphasis to the primacy of the environment and the mother's influence, and away from the infant's internal fantasy life that is so emphasized by Klein. Unless good-enough mothering occurs, the infant takes flight more and more into the inner world of fantasy objects. But what about the superego?

*Richard:* For Fairbairn, the superego is a sub-aspect of the ego based, as I said, on the idealization of the parents. Libido for Fairbairn, in a totally non-Freudian definition, is object-seeking rather than seeking discharge. It is the energy of the search for good objects, which makes ego growth possible. For Fairbairn, just as later on for Kohut, aggression is a reaction to frustration of the libidinal drives, not an instinct! Treatment is therefore based on a good object relation, which is possible after transference projections are analyzed and the analyst survives these projections. This enables the patient to find his or her own true self. For Fairbairn psychoses, neuroses, and repression are all defenses against internalized bad objects, not against the id, and the British school of object relations in general tends to approach all disorders with the same sort of interpretations. This has been an important source of criticism.

*Donald:* What pleases me is that for Fairbairn psychoanalysis is not biology and it is not proposed to be, as Hartmann (1958) believed it was, a universal psychology. What about the relationship *between* these split-off parts, the central ego, the libidinal ego, and the anti-libidinal ego? It gets quite complicated.

*Richard:* The central ego attempts to repress the libidinal and anti-libidinal ego. The anti-libidinal ego attacks the libidinal ego along with the help of the central ego, and therefore the libidinal ego is more repressed. So much threat to the libidinal ego reinforces the link between the libidinal ego and its exciting object, and this forms a crucial source of resistance to the uncovering and working through of this aspect of the psyche in psychoanalytic treatment. Furthermore, all these developments occur early in the first year of life, during what Klein called the paranoid-schizoid position. Summers (1994) points out that, "Like Klein, Fairbairn conceptualized the depressive position as the intent to injure the loved object" (p. 29). But he goes on to say,

> While Fairbairn theoretically recognized two pathological positions, the schizoid and the depressive, his discussion of pathology (and especially his limited case material), focused exclusively on the schizoid fear of destroying the object with love. . . . Ultimately, Fairbairn and Guntrip reduced all human problems to a single issue. The drug addict, the demanding borderline patient, the anxiety neurotic, and the depressive all suffer from the same "disease"—fear of object love. [p. 71]

There is a remarkable summary of his position published by Fairbairn (1963), consisting of a one-page synopsis of his rather complex theory. Remember that for Fairbairn the relationship with the object, not gratification of the impulse, is the aim of libidinal striving. What is repressed are relationships with bad internalized objects, not impulses or memories; but significant internalization only occurs when it is necessary to survive in the system of the family and to maintain the myth of the purified pleasuring mother by introjecting and identifying with her unpleasuring aspects, either her enticing and disappointing or her rejecting aspects. This is in sharp contrast to Klein's theories.

The greatest of all sources of resistance according to Fairbairn (1958) is the maintenance of the patient's internal world as a closed system. It becomes an aim of psychoanalytic treatment to breach this "closed system which constitutes the patient's inner world and thus to make this world accessible to the influence of the outer reality" (p. 380). I believe this is the main clinical contribution of Fairbairn.

In the transference one perceives the enactment first of the conscious central ego to the analyst as an ideal object. This may be tenaciously maintained to avoid the transference of the relation between the rejecting object and the anti-libidinal ego, which would cause a need for a masochistic dependency on the sadistic persecutory object projected onto the analyst, and/or an even more threatening activation of the libidinal ego relating to the exciting object. This activation is so frightening because a true investment of others reminds the individual of the lack of response to his or her original libidinal investment.

*Maria:* According to Grotstein and Rinsley (1994), "Fairbairn conceptualized penis envy, castration anxiety, and genital longings for both parents in the positive and negative oedipal situation as expressions of deterioration of the object relations to the parents" (p. 51). So the various libidinal phases and even the longing for mature heterosexual relations are not instinctually determined but are manifestations of various kinds of object relations. Furthermore, efforts to avoid giving, which becomes equivalent to being emptied out, may reinforce the need to repress all affects to avoid affective investment.

*Donald:* Why does giving become equivalent to being emptied out?

*Maria:* It is a reminder of the sense of depletion derived from previous libidinal investment not responded to! Grotstein and Rinsley (1994) write, "In order to avoid a sense of loss, the patient may curtail his links with his own artistic products, stifle his creativity, and take active measures to drive away those who potentially threaten him with love" (p. 47).

*Donald:* It follows then that for Fairbairn the reality aspects of the analyst's personality are the most important therapeutic factor: "Therapeutic effects do not derive only from the analyst's interpretations . . . but also . . . from the analyst's capacity to provide, by means of his real interest and concern, the necessary counterbalance to the activation of bad repressed object relations in the transference" (p. 56), an activation that manifests itself by projection of them onto the analyst. But Fairbairn, like certain other object relations theorists, seems to have a "characteristic tendency to become absorbed in schematic, intricate theoretical constructs which drift away from their clinical and developmental referents" (p. 80). And what is Fairbairn's "moral defense"?

*Maria:* In this defense, the central ego attempts to live up to the ideals of the ideal object and maintain external contact in relationship with others. The patient places the badness of the abusive parent in himself or herself. For example, this can occur in the transference and serve as a defense against the cathexis and projection of the internal objects, that is to say, the libidinal ego-exciting object relationship, and the antilibidinal ego-rejecting object relationship. External objects must be kept "good" by the child at all costs.

*Donald:* But why does the patient remain loyal to the bad internal object? Why not just drop it and substitute a better object, such as a good friend or a good therapist?

*Maria:* Grotstein and Rinsley (1994) explain that such loyalty comes from the child's unconscious conviction that a bad object is preferable to no object. Loyalty to a bad internal object protects the person from the terror of impending annihilation, which occurs when one "feels that all external and internal object ties are being severed" (p. 104). So the person "clings desperately to any object tie (external or internal) . . . when that is all that is available" (p. 104). This explains the resistance in treatment arising from the fear of giving up a particular internal object relationship.

*Donald:* I take it then that the infant undergoes this splitting in order to repair the image of the parents. The infant identifies itself as the owner of the bad objects, which soon become indistinguishable from his or her "self." Either physical or psychological maternal absence is the primordial bad situation for Fairbairn. The bad situation is internalized and then reenacted as "the allure of the bad object," an obsessive love for the exciting object. The patient finds an individual who is similar to the frustrating and rejecting aspects of the original whole object; current interactions of the patient and this individual then mirror the initial trauma.

*Richard:* You must realize that this compulsive tie to the object, even if it is a bad object, is not explained in the same way by Fairbairn and Klein. Maria, do you understand how their views differ in this matter? This "compulsive tie to the object" is one of the thorniest problems we have to encounter in our clinical work!

*Maria:* For Klein, it is not a manifestation of an early need for an object as Fairbairn described it, but rather it is due to projective mechanisms initiated by the anxiety produced through the infant's inborn oral sadism. This, as Summers (1994) points out, "sets Klein's views in direct opposition to the theories of Fairbairn and Guntrip" (p. 83). For Klein, it is excessive aggressiveness or sadism that ties the person to the object. The underlying force or motivation comes from either persecutory anxiety arising from projection in the paranoid-schizoid position, or depressive anxiety arising from guilt over the potential destructiveness of the love object threatened in the depressive position.

*Richard:* Klein's theories are also useful in a similar fashion to explain the common clinical phenomena of eating disorders and hypochondriasis. In some types of eating disorders, food is thought of as a sort of poison, the ingestion of which represents an attack on the body, and therefore food must be avoided at all costs. An example of this would be a severely paranoid anxiety on the part of someone who has suffered a myocardial infarction about any food containing cholesterol or saturated fats. Here the patient has regressed to the paranoid-schizoid position as a consequence of the narcissistic blow involved in a heart attack; other patients use dangerous manic denial in this situation. In the more depressive types of anxiety underlying eating disorders, food is thought of as the good object that is endangered by being chewed and bitten into, and therefore must not be eaten. In hypochondriasis, we also see two similar clinical types of phenomena. In some forms, the patient is frightened of various environmental factors such as fumes, chemicals, gases, and so forth, which represent projected persecutory bad objects attacking the patient from outside the patient's body. Other forms of hypochondriasis emphasize attack from the inside of the body, such as imaginary cancers and various allegedly "undiagnosed" diseases within; these represent a depressive type of anxiety over the aggressive wish to destroy the internalized good object.

*Donald:* It seems to me that Klein and Fairbairn have produced theories that are fundamentally irreconcilable.

*Richard:* The issue of whether the child is a victim or a villain is central to the debate between Klein and Fairbairn, a debate repeated in the contrasting systems devised by Kernberg and Kohut. For Klein it is the child's own greed, envy, jealousy, and murderous sadism that creates early anxiety situations and generates bad internal objects. Other people can only ameliorate or exacerbate the situation. To Fairbairn it is the other way around, for a neurosis derives from parental failure. The rage that arises is secondary to disappointment and necessitates along with excess ungratified need, "the internalization of 'bad' objects and consequent pathogenic ego-splitting" (Grotstein and Rinsley 1994, p. 85). Notice that for Fairbairn object relationships, not objects, are internalized; transference can be explained in these terms as the interpersonal externalization or actualization of an internal object relationship. This allows us through examination of our countertransference to study what internal object relationship is being externalized in the transference at any given time. Ogden (1979) adds projective identification as carrying an additional interpersonal pressure on the therapist to behave in a manner that corresponds to the externalized object assigned to him in the object relationship that is being enacted.

*Donald:* I know that Winnicott was much influenced by the work of Klein. Where does his approach stand in relation to the theories of Klein and Fairbairn?

*Richard:* Summers (1994) points out that "Winnicott's views on early aggression bear a similarity to those of Klein, by whom he was influenced, and yet they are decidedly different" (p. 142). Winnicott believed the early split in life was between excited states (including aggression) and quiescence. The splitting of good and bad objects that Klein postulates is for Winnicott, a defensive pathological reaction that takes place when maternal holding is not good enough. So for Winnicott aggressive and libidinal drives are not directed toward different objects initially as Klein thought, but are initially fused. Also, for Winnicott, aggression has a more constructive role than it does for Klein because it helps in the development of the self as well as in the development of the sense of reality and the recognition and use of objects. Winnicott's theories are not that much different from the work of Fairbairn in many respects. His concepts are more genial and clinical but his weakness is in metapsychology. For Winnicott (1958, 1965), preoedipal cases require "management," providing an "ego-adaptive" environment of holding. He was an intuitive, magnificent clinician using very sloppy terminology and there is a certain vagueness to his conceptions that is generally recognized. His most famous clinical contributions are those of the "false self," the "transitional object," and the "facilitating environment."

*Maria:* The false self develops in response to early nonempathic mothering and has to do with learning to be compliant, never exploring one's own authentic self and its needs. This leads to a certain inherent rigidity and a lack of autonomy or spontaneous feeling. The patient is really disengaged and the false self functions to keep the true self hidden. It has to be broken down through therapeutic regression, so that the pathological false self compliance can disappear and a real exchange of affect and feeling can emerge into the therapeutic situation. Easier said than done!

*Richard:* Like Kohut, Winnicott (1965) emphasizes that the patient makes use of the "analyst's failures" (p. 258). These are used and treated as past failures to be angry about. The psychoanalytic treatment facilitates the patient's finding his or her true self in the analytic situation. There is a schizoid subvariant in which the real or true self is disassociated from the false self. The latter is caught up in compliance or submission to the demands of external reality. Patients like this are the focus of the theories of Fairbairn and Guntrip, rather than borderline patients where compliance is not the major problem. Yet, as you have mentioned, Donald, Fairbairn's concepts can be applied to the treatment of the borderline patient also (for example, Celani 1993), and I think to most preoedipal disorders.

*Donald:* Clearly for Winnicott the setting of the treatment becomes more important than interpretation. Management of the patient seems to put a special strain on the countertransference and sensitivity of the analyst.

*Maria:* Maturation requires and depends on the quality of the facilitating environment. The infant, under the aegis of this environment, creates and re-creates the object, says Winnicott. This object is at first a subjective phenomenon, the "subjective object." Later it becomes an object objectively perceived; this is a function, in turn, of the formation of an "objective subject." This "objective subject" represents the individual having a self and the feeling of being real that springs from having an identity. Notice that for Winnicott, as for Kohut later, the self is not equated with the ego. The self for Winnicott (1965) is defined as the person who is me, who is only me, who has a totality based on the operation of the maturational process. Winnicott clearly used the self in an idiosyncratic way, as some kind of inarticulate ultimately unknowable essence, as Phillips (1988) points out.

*Richard:* It is important to remember that for Winnicott there is not a baby, but a "nursing couple." The mother must actively adapt to the needs of the baby and there is a reciprocity. If the mother fails to adapt and is herself intrusively demanding, it fosters a precocious compliance in the child. Remember that Winnicott began as pediatrician! Our sense of life being worth living, of being alive, of being real comes not from instinctual satisfaction but from proper maternal care. Similarly, the "capacity to be alone" begins with the child's experience of being alone with the mother. If she is there and undemanding, the child does not have to be preoccupied with her and can lose itself in play. The implications of this for what needs to occur in the psychoanalytic treatment room are obvious.

*Donald:* In contrast to Klein then, Winnicott must avoid deep interpretations and facilitate self-discovery through an attitude of the therapist free from anxiety. Contrary to Klein, with average expectable mothering the ordinary baby is not mad, and not terrified by innate sadism! The paranoid-schizoid position of Klein would occur only in a baby kept waiting too long by an inattentive mother. Clearly for Winnicott the crucial drive is not for pleasure but for development, a powerful rival theory to that of Freud and Klein that he worked out in the 1940s, although his best known papers were in the 1950s and 1960s. Kohut continued on this foundation, I believe.

*Richard:* To summarize—the core catastrophe for Freud is castration, for Klein it is the triumph of the death instinct, and for Winnicott it is the annihilation of the core self by intrusion and a failure of the holding environment. There are some obvious implications of Winnicott's (and later Kohut's) theories for psychoanalytic treatment. What the therapist calls "resistance" can simply reflect the untimeliness of an interpretation and therefore its irrelevance. The patient can come to himself or herself only in his or her own time; the patient has to set the pace. Psychoanalysis for Winnicott is connecting dissociated parts of the self, not modifying the repression of the instincts.

Winnicott's emphasis on the quality of mothering brings up the crucial questions of what are the analyst's desires from the patient, and how is the analyst using the patient. We must always ask ourselves such questions. Treatment involves noninterference, the providing of a holding environment that allows natural growth processes to reassert themselves. The analytic setting is a transitional space for collaborative exchange, an intermediate area of experiencing to which inner reality and external life contribute. The patient needs this to recognize and accept reality. Interpretation comes out of empathy, with the therapist's commitment just like primary maternal preoccupation. Psychoanalysis for Winnicott comes down to a special form of play in the service of communication with one's self and others.

*Maria:* This is not far from Balint's (1952) concept of primary love. Following Fairbairn, Balint maintains that the individual is born with "primary object love," the kind of seeking for an object that will gratify the person without even having to first communicate the need to the object. It is the wish for the intuitive, empathic, all-loving maternal object. There is no room in the theory of Balint for primary narcissism; he conceives of development as progressing strictly along the line of object relations, from primary object relations to mature object love.

It follows from this that the task of the psychotherapist with patients who are not classical neurotics is essentially to supply a "new beginning" to the patient so as to correct a "basic fault." He attempts to provide an atmosphere in the psychotherapy that in a sense is a corrective emotional experience to the early nonempathic mothering the patient had, similar to Winnicott's notion of the holding environment. Those who follow Balint emphasize the patient's absolute need for empathy from the therapist, and stress the danger that inappropriate verbal interpretations may produce because it is the empathic interactions that are essential for the successful treatment of such patients rather than interpretations of a transference.

*Richard:* That is correct, but you should add that Balint distinguishes between two important clinical types of regressions, which he calls malignant and benign. Regression for the sake of gratification—which has the qualities of despair and passion and aims at gratification by external action with a suspiciously high intensity of demands and needs—is Balint's concept of malignant regression. He sharply distinguishes this from a regression in which what the patient needs is the "arglos" state. What is desired in this state is the analyst's recognition of the patient's needs and longings for satisfaction, which are the essence of a "new beginning" and the patient's recovery from his or her basic fault. The arglos state, which Balint considers to be an absolutely necessary precondition for the new beginning, is explained by the craving of the patient for primary love. It is clear that the special atmosphere provided during this state has more to do with recognition than massive gratification; only token satisfaction of need is provided—and there was a slow evolution of Balint's views so that the tokens of direct gratification become less and less.

*Donald:* Then the recognition of the patient's need and the unobtrusiveness of the therapist are the essential ingredients? Recognition? Gratification? Token satisfaction?

*Richard:* Beware; deliberate attempts to provide a special atmosphere to certain patients have the disadvantage of being manipulative, overly dramatic, and mystical. All patients should be presented with a physicianly vocation and the authentic self of the therapist. It is not at all clear what special techniques are really involved in somehow trying to provide the patient with totally empathic mothering. It is perhaps more realistic and practical to turn to Modell's (1968, 1975, 1976) suggestion of allowing a transitional object transference to take place so that the development of the patient can resume. The concept of the transitional object, first introduced by Winnicott and later referred to by Modell, can be utilized through Modell's definition of a "traditional object phase" of the development of object love. During this phase there is a clinging, dependent relationship to the external object, which is given magical powers to produce well-being and protection. This stands between primary narcissism—where there is no recognition of the object as separate—and true object love where there is the capacity to relate to the object as separate, human, and having needs of its own.

Modell believes that borderline patients have endured a developmental arrest at the transitional object phase. He emphasizes Winnicott's good-enough holding environment, that leads to a transitional object transference in the therapy. By emphasizing the transitional object transference, he tries to maintain the distinction between the classical type of psychoneuroses, and patients who are suffering from preoedipal disorders. Most authors agree that healing, especially in the preoedipal disorders, is facilitated by the analytic setting serving as a holding environment. There is a gratification implicit in the constancy and reliability of the analyst's judgment and the analyst's capacity to perceive the patient's unique identity, as well as in the constancy and reliability of the person of the analyst.

*Donald:* It is getting late. We have not yet discussed the concept of splitting as it is used by Kernberg. Since Kernberg's (1975, 1976, 1980) theories are so popular today, especially in the treatment of preoedipal disorders, wouldn't it be worthwhile to turn to his conceptions now?

*Richard: Splitting* is a term used differently by authors in various object relations theories (Pruyser 1975). It represents a failure in the synthesizing function of the ego and is crucial to the turning away from reality in any condition. The concept of splitting lies at the basis of Kernberg's theories of development and is central to his long experience with, understanding of, and treatment of borderline patients. Kernberg (1976) postulates five stages of development of internalized object relations. Let's review these. Maria, what do you remember from this complicated theory?

*Maria:* The first, or primary undifferentiated stage resembles Mahler's (Mahler et al. 1975) phase of normal autism. During this time there are no self or object representations, or *images* as they are called by Kernberg. This stage lasts about a month or two and leads to the second stage, which corresponds to Mahler's symbiotic phase between the ages of two and six months, plus her first or "differentiation" subphase of separation-individuation from six to nine months of age.

*Richard:* In this second stage there are representations, but these are roughly undifferentiated self and object constellations separated only into good and bad; consequently there is no differentiation between self and object. Kernberg here postulates a primary undifferentiated "good" self-object representation or constellation associated with pleasurable experiences (pure pleasure ego) and invested with libido, and a primary undifferentiated "bad" self-object representation or constellation associated with pain and frustration and invested with aggression. Do not mix this up with Kohut's (1977) notion of a "selfobject"!

*Donald:* I know that the borderline patient suffers from pathological fixation and/or regression to the third stage of development as postulated by Kernberg. In this stage self and object representations have been differentiated within the two primary constellations (good and bad) that predominate in the second stage. It ends somewhere in the third year of life with the eventual integration of good and bad self representations into an integrated self-concept, and the integration of good and bad object representations into total object representations. The achievement of object constancy and the firm capacity to distinguish the inner from the outer world, what Freud would call stable ego boundaries, depends on this stage. How does splitting come in here?

*Maria:* Kernberg (1976) explains that in this third stage, "The separation of libidinally invested and aggressively invested self- and object-representations becomes strengthened by active utilization of the mechanism of splitting, which is geared to protect the ideal, good relationship with the mother from 'contamination' by bad self-representations and bad representations of her" (p. 67). Normally this splitting decreases, but Kernberg continues with a statement meant to specifically delineate the intrapsychic pathology that predominates in the borderline personality: "The main objective of the defensive constellation centering on splitting in borderline personality organization is to keep separate the aggressively determined and the libidinally determined intrapsychic structures stemming from early object relations" (p. 67).

*Richard:* The fourth stage, beginning in the latter part of the third year of life and lasting through the oedipal period, is characterized by the integration of these libidinally invested and aggressively invested self-representations into a definitive self-system and similarly, of libidinally invested and aggressively invested object-images into total object representations. In this phase the ego and superego as intrapsychic structures are consolidated and the typical pathology is represented by a neurosis and what Kernberg calls higher-level character pathology. This stage fails in the borderline patient due to either a congenital ego defect or excessive aggression, fixing the patient in the third stage. The final developmental stage, from age 5 to 7, is the resolution of the oedipal phase, the consolidation of the superego, a diminished sharp opposition between the ego and the superego leading to more internal harmony, and finally the formation and consolidation of ego identity. Notice, Donald, that in normal development, according to Kernberg, splitting begins around the third month, peaks several months later, and gradually disappears at the end of the second year and beginning of the third year of life, after which there is the development of repression and higher level defenses.

*Donald:* What about the formation of the superego?

*Maria:* According to Kernberg (1976), the main components of the superego are built during the second to fifth year, earlier than Freud thought. They are integrated in the fourth to the sixth years and toned down and consolidated during the fifth through seventh years. The earliest superego structure is from "the internalization of fantastically hostile, highly unrealistic object-images reflecting 'expelled', projected and reintrojected 'bad' self-object representations" (pp. 71–72). The stronger the pregenital frustration and constitutional aggression, the more predominant the sadistic superego forerunners; the sadistic superego peaks at the beginning of the fourth stage of development.

*Donald:* It seems that Kernberg has borrowed a lot from Melanie Klein and used it in his own way, but he moved away from drive theory. According to Summers (1994), "the primary motivational system for Kernberg consists of inborn affect dispositions . . . the affect is always embedded within a relationship between self- and object images and these object relations units are stored as 'affective memory'" (p . 192). Drives for Kernberg are not inborn motivational units as they are for Klein. Affective dispositions are inborn, but the drive organization is conceptualized as an outcome of developmental experience that begins as undifferentiated object relations units.

*Richard:* That is correct. There is also a second primitive superego structure—the condensed, ideal, "all-good" self- and object-representations that form the kernel of the ego-ideal through primitive idealization.

*Maria:* In the fourth stage of development these two aspects of the precursors of the superego are "integrated," leading to decreased defensive projection and permitting the internalization of more realistic demands and prohibitions of the parents during the oedipal period. Integration and internalization perform the function of toning down the superego from primitive and archaic to more modulated and reasonable functioning. In the fifth stage of development the toned-down superego becomes more integrated and harmonious with the ego, leading to consolidation of ego identity and the superego becomes more abstract and depersonified.

*Richard:* In Kernberg's theory two types of superego failure can occur. In the first type, there is a failure in the integration of the sadistic precursors of the superego with the benign or primitively idealized precursors, which interferes with the internalization of more realistic oedipal parental images and so perpetuates the primitive sadistic superego forerunners and fosters excessive reprojection, leading to paranoia.

In the second type, as in the borderline personality, there is a similar type of failure of integration of these precursors due to a dangerous primitive idealization. External objects are seen as totally good in order to be sure they cannot be destroyed by projected bad objects. Remember our discussion of Melanie Klein! This phenomenon occurs too early and in too extreme a fashion as a result of the need to defend against so much aggression. Idealization is seen here as a defense against aggression. The internalization of primitively idealized early object images creates impossible internalized demands, causing an impasse. What Kernberg calls a "catastrophic fusion" between these unrealistic ideal objects, and the external persecutors or projected bad objects, then forms. This leads to introjecting a sadistic superego nucleus that is perpetuated by reprojection and reintrojection. It also leads to an interference with the toning down of the superego by the internalization of more realistic parental prohibitions, with the integration of the superego itself, and with the development of harmony between the superego and the ego. The latter causes interference with the formation of ego identity, leading to the lack of a consistent, solid, integrated self-concept.

*Donald:* I am exhausted!

*Maria:* We have come a long way from Freud indeed. Kernberg's classification of character pathology consists of "low-level" character disorders organized around splitting and related defenses, with a fixation point in the third stage of development (positive and negative self- and object-representations have not been integrated) and both an intermediate and a higher level set where the integration of self- and object-representations has been achieved and object relationships are stable. In this latter group, pathology results from conflict between ego and superego structures. The low-level disorders include borderline personality disorders; narcissistic personality disorders; sexual deviancy; hypomanic disorders; infantile personalities; antisocial, impulse-ridden, "as if," and inadequate personalities; and prepsychotic character disorders. Is such precise systemization possible? I feel like I've been going through mental acrobatics! Clearly Freud's tripartite structural theory is being replaced by, and is not reconcilable with, object relations theories.

*Richard:*  Beware viewing the patient through a prism of prefabricated ideas based on what is believed to be contained within a given diagnostic label. There is much argument in the literature about whether Kernberg's assumptions and complex terminology as well as his complicated ideas are clear and necessary. One of the disadvantages of these extreme examples of object relations theories is that the person described by these theories does not seem to think. He or she lives more or less by, or is lived by, his or her introjects or internal representations. There is no resolution in the literature about whether these theories are universally acceptable or not.

On the other hand it is true, as Kernberg indicates, that the analyst must realize patients "will not only enact themselves as their childhood selves, with the analyst as the parental figure, but will also enact the parental figure, with the analyst as the childhood self. Often the analytic material appears not to make sense because the patient is enacting an internalized object relations unit with the roles reversed" (Summers 1994, pp. 216–217). For Kernberg, the therapist "must continually search for the object relations unit enacted at each phase of the treatment, label for the patient the self- and object images enacted, and identify the connecting affective link" (p. 222). Also, the therapist must point out the existence of contradictory self- and object images and their connection, which Kernberg alleges will bring them together into integrated whole object representations.

Object relations theories emphasize that patients communicate by projective identification rather than by verbalizing. In formulating transference interpretations, therapists must sort out and understand their own affective responses, identify the actors in the drama that is being enacted with the patient, and communicate verbally to the patient. This is a fundamentally different kind of emphasis than the traditional reliance on reconstruction, dream interpretation, and the ego's role in compromise formations and defenses against the drives.

*Donald:*  This of course leaves us where we began. Certainly all of these theorists are brilliant and if one follows their contentions, in each instance one has a rather comprehensive notion of what to interpret and how to behave optimally in the analytic situation!

*Richard:* That's true, but I often worry that these brilliant theories, which perhaps work so well in the hands of clinicians like Kernberg and Kohut, may be used in a stereotyped and even destructive fashion by ordinary and less-talented therapists. Personally I prefer to be somewhat skeptical of all theories, and to use them as tools rather than dogma that prescribes how I am to conduct analytic treatment. Perhaps this is because I have seen in second analyses too many patients who were treated by rigid adherents of one theory or another; in these situations the theoretical conceptions are more or less forced on the patient, who identifies with the aggressor in order to put an end to the assault. Kohut's (1979) description of the "two analyses of Mr. Z." is a good example of this.

*Maria:* It is getting late and I am getting tired.

*Donald:* We have not discussed self psychology! Of course we referred to it in previous discussions, but you haven't reviewed it today. Is it not an object relations theory?

*Richard:* I think it *is* a form of object relations theory, because it hinges on the early relationship of the mother and the infant as primary in the formation or development of the self. Self psychologists disagree among themselves as to whether or not it is an object relations theory. It has been discussed and compared with the other object relations theories elsewhere (see Chessick 1985).

*Donald:* Perhaps it is best that we adjourn for today and clear our heads. Tomorrow we can review our discussions and get an idea of where we are heading with all these conflicting theories, and perhaps of the future of psychoanalysis and psychodynamic psychotherapy altogether, if any. And do not forget Lacan!

*Maria:* Enough! Cocktails, and then the dinner I have prepared for you.

*Donald and Richard:* Thank you. Let us drink to your health, Maria!

# 11

## The Eleventh Day:
## The Future

*Donald:* Well, I had another bad night. This is not the way I thought we would be concluding our discussions. Since you interested me in the Kleinians, I have been reading the *Freud-Klein Controversies* (King and Steiner 1991), and it has left me rather discouraged and disappointed. There seem to be so many oppositions between the traditional school of Anna Freud and the object relations school of Melanie Klein and her subsequent followers and successors!

*Richard:* Currently, as Kernberg (1993) points out, there are "certain areas of major convergences of technique," and growing divergences in other areas of technique (p. 659).

*Maria:* Perhaps it would be wise to have a look at what Anna Freud herself said in her controversy with Melanie Klein. Anna Freud's presentation offers about ten areas of disagreement. For Klein, object relations begin at birth, "whereas I consider there is a narcissistic and autoerotic phase of several months' duration, which precedes what we call object relationship in its proper sense, even though the beginning of object relation [sic] are slowly built up during this initial stage" (p. 418). All Klein's attributions to the newborn infant of loving, hating, desiring, attacking, and attempting to destroy and dismember the mother, and so forth, as well as feelings of guilt about all this and the wish to do reparation constitutes a far different theory than that of Anna Freud who considers the infant in the first few months of life "exclusively concerned with his own well-being" (p. 418). The mother, according to Anna Freud, is important simply if she either disturbs or serves this well-being. For example, I was at Richard's house during a supervisory session the other day and noticed his daughter trying to fill out her income tax form and soothe her baby at the same time. The baby would not be soothed; it cried incessantly. The minute the mother was finished filling out the income tax form and ready to relax, the baby stopped crying.

*Richard:* Anna Freud utilized Freud's pleasure principle in her understanding of the intraphysic processes of the child. That is to say, she believed that the psychic activity of the child was aimed at satisfaction or discharge of instinctual tensions and not ruled by fantasies or internalized object relations. For Freud the infant simply desires and hallucinates satisfaction.

*Maria:* So, Anna Freud writes, "according to analytic concepts an object relationship is built up slowly during a period of several months. Perception and reality testing in connection with experiences of satisfaction and frustration of wishes furnish the means by which the object becomes the centre of interest and, during the next year of life, equals in importance, sometimes even supersedes in importance, the gratification received" (p. 419). This occurrence marks an end to the era of infantile narcissism, according to Anna Freud. She allows only for the crudest rudiments of object relations in the earliest months of life, a rather dark and perhaps otherwise empty period that the Kleinians attempt to fill with this active fantasy process. Chessick (1996a) has attempted to delineate what it feels like during the regression that occurs in adult psychoanalysis when the patient approaches this so-called empty period.

*Donald:* It's very distressing because there is simply no direct evidence that can possibly be gathered about alleged fantasies in the first year of life; as we have seen this is all extrapolation from Klein's study of children 3 or 4 years old. The dating of these fantasies and the nature of them remains a highly controversial issue, and this is very important because it has great influence on the technique and practice of psychoanalytic treatment, as Anne Freud says: "An analyst who is not convinced of the existence of a synthetic function in the first year of life will not date back to that period fantasies which include elements of guilt and reparation" (p. 423).

*Richard:* There is indeed a serious difference of opinion in views about the sequence and mode of psychic development and about the dating of all important events and origins of various aspects of psychic functioning. Beside the debate about when object relations begin, there are also arguments about the timing and nature of the onset and climax of the Oedipus complex, the formation of the superego, and various ego functions. There is in addition a tremendous difference of opinion on the origin of violently aggressive fantasies, which are thought to be most fundamental by the Kleinians and yet are viewed as secondary disintegration products by those who follow Fairbairn or Kohut.

*Donald:* What about a clinical example?

*Maria:* Payne asks Anna Freud about the following situation: A child may be given the bottle by a stranger and refuse it, or refuse to take the breast from a wet nurse, whereas it will immediately accept these items from its customary mothering one. Does that not suggest that the child differentiates between objects? Anna Freud answers,

> There is no doubt that the child notices differences and even the slightest differences in atmosphere, position, behaviour, mood of the person who gives the bottle. . . . These differences reach the child because there is a change of the form in which the satisfaction is presented. . . . What we call change of atmosphere, change of mood, is not the tie to the person. If one could imitate the form in which the satisfaction is given completely, the child would accept it. Experience shows that it is surprisingly easy to interchange objects at that time, just as it is surprising how difficult it is later." [p. 435]

*Donald:* I find it most frustrating that the views of various brilliant clinicians and theoreticians like this cannot be reconciled, nor can I think of any way in which experimental data could really lead to validation or negation of these views. For example, Couch (1995) summarizes Anna Freud's recommendations for adult technique:

> (1) to analyze ego resistance before id content; (2) to proceed from surface to depth; (3) to offer the analyst as a transference object for the unforced natural growth of unconscious feelings, fears, wishes, memories, fantasies, and expectations about childhood figures; (4) to analyze impulses in a state of frustration as created by the analytic boundaries; (5) to lift material from the level of primary-process functioning to secondary-process thinking; in short, turn id into ego." [p. 157]

This seems quite reasonable to me, and yet there is so much controversy about it!

*Richard:* In addition to her position, as Couch describes it, which was certainly that established by Sigmund Freud, transference for both Freud and his daughter was used as only one of several important roads for learning about the patient's unconscious. Dreams remained the "royal road" to the unconscious. In addition there are free associations, memories, fantasies, affects, defenses, resistance, and nonverbal behavior utilized to explore the unconscious by the Freuds. Today the emphasis has shifted predominantly to the transference and countertransference, and the interpersonal exchange between the patient and the analyst.

*Maria:* I was impressed with Couch's explication of Anna Freud's practice of adult psychoanalysis. He remarks on the fact that she employed no strict system or rules and she retained her natural manner during sessions. Rather surprisingly, according to Couch, "She was responsive to my realistic questions and answered them in an ordinary way. . . . She also made commonsensical and realistic comments about some of the things I told her" (p. 158). I wonder if traditional classical analysts these days do that very much.

*Donald:* Are there any "traditional classical analysts" left?

*Maria:* The point is that Anna Freud was a naturally helpful person who had a "physicianly vocation" (Stone 1961) and her patients were fortunate to experience that vocation. I believe the same was true of Freud, in spite of his various published strictures on what the analyst should or should not say.

*Richard:* Certainly feel free and natural with a patient, but be ready to analyze whatever the patient's responses are, even in their exit lines (Gabbard 1982) as they leave the office, and in your reply to such exit lines be alert for any countertransference manifestations. This is of crucial importance.

*Donald:* But there are new controversies and approaches in psychoanalysis and psychoanalytic treatment today as a result of the work of object relations theorists, self psychologists, and others. Couch describes their technique as involving a total central focus on transference interpretations, and, for some authors (Gill 1982, 1984, 1994), on the here-and-now interaction of the patient and analyst under the influence of transference and countertransference. Couch claims that for object relations theorists an internal object model takes the place of the traditional drive/defense model, and they certainly make extensive use of concepts such as projective identification with a corresponding diminution of the older traditional attention to reconstructions.

*Richard:* One reason for this shift is that analytic treatment has a widening scope today, since we're dealing much more frequently with preoedipal disorders than with classical oedipal neurotics. Anna Freud had little hope for the analysis of narcissistic, borderline, and other personality disorders, or of the perversions or psychoses, in agreement with her father. She believed such patients could be helped only by ego building, whereas Kleinians and their subsequent followers have attempted to treat them using regular analytic techniques. Similarly, interpretive work has shifted from emphasis on childhood conflicts that appear after children are able to speak, to the earliest preoedipal periods, the so-called preverbal years of life. The current belief by the neo-Kleinians and many object relations theorists is that these earliest experiences can be relived and reexperienced in the analytic setting and interpreted, and that such interpretation would lead to ego integration and maturation or the resumption of development. There is more emphasis on the analyst's countertransference *pari passu* with the emphasis on projective identification, as we have discussed it earlier, and at least the orthodox Kleinians focus much more exclusively on internal psychic reality rather than the external reality confronting the patient.

*Donald:* Here we go again! Couch asks what we gain by replacing Freud's structural concepts "with a new metapsychology of internal object relationships and primitive unconscious fantasies of the infant as the basis of mental functioning?" (p. 169). He argues that the humane or humanistic aspect of psychoanalysis is lost if there is so much emphasis on transference interpretation of every communication between patient and analyst. He feels this undermines the "very authenticity of the analytic relationship" (p. 169), and he ends on a very pessimistic note. He worries that claims of success in the psychoanalytic treatment of very disturbed patients, in which only transference interpretations are focused upon, will result in the final loss of respect for psychoanalytic therapy.

*Richard:* I believe that is too gloomy, Donald. In the first place, psychoanalysis is on the rise as a respected therapy in South American countries and certain other parts of the world. It has declined only in the United States and England, primarily—very pragmatic countries that demand statistical studies to demonstrate the efficacy of any procedure. The difficulties involved in producing experimental data and statistical studies of the results of psychoanalysis have made it impossible, so far, for convincing data to be produced. This has been seized upon by the insurance companies—who now, at great profit, control the whole of medical practice in the United States—to eliminate long-term psychoanalytic or psychotherapeutic treatment. And already they have succeeded in this to a great extent. But this profit motive has nothing to do with the efficacy of that treatment or the importance of it. Psychoanalytic therapy will go on because it is needed, and there is a wide accumulation of anecdotal knowledge that indicates the power and effectiveness of psychoanalytic techniques. Scientific proof in the traditional sense of statistical analysis is still lacking, and the wide variety of disagreement in the field does not by itself vitiate the entire field; in fact it may be a sign of fertility and growth in a field!

*Donald:* Hale (1995) writes:

> Between 1960 and 1985 nearly all the factors that had contributed to the rise of psychoanalytic psychiatry were in part reversed: doubts grew about the scientific validity and effectiveness of psychoanalysis; alternatives to the psychoanalytic psychodynamic style arose; psychoanalysis lost its identifi-

cation with psychiatric reform; social conditions for psychoanalytic practice changed; partly because of a lack of demonstrable results, government and private funding for psychoanalytic training and research dwindled; some psychoanalysts retreated from the new therapeutic fields they had staked out, among them, psychosomatic medicine and the treatment of schizophrenia." [p. 300]

That is one sentence! If psychoanalysis were a science, or "our science" as psychoanalysts beginning with Freud have arrogantly tended to call it, would this happen?

*Maria:* That's too strong, Donald. The definition of science is not so simple. Feyerabend, that brilliant iconoclast, made quite a name for himself by challenging the smugness of positivists, scientists, and philosophers who considered themselves experts on the so-called philosophy of science. For example, he (1995) points out that "Science itself has conflicting parts with different strategies, results, metaphysical embroideries. It is a collage, not a system. . . . Scientific institutions are not 'objective'; neither they nor their products confront people like a rock, or a star. They often merge with other traditions, are affected by them, affect them in turn" (p. 143). Psychoanalysis, "our science," is in the same boat with all the other sciences.

*Richard:* The decline of psychoanalysis in the United States, which has rapidly precipitated over the past twenty years, has more to do with the general decline of the cultural level and the regression from civilized behavior to barbaric behavior that has permeated our country. But the pendulum swings back and forth, and the current search for "fast-fast-fast" relief, aided and abetted by the huge pharmaceutical corporations which are urging psychiatrists to give drugs to everybody for everything, will eventually lead to a new phase of disillusionment. The real question as I see it is whether American civilization can turn around the decline of civility and the loss of the dignity of the individual that has taken place in such tragic proportions in our generation. The loss of respectability of long-term psychoanalytic treatment is a function of that decline.

*Maria:* This is the place to talk about Lacan. His controversial work led to an explosion of interest in psychoanalysis in France and it's my understanding that Lacanian concepts are replacing Kleinian concepts in a rapidly growing psychoanalytic renaissance in South America! We have managed to hardly mention Lacan in these discussions!

*Donald:* Of course one could comment that moving from Kleinian to Lacanian psychoanalysis is moving in an increasingly mystical and unverifiable and unscientific direction!

*Richard:* It is moving in a hermeneutic direction and away from psychoanalysis as a natural science. Will this be the future of psychoanalysis? What will be the impact of the growing influence of psychologists in the United States on the practice of psychoanalysis? It is no longer a standard, exclusively medical discipline in our country and in that sense it has become much less respectable, and probably less remunerative. This mention of Lacan brings us to the postmodern era. The implications of postmodernism for psychoanalysis are very important. If the postmodernist view is to be followed, each of us consists of many voices, many selves, and all in different contexts. The presentation of homogeneity, of the integrated subject, can be thought of as a mask, a masquerade that falsely unifies diverse aspects of experience and marginalizes or forecloses other aspects. Concepts of the unified and well-integrated self are no longer viewed as ideals. They are considered to be dangerous ideological fictions used to erase the awareness of differences between and within human beings.

*Maria:* Postmodernists argue that if we do not have an understanding of this multiplicity, we are going to wind up missing those dimensions of our patients' experiences that enable them to grow, and we will be unable to re-create the patterns that got our patients into trouble in the first place. So, for example, postmodernist discourses open up spaces to hear the voices of the marginalized experiences of the family. Psychoanalysts need to listen attentively for multiple voices—not as a unified choir but to tease out singular voices that have been drowned out through years of oppression, demand for conformity, submission, and pain. The individual—often the patient—who dares to challenge the demand for conformity and submission to the family system is labeled as either bad or mad.

*Donald:* But as I understand it, from the postmodernist point of view cultural differences and conflicts are no longer erased and collapsed into a psychiatric diagnosis! A dialogue is created whereby these positions with all their histories, peoples, and affects, become signified in language. We no longer encounter patients who fall into theoretical categories, our dominant psychoanalytic paradigms, the psychiatric labels in *DSM-IV*, and all that, but instead we experience individuals who are constructed through a variety of cultural, class, historical, racial, and gendered experiences, all coded in available language and discourse. I don't know if, as a scientific psychiatrist and physician, I can accept this proposed revolutionary change. According to this new orientation, we enter into a dialogic discourse with our patients rather than occupying a monologic position of dispensing knowledge in the guise of true interpretations. To some this represents nihilism and anarchy; to others, free-

dom and options. To some it represents the decline in scientific objec-
tivity and technological confidence, to others a rooting of scientific
knowledge in a particular history and cultural setting. Different viewpoints depend on where you are standing, and utilizing Foucault's power/
knowledge discourse, on where you are situated in the cultural context
and the politics of psychoanalysis. Again my head is spinning around!

*Richard:* For postmodernists language is anything but neutral and our
speaking parts have been scripted in ways that implicitly represent the
standpoint of dominant social groups. We as analysts are in paradoxical
positions because we are constantly attempting to deconstruct and challenge people's discourse, and yet all the time we ourselves are constituted by the available and general social, cultural, and historical discourses of knowledge. Still, argue the postmodernists, only by listening
to one's multiples voices can the apparent and fictive "natural order of
things" be contested and aid us in not complying with the domination
of ourselves or others.

*Maria:* In its de-privileging of the analyst as the oracle of truth,
postmodernism stands in contrast to a positivist interpretation of experience. It moves the psychoanalyst from the place of a scientist uncovering facts to a collaboration in developing personal narratives that are
concerned with the relativism and the interpretive nature of all clinical
understanding.

*Richard:* This hermeneutic trend is not anything to be afraid of, for
interpretation is what we do best. The attempt to justify our interpretations in the name of scientific explanations actually leads to a loss of
authority, for this demeans and neglects our hermeneutic skills and real
power. The presentation of psychoanalysis as a science may have been
necessary for Freud to legitimize a new, highly revolutionary and brilliant discourse, but today we are in a new context, in a new history that
does not demand these rhetorical strategies. The new focus on a two-
person psychology in the consulting room creates spaces whereby two
subjectivities are legitimized, each with its own histories, scripts, and cast
of characters. We're interested in the influence of one on the other.
Postmodernism goes to the extreme of arguing that the idea of the sig-
nifier implies that true meaning can never be discovered, and that which
is signified is forever elusive, leaving us only with a continuous chain of
signifiers. This chain of signification is saturated with multiple meanings, and essential meaning exists only in the realm of the imaginary.

*Maria:* The postmodern emphasis is on the present and the unfolding moment in the consulting room. It diverts attention from that which
allegedly endures in persons to social transactions and the world in which
they occur. This is an inevitable consequence for example, of Hoffman's

(1983, 1991, 1992) social constructivist and other narrative theories. I think this is an unfortunate development.

*Richard:* I am against the extreme relativism inherent in attempts to develop a thoroughly "postmodern" psychoanalysis. My (Chessick 1995b) argument is that such postmodern psychoanalysis, which postulates that meaning is uniquely generated out of the interaction between each specific therapist–patient pair and has no correlation with empirical facts, has become a fashionable but dangerous and unsupportable stance. The postmodern view that even partial truth does not exist suggests an approach that could easily degenerate into wild analysis, interpretations without effort to base them on any sense of reality, and ultimately a collusion between patient and analyst to avoid whatever makes either of them anxious.

*Donald:* Yet all of this has immediate application to the clinical practice of psychoanalysis and intensive psychotherapy because of the unresolved issue of whether these procedures represent science or hermeneutics, and the debate continues! If postmodernists are to be believed, the human "sciences," to whatever extent they rely on "text" or "narratives" that arise in the psychoanalytic situation, are subject to deconstruction and continuing reinterpretation. In this sense it is no longer possible to speak of truth or reality as Freud once did when he repeatedly and insistently presented psychoanalysis as uncovering scientific facts.

*Richard:* At the same time it is important to realize that psychoanalytic treatment does indeed involve two people in the same room who interact with one another, that one should always be skeptical about theoretical formulations, and that descriptions of treatments in the literature need to be made more precise by giving specific details of the verbal and nonverbal interaction between the analyst and the patient. For example, Ogden (1994) points out how sometimes the analyst uses action instead of words to convey his or her understanding of the transference-countertransference manifestations.

*Donald:* But he adds that this also requires a silent formulation in words by the analyst!

*Richard:* Nevertheless, as he says, "I take it for granted that interpretation is a form of object relationship and that object relationship is a form of interpretation" (p. 222). So-called clinical material—how I dislike that inhuman phrase!—often ignores this when presented as part of a paper that is intended to make a metapsychological point or support a generalization from the author's clinical experience. So many of these anecdotal clinical examples simply represent an illustrative formulation by the author meant to buttress a theoretical point of view and are not reliable as narratives for hermeneutic investigation or even as clinical data. As such they are tendentious and not to be trusted. It requires only a simple perusal of Freud's wonderfully written case histories to see to what an enormous extent Freud's behavior, prejudices, and cultural style influenced the production of his patient's material. Yet again it should be kept in mind that in spite of these peccadilloes and Freud's commanding presence, certain basic transference paradigms took place and could be analyzed. In that sense the patient's urge toward health and drive to resume development triumphs over the obstacles presented by the individual foibles of the analyst if there is a basically analytic stance on the part of the analyst and a genuine concern for the patient, free of the need to use the patient for one's own purposes.

*Donald:* Let me write this down so I can remember it: The patient's urge toward health, and his or her drive to resume development, triumphs over the inevitable obstacles presented by the individual foibles of the analyst—*if* there is on the part of the analyst a basically analytic stance and a genuine concern for the patient, free of the need to use the patient for one's own purposes.

*Maria:* An unfortunate negative example of the latter is the failed case of Dora presented by Freud (1905), in which he attempted to use the treatment as a demonstration of his theories of infantile sexuality rather than pay attention to Dora's realistic plight. One might uncharitably say that Freud in this procedure rammed his theoretical interpretations down Dora's throat, as the metaphor goes. We can forgive Freud for this treatment failure because his whole procedure was in its infancy in the autumn of 1900 when it was carried out, but it is harder to forgive some of our contemporary colleagues who abuse patients in this fashion.

*Donald:* Speaking of abusing patients, what about Lacan?

*Maria:* Certainly his "five-minute hour" lends itself easily to the abuse and exploitation of patients. It's interesting that we began our discussion on the first day, Donald, with your question about *Nachträglichkeit*, or in French *après-coup*, and Laplanche and Pontalis (1973), in their discussion of Freud's ambiguous use of this term give Lacan the credit for first pointing out its importance! His reason for emphasizing the concept is related to his notion that truth is a function of speech, and "the analysand's truth is essentially shaped by the temporality of his telling of his life story" (Lee 1990, p. 43). It is no secret that Lacan had many unresolved narcissistic problems, yet a study of Lacan's work seems to stir up a great deal of thinking and, if nothing else, motivates one to return to a study of Freud.

*Richard:* I believe that one cannot review and study Freud's writings over and over enough times in one's lifetime (Chessick 1980). This is true for all psychodynamically oriented psychotherapists, not just for psychoanalysts. Every time one reads or works through the corpus of Freud's productions, one comes up with new ideas and differences in emphasis as one gains experience in the clinical consulting room. Freud, like Marx, was one of those "founders of discursivity," as Foucault (1984) calls them in the human sciences, who have "produced something else: the possibilities and the rules for the formation of other texts. . . . They . . . have established an endless possibility of discourse" (p. 114). One returns repeatedly to their writings even if there are errors in them, and each reexamination modifies one's thought and practice, and consequently their human science itself. For over forty years in this psychoanalytic psychotherapeutic field I have found this to be quite true of Freud's work. None of this is vitiated by the fact, as Freud's enemies love to point out, that Freud made a variety of culture-bound errors and manifested personal prejudices Who does not?

Lacan is a far more difficult writer to appraise. The greatest value to the study of Lacan, it seems to me, is to increase our sensitivity to spoken language and hidden meanings that are signified in it when we listen properly to the patient. Lacan (for a review of his concepts see Chessick 1992a, Lee 1990) repeatedly warns us of the existence of the "Other," which is consistent with the postmodern position that we have already discussed today. The more we become aware of this "Other" in ourselves, our patients, and our culture, the more tolerant, mature, and understanding we may become in our relationships with all individuals, including patients. And there is certainly a desperate need for mutual understanding in today's troubled and violent world.

*Donald:* In a way it is sad to end our discussions on such a dark note, a note of unresolved disagreement, and of difficulties even in the establishment of mutual tolerance of political, scientific, philosophical, and religious points of view. We can only wait and hope that the pendulum will swing in the other direction for the next generation.

*Richard:* I disagree with that last statement, Donald, which too much echoes Heidegger's (1966) view. I believe a person is not mature unless he or she is willing to take an *active* role in the various organizations and movements that exist for the purpose of improving the health and well-being of the people of the world and fostering mutual tolerance between cultural, ethnic, racial, and sexually diverse groups. The era in which the doctor or the "scientist" can immerse himself or herself in a laboratory or consulting room and pay no attention to what is going on outside has come to an end. The entire history of the twentieth century shows what happens when the more intelligent voices of a generation are muted, or turned inward, and the fanatic and paranoid voices are allowed to gain dominance. No psychotherapist or psychoanalyst can consider herself or himself to be free of a major ego or superego defect if the therapist withdraws from the never-ending struggle to improve the human condition and make life gracious, even in a barbaric, dark, and nuclear age.

*Maria:* Part of this depends on the reemergence of the maternal or nurturing principle in both men and women. I hope that this aspect of feminist thinking gains predominance in postmodern dialogue. I believe that our species is in danger and it has a long way to go to reverse the brutal and exploitative trends that have become dominant in today's world.

*Donald:* Yes, humans are an endangered species!

*Richard:* This is a crucial aspect of our psychoanalytic work; as the future generations of psychoanalysts explore the psyche and gain greater and greater understanding of its limitations and the forces that bend it out of shape from the early beginnings of life, there is greater hope for the amelioration and prevention of the kind of damage that leads to brutal, fanatic, violent, barbaric adults. The diversity of views in our field is an asset rather than a liability at this point, for, if the narcissistic investments in these various views can be kept under control, an important cross-fertilization can take place, even with views as provocative and esoteric or obscurantist as those of Lacan. And it is this cross-fertilization and stimulation to dialogue and discussion that holds the greatest hope for the improvement of our understanding and eventual betterment of the human condition.

*Donald:* I am getting sleepy. Thank you, Maria, for being the generous hostess of these discussions. I hope we may continue again at some future time.

*Maria:* Thank you Richard and Donald for being such stimulating and rewarding guests.

*Richard:* I will end where I began. Franz Alexander taught me a lot about psychodynamic psychotherapy and psychoanalysis, which I hope I have handed down to you today. He explains,

> When I was asked to speak about the social significance of psychotherapy, I came, after serious consideration, to the conclusion that it lies in giving an operational meaning to the motto of the Renaissance humanists, "respect for the dignity of the individual." Psychotherapy aims not only at enabling a person to adjust himself to existing conditions, but also to realize his unique potentials. Never was this aim more difficult and at the same time more essential. Psychoanalysis and psychotherapy in general are among the few still existing remedies against the relentlessly progressing levelization of indus-

trial societies which tend to reduce the individual person to becoming an indistinguishable member of the faceless masses." [1964, p. 243]

Maria and Donald, you are the next generation. The hope of the mentally ill, in their vital continuing struggle to obtain the treatment they need against the greed of huge insurance companies and the profit motive of the multinational corporations they represent, as well as the self-serving political bureaucracy that their wealth supports, rests on your tireless energy and empathic understanding of the underprivileged in our rich Western societies and in the rest of the world. May we meet again soon!

# References

Abend, S. (1989). Countertransference and psychoanalytic technique. *Psychoanalytic Quarterly* 58:374–395.

Abend, S., Porder, M., and Willick, M. (1983). *Borderline Patients: Psychoanalytic Perspectives*. New York: International Universities Press.

Adler, G. (1980). Transference, real relationship and alliance. *International Journal of Psycho-Analysis* 61:547–558.

Akiskal, H. (1981). Subaffective disorders: dysthymic, cyclothymic and bipolar II disorders in the "borderline" realm. *Psychiatry Clinics of North America* 4:25–46.

Alexander, F. (1956). *Psychoanalysis and Psychotherapy: Developments in Theory, Technique and Training*. New York: Norton.

—— (1964). Social significance of psychoanalysis and psychotherapy. *Archives of Psychiatry* 11:235–244.

Arlow, J. (1980). Object concept and object choice. *Psychoanalytic Quarterly* 49:109–133.

—— (1985a). Some technical problems of countertransference. *Psychoanalytic Quarterly* 54:164–174.

—— (1985b). The concept of psychic reality and related problems. *Journal of the American Psychoanalytic Association* 33:521–535.

—— (1991a). *Psychoanalysis: Clinical Theory and Practice*. Madison, CT: International Universities Press.

—— (1991b). Methodology and reconstruction. *Psychoanalytic Quarterly* 60:539–563.

Bak, R. (1973). Being in love and object loss. *International Journal of Psycho-Analysis* 54:1–7.

Balint, M. (1952). *Primary Love and Psychoanalytic Technique*. New York: Liveright.

Basch, M. (1992). *Practicing Psychotherapy: A Case Book*. New York: Basic Books.

Benjamin, W. (1968). *Illuminations: Essays and Reflections*, trans. H. Zohn. New York: Schocken.

Bettelheim, B. (1983). *Freud and Man's Soul*. New York: Knopf.

Bion, W. (1963). *Elements of Psycho-Analysis*. New York: Basic Books.

—— (1976). *Second Thoughts: Selected Papers on Psycho-Analysis*. London: Heinemann.

Bléandonu, G. (1994). *Wilfred Bion: His Life and Works 1897–1979*, trans. C. Pajaczkowska. New York: Guilford.

Blum, H. (1973). The concept of eroticized transference. *Journal of the American Psychoanalytic Association* 21:61–76.

—— (1994). Discussion on the erotic transference: contemporary perspectives. *Psychoanalytic Inquiry* 14:622–635.

Boesky, D. (1988). Comments on the structural theory of technique. *International Journal of Psycho-Analysis* 69:303–316.

Brenner, C. (1982). *The Mind in Conflict*. New York: International Universities Press.

Calef, V. (1971). Concluding remarks. *Journal of the American Psychoanalytic Association* 19:89–97.

Cavell, M. (1993). *The Psychoanalytic Mind: From Freud to Philosophy*. Cambridge, MA: Harvard University Press.

Celani, D. (1993). *The Treatment of the Borderline Patient: Applying Fairbairn's Object Relations Theory in the Clinical Setting*. Madison, CT: International Universities Press.

Cheshire, N., and Thomä, H. (1991). Metaphor, neologism and "open texture": implications for translating Freud's scientific thought. *International Review of Psycho-Analysis* 18:429–455.

Chessick, R. (1971). The use of the couch in the psychotherapy of borderline patients. *Archives of Psychiatry* 25:306–131.

—— (1972). Externalization and existential anguish. *Archives of Psychiatry* 27:764–770.

—— (1977). *Intensive Psychotherapy of the Borderline Patient*. Northvale, NJ: Jason Aronson.

—— (1980). *Freud Teaches Psychotherapy*. Indianapolis: Hackett.

—— (1982). Intensive psychotherapy of a borderline patient. *Archives of General Psychiatry* 39:413–419.

—— (1983a). *How Psychotherapy Heals*. Northvale, NJ: Jason Aronson.

—— (1983b). *Why Psychotherapists Fail*. Northvale, NJ: Jason Aronson.

—— (1984). A failure in psychoanalytic psychotherapy of a schizophrenic patient. *Dynamic Psychotherapy* 2:136–156.

—— (1985). *Psychology of the Self and the Treatment of Narcissism*. Northvale, NJ: Jason Aronson.

—— (1987). *Great Ideas in Psychotherapy*. Northvale, NJ: Jason Aronson.

—— (1989). *The Technique and Practice of Listening in Intensive Psychotherapy*. Northvale, NJ: Jason Aronson.

—— (1990). Self-analysis: A fool for a patient? *Psychoanalytic Review* 77:311–340.

—— (1991). *The Technique and Practice of Intensive Psychotherapy*, 3rd ed. Northvale, NJ: Jason Aronson.

—— (1992a). *What Constitutes the Patient in Psychotherapy: Alternative Approaches to Understanding.* Northvale, NJ: Jason Aronson.

—— (1992b). The death instinct revisited. *Journal of the American Academy of Psychoanalysis* 20:3–28.

—— (1993). *A Dictionary for Psychotherapists: Dynamic Concepts in Psychotherapy.* Northvale, NJ: Jason Aronson.

—— (1994). The dead self. *American Journal of Psychoanalysis* 54:266–273.

—— (1995a). Psychosis after open heart surgery: a phenomenological study. *American Journal of Psychotherapy* 49:171–179.

—— (1995b). Postmodern psychoanalysis or wild analysis? *Journal of the American Academy of Psychoanalysis* 23:47–62.

—— (1996a). Nothingness, meaninglessness, chaos and the "black hole" revisited. *Journal of the American Academy of Psychoanalysis* 23: in press.

—— (1996b). Impasse and failure in psychoanalysis. *Journal of the American Academy of Psychoanalysis* 24: in press.

Coen, S. (1994). Report of a panel on impasses in psychoanalysis. *Journal of the American Psychoanalytic Association* 42:1225–1235.

Couch, A. (1995). Anna Freud's adult psychoanalytic technique: a defense of classical analysis. *International Journal of Psycho-Analysis* 76:153–171.

Dowling, S. (1990). Fantasy formation: a child analyst's perspective. *Journal of the American Psychoanalytic Association* 38:93–112.

Einstein, A. (1974). Preface to *Dialogue Concerning the Two Chief World Systems,* trans. S. Drake. Berkeley, CA: University of California Press.

Eisenberg, L. (1995). The social construction of the human brain. *American Journal of Psychiatry* 152:1563–1575.

Eisold, K. (1994). The intolerance of diversity in psychoanalytic institutes. *International Journal of Psycho-Analysis* 75:785–800.

Eissler, K. (1953). The effect of the structure of the ego on psychoanalytic technique. *Journal of the American Psychoanalytic Association* 1:104–143.

Etchegoyen, R. (1991). *Fundamentals of Psychoanalytic Technique.* London: Karnac.

Fairbairn, W. (1958). On the nature and aims of psychoanalytic treatment. *International Journal of Psycho-Analysis* 39:374–385.

—— (1963). Synopsis of an object-relations theory of the personality. *International Journal of Psycho-Analysis* 44:224–225.

Fenichel, O. (1945). *Psychoanalytic Theory of the Neuroses.* New York: Norton.

Ferenczi, S. (1933). Confusion of tongues between adults and the child. In *Final Contributions to the Problems and Methods of Psychoanalysis: Selected Papers of Sándor Ferenczi,* vol. 3. New York: Basic Books.

—— (1988). *The Clinical Diary of Sándor Ferenczi,* trans. M. Balint and N. Jackson. Cambridge, MA: Harvard University Press.

Feyerabend, P. (1995). *Killing Time: The Autobiography of Paul Feyerabend.* Chicago: University of Chicago Press.

Foucault, M. (1984). *The Foucault Reader,* ed. P. Rabinow. New York: Pantheon.

Freud, S. (1900). The interpretation of dreams. *Standard Edition* 4/5:1–626.

—— (1901). The psychopathology of everyday life. *Standard Edition* 6:1–289.
—— (1905a). Fragment of an analysis of a case of hysteria. *Standard Edition* 7:3–122.
—— (1905b). Three essays on the theory of sexuality. *Standard Edition* 7:125–248.
—— (1910). "Wild" psycho-analysis. *Standard Edition* 11:219–230.
—— (1911). Formulations on the two principles of mental functioning. *Standard Edition* 12:218–226.
—— (1912). Recommendations to physicians practicing psychoanalysis. *Standard Edition* 12:109–120.
—— (1915a). Observations on transference love (further recommendations on the technique of psychoanalysis III). *Standard Edition* 12:157–171.
—— (1915b). Instincts and their vicissitudes. *Standard Edition* 14:109–140.
—— (1915–1916). Introductory lectures on psychoanalysis. *Standard Edition* 15/16:1–496.
—— (1917). Mourning and melancholia. *Standard Edition* 14:237–258.
—— (1918). From the history of an infantile neurosis. *Standard Edition* 17:7–122.
—— (1920). Beyond the pleasure principle. *Standard Edition* 18:3–66.
—— (1930). Civilization and its discontents. *Standard Edition* 21:59–148.
—— (1933). New introductory lectures on psychoanalysis. *Standard Edition* 22:3–184.
—— (1937). Analysis terminable and interminable. *Standard Edition* 23:209–254.
—— (1950). Project for a scientific psychology. *Standard Edition* 1:295–343.
Fromm-Reichmann, F. (1950). *Principles of Intensive Psychotherapy*. Chicago: University of Chicago Press.
Frosch, J. (1991). The New York psychoanalytic civil war. *Journal of the American Psychoanalytic Association* 39:1037–1064.
Gabbard, G. (1982). The exit line: heightened transference–countertransference manifestations at the end of the hour. *Journal of the American Psychoanalytic Association* 30:579–598.
——, ed. (1989). *Sexual Exploitation in Professional Relationships*. Washington, DC: American Psychiatric Press.
Galileo, G. (1629). *Dialogue Concerning the Two Chief World Systems*, trans. S. Drake. Berkeley, CA: University of California Press, 1974.
Gedo, J. (1977). Notes on the psychoanalytic management of archaic transferences. *Journal of the American Psychoanalytic Association* 25:787–803.
—— (1979). *Beyond Interpretation: Toward a Revised Theory for Psychoanalysis*. New York: International Universities Press.
—— (1981). *Advances in Clinical Psychoanalysis*. New York: International Universities Press.
—— (1984). *Psychoanalysis and Its Discontents*. New York: Guilford.
—— (1986). *Conceptual Issues in Psychoanalysis*. Hillsdale, NJ: Analytic Press.
Gedo, J., and Gehrie, M., eds. (1993). *Impasse and Innovation in Psychoanalysis: Clinical Case Seminars*. Hillsdale, NJ: Analytic Press.
Gedo, J., and Goldberg, A. (1973). *Models of the Mind: A Psychoanalytic Theory*. Chicago: University of Chicago Press.

Gill, M. (1982). *Analysis of Transference*. New York: International Universities Press.

—— (1984). Psychoanalysis and psychotherapy: a revision. *International Review of Psychoanalysis* 11:141–179.

—— (1994). *Psychoanalysis in Transition: A Personal View*. Hillsdale, NJ: Analytic Press.

Gray, P. (1994). *The Ego and Analysis of Defense*. Northvale, NJ: Jason Aronson.

Greenberg, J., and Mitchell, S. (1983). *Object Relations in Psychoanalytic Theory*. Cambridge, MA: Harvard University Press.

Greenson, R. (1967). *The Technique and Practice of Psychoanalysis*. New York: International Universities Press.

—— (1974). The decline and fall of the fifty-minute hour. *Journal of the American Psychoanalytic Association* 22:785–791.

Groddeck, G. (1961). *The Book of the It*. New York: Mentor.

Grotstein, J. (1990). The "Black Hole" as the basic psychotic experience: some newer psychoanalytic and neuroscience perspectives on psychosis. *Journal of the American Academy of Psychoanalysis* 18:29–46.

—— (1990a). Nothingness, meaninglessness, chaos, and the "black hole" I. *Contemporary Psychoanalysis* 26:257–290.

—— (1990b). Nothingness, meaninglessness, chaos, and the "black hole" II: The black hole. *Contemporary Psychoanalysis* 26:377–407.

—— (1991). Nothingness, meaninglessness, chaos, and the "black hole" III: Self- and interactional regulation and the background presence of primary identification. *Contempoarary Psychoanalysis* 27:1–33.

Grotstein, J., and Rinsley, D., eds. (1994). *Fairbairn and the Origins of Object Relations*. New York: Guilford.

Gunderson, J., and Elliott, G. (1985). The interface between borderline personality disorder and affective disorder. *American Journal of Psychiatry* 142:277–288.

Gunther, M. (1976). The endangered self: a contribution to the understanding of narcissistic determinants of countertransference. *Annual of Psychoanalysis* 4:201–224.

Guntrip, H. (1974). Psychoanalytic object relations theory: the Fairbairn-Guntrip approach. In *American Handbook of Psychiatry*, vol. 1, 2nd ed., ed. S. Arieti, pp. 828–842. New York: Basic Books.

Gutheil, T. (1989). Borderline personality disorder, boundary violations, and patient–therapist sex: medical legal pitfalls. *American Journal of Psychiatry* 146:597–602.

Halberstam, D. (1993). *The Fifties*. New York: Villard.

Hale, N. (1995). *The Rise and Crisis of Psychoanalysis in the United States: Freud and the Americans 1917–1985*. New York: Oxford University Press.

Hartmann, H. (1958). *Ego Psychology and the Problem of Adaptation*. New York: International Universities Press.

Hayman, A. (1994). Some remarks about the "controversial discussions." *International Journal of Psycho-Analysis* 75:343–358.

Heidegger, M. (1966). "Only a god can save us": the *Spiegel* interview. In *Heidegger: The Man and the Thinker*, ed. T. Sheehan, pp. 45–72. Chicago: Precedent.

Hoffman, I. (1983). The patient as interpreter of the analyst's experience. *Contemporary Psychoanalysis* 19:389–422.

—— (1991). Discussion. Towards a social-constructivist view of the psychoanalytic situation. *Psychoanalytic Dialogues* 1:74–105.

—— (1992). Some practical implications of a social-constructivist view of the psychoanalytic situation. *Psychoanalytic Dialogues* 2:287–304.

Jacobson, E. (1964). *The Self and the Object World*. New York: International Universities Press.

Jaspers, K. (1972). *General Psychopathology*, trans. J. Hoenig and M. Hamilton. Chicago: University of Chicago Press.

Jones, E. (1953). *The Life and Work of Sigmund Freud: 1856–1900. The Formative Years and the Great Discoveries*. New York: Basic Books.

Kernberg, O. (1975). *Borderline Conditions and Pathological Narcissism*. Northvale, NJ: Jason Aronson.

—— (1976). *Object Relations Theory and Clinical Psychoanalysis*. Northvale, NJ: Jason Aronson.

—— (1980). *Internal World and External Reality*. Northvale, NJ: Jason Aronson.

—— (1987). Projection and projective identification: developmental and clinical aspects. *Journal of the American Psychoanalytic Association* 35:795–819.

—— (1993). Convergences and divergences in contemporary psychoanalytic technique. *International Journal of Psycho-Analysis* 74:659–673.

Kernberg, O., Selzer, M., Koenigsberg, H., et al. (1989). *Psychodynamic Psychotherapy of Borderline Patients*. New York: Basic Books.

King, P., and Steiner, R., eds. (1991). *The Freud–Klein Controversies 1941–45*. London: Tavistock/Routledge.

Klein, M. (1946). Notes on some schizoid mechanisms. In *Envy and Gratitude and Other Works 1946–1963*. New York: Delta, 1975.

Kohut, H. (1971). *The Analysis of the Self*. New York: International Universities Press.

—— (1977). *The Restoration of the Self*. New York: International Universities Press.

—— (1979). The two analyses of Mr. Z. *International Journal of Psycho-Analysis* 60:3–27.

—— (1984). *How Does Analysis Cure?* Chicago: University of Chicago Press.

—— (1987). *Rilke and Benvenuta: An Intimate Correspondence*, trans. J. Agee. New York: Fromm International.

Lacan, J. (1978). *The Four Fundamental Concepts of Psycho-Analysis*, trans. A. Sheridan. New York: Norton.

Langs, R. (1979). *The Therapeutic Environment*. Northvale, NJ: Jason Aronson.

—— (1982). *Psychotherapy: A Basic Text*. Northvale, NJ: Jason Aronson.

Laplanche, J., and Pontalis, J. (1973). *The Language of Psycho-Analysis*, trans. D. Nicholson-Smith. New York: Norton.

Lee, J. (1990). *Jacques Lacan*. Amherst: University of Massachusetts Press.

Lipton, S. (1977). The advantages of Freud's technique as shown in his analysis of the Rat Man. *International Journal of Psycho-Analysis* 58:255–274.

—— (1979). An addendum to "The advantages of Freud's technique as shown in his analysis of the Rat Man." *International Journal of Psycho-Analysis* 60:215–216.

—— (1983). A critique of so-called standard psychoanalytic technique. *Contemporary Psychoanalysis* 19:35–46.

Loewald, H. (1980). On the therapeutic action of psychoanalysis. In *Papers on Psychoanalysis*, pp. 221–256. New Haven: Yale University Press.

Loewenstein, R., Newman, L., Schur, M., and Solnit, A., eds. (1966). *Psychoanalysis: A General Psychology*. New York: International Universities Press.

Maguire, J. (1990). Notes on stalemate: a particular negative reaction affecting therapeutic outcome. *Annual of Psychoanalysis* 18:63–83.

Mahler, M., Pine, F., and Bergman, A. (1975). *The Psychological Birth of the Human Infant*. New York: Basic Books.

Maltsberger, J., and Buie, D. (1974). Countertransference hate in the treatment of suicidal patients. *Archives of General Psychiatry* 30:625–633.

McGlashan, T. (1983). The borderline syndrome II: Is it a variant of schizophrenia or affective disorder? *Archives of General Psychiatry* 40:1319–1323.

Meissner, W. (1984). *The Borderline Spectrum: Differential Diagnosis and Developmental Issues*. Northvale, NJ: Jason Aronson.

Menninger, K. (1958). *The Theory of Psychoanalytic Technique*. New York: Basic Books.

Modell, A. (1968). *Object Love and Reality*. New York: International Universities Press.

—— (1975). A narcissistic defense against affects and the illusion of self-sufficiency. *International Journal of Psycho-Analysis* 56:132–146.

—— (1976). "The holding environment" and the therapeutic action of psychoanalysis. *Journal of the American Psychoanalytic Association* 24:285–308.

Nacht, S. (1962). The curative factors in psychoanalysis. *International Journal of Psycho-Analysis* 43:206–211.

Nadelson, T. (1977). Borderline rage and therapist's response. *American Journal of Psychiatry* 134:748–751.

Newman, K. (1988). Countertransference: its role in facilitating the use of the object. *Annual of Psychoanalysis* 5:329–370.

—— (1992). Abstinence, neutrality, edification: new trends, new climates, new implications. *Annual of Psychoanalysis* 20:131–144.

Ogden, T. (1979). On projective identification. *International Journal of Psycho-Analysis* 60:357–373.

—— (1994). The concept of interpretive action. *Psychoanalytic Quarterly* 63:219–245.

—— (1995). Analyzing forms of aliveness and deadness of tranference–countertransference. *International Journal of Psycho-Analysis* 76:695–709.

Ornstein, P., and Ornstein, A. (1977). On the continuing evolution of psychoanalytic psychotherapy: reflections and predictions. *Annual of Psycho-Analysis* 5:329–370.

Ornston, D. (1982). Strachey's influence: a preliminary report. *International Journal of Psycho-Analysis* 63:409–426.

—— (1985a). Freud's conception is different from Strachey's. *Journal of the American Psychoanalytic Association* 33:379–412.

—— (1985b). The invention of "cathexis" and Strachey's strategy. *International Review of Psycho-Analysis* 12:391–412.

Pao, P. (1979). *Schizophrenic Disorders.* New York: International Universities Press.

Phillips, A. (1988). *Winnicott.* Cambridge, MA: Harvard University Press.

Pruyser, P. (1975). What splits in "splitting"? *Bulletin of the Menninger Clinic* 39:1–46.

Reich, A. (1973). *Psychoanalytic Contributions.* New York: International Universities Press.

Rosenblum, S. (1994). Report of a panel on analyzing the "unanalyzable" patient: implications for technique. *Journal of the American Psychoanalytic Association* 42:1251–1259.

Rothstein, A., ed. (1988). *How Does Treatment Help? On the Modes of Therapeutic Action of Psychoanalytic Psychotherapy.* New York: International Universities Press.

Sandler, J., Dare, C., and Holder, A. (1992). *The Patient and the Analyst: The Basis of the Psychoanalytic Process.* 2nd ed. Madison, CT: International Universities Press.

Schafer, R. (1968). *Aspects of Internalization.* New York: International Universities Press.

—— (1985). Wild analysis. *Journal of the American Psychoanalytic Association* 33:275–300.

—— (1993). Five readings of Freud's "Observations on transference-love." In *On Freud's "Observations on Transference-Love"* ed. E. Person, A. Hagelin, and P. Fonagy. New Haven: Yale University Press.

Schlessinger, N., and Robbins, F. (1974). Assessment and follow-up in psychoanalysis. *Journal of the American Psychoanalytic Association* 22:542–567.

Schwartz, L. (1978). Review of *The Restoration of the Self. Psychoanalytic Quarterly* 47:436–443.

Segal, H. (1967). Melanie Klein's technique. In *Psychoanalytic Techniques: A Handbook for the Practicing Psychoanalyst,* ed. B. Wolman. New York: Basic Books.

—— (1974). *Introduction to the Work of Melanie Klein.* New York: Basic Books.

—— (1980). *Melanie Klein.* New York: Viking.

Solof, P., and Millward, J. (1983). Psychiatric disorders in the families of borderline patients. *Archives of General Psychiatry* 40:36–44.

Spillius, E., ed. (1990). *Melanie Klein Today: Developments in Theory and Practice, vol. 1: Mainly Theory.* New York: Routledge.

—— (1992). *Melanie Klein Today: Developments in Theory and Practice, vol. 2: Mainly Practice.* New York: Routledge.

—— (1994). Developments in Kleinian thought: overview and personal view. *Psychoanalytic Inquiry* 14:324–364.

Spira, D. (1988). The defensive function of psychoanalytic theories. *Annual of Psychoanalysis* 16:81–92.

Stern, D. (1985). *The Interpersonal World of the Infant: A View from Psychoanalysis and Developmental Psychology.* New York: Basic Books.

Stone, L. (1961). *The Psychoanalytic Situation.* New York: International Universities Press.

—— (1981). Notes on the noninterpretive elements in the psychoanalytic situation and process. *Journal of the American Psychoanalytic Association* 29:89–118.

Stone, M. (1990). *The Borderline Syndromes: Constitution, Personality and Adaptation.* New York: McGraw-Hill.

Strachey, J. (1934) The nature of the therapeutic action of psychoanalysis. *International Journal of Psycho-Analysis* 15:117–126.

Sullivan, H. (1947). *Conceptions of Modern Psychiatry.* Washington, DC: William Alanson White Psychiatric Foundation.

—— (1953). *The Interpersonal Theory of Psychiatry.* New York: Norton.

Summers, F. (1993). Implications of object relations theories for the psychoanalytic process. *Annual of Psychoanalysis* 21:225–242.

—— (1994). *Object Relations Theories and Psychopathology: A Comprehensive Text.* Hillsdale, NJ: Analytic Press.

Tarachow, S. (1963). *An Introduction to Psychotherapy.* New York: International Universities Press.

Thomä, H., and Cheshire, N. (1991). Freud's *Nachträglichkeit* and Strachey's "Deferred Action": trauma, constructions and the direction of causality. *International Review of Psycho-Analysis* 18:407–427.

Thomä, H., and Kächele, H. (1987). *Psychoanalytic Practice 1: Principles,* trans. M. Wilson, and D. Roseveare. Berlin: Springer-Verlag.

—— (1992). *Psychoanalytic Practice, 2: Clinical Studies,* trans. M. Wilson. Berlin: Springer-Verlag.

Turkle, S. (1978). *Psychoanalytic Politics.* New York: Basic Books.

Weiss, J., and Sampson, H. (1986). *The Psychoanalytic Process: Theory, Clinical Observation and Empirical Research.* New York: Guilford.

Widlöcher, D. (1994). A case is not a fact. *International Journal of Psycho-Analysis* 75:1223–1244.

Winnicott, D. (1958). *Collected Papers.* New York: Basic Books.

—— (1965). *The Maturational Processes and the Facilitating Environment.* New York: International Universities Press.

Wolf, E. (1992). On being a scientist or a healer: reflections on abstinence, neutrality, and gratification. *Annual of Psychoanalysis* 20:115–129.

# Index

# About the Author

Richard D. Chessick, M.D., Ph.D., is Professor of Psychiatry at Northwestern University and Senior Attending Psychiatrist at Evanston Hospital. Dr. Chessick is the 1989 recipient of the American Society of Psychoanalytic Physicians' Sigmund Freud Award for outstanding contributions to psychiatry and psychoanalysis, and he is also the current president of that organization. He is a Fellow of the American Academy of Psychoanalysis, a Life Fellow of the American Psychiatric Association and the American Orthopsychiatric Association, a Fellow of the Academy of Psychosomatic Medicine and the American Society for Adolescent Psychiatry, a Councillor of the American Association for Social Psychiatry, a corresponding member of the German Psychoanalytic Society, and a member of eighteen other professional societies.

Dr. Chessick is on the editorial board of three major journals and has published more than 200 papers since 1953 in the fields of neurology, psychiatry, philosophy, and psychoanalysis. He is the author of *How Psychotherapy Heals, Why Psychotherapists Fail, Technique and Practice of Intensive Psychotherapy, Agonie: Diary of a Twentieth-Century Man, Great Ideas in Psychotherapy, Intensive Psychotherapy of the Borderline Patient, Freud Teaches Psychotherapy, A Brief Introduction to the Genius of Nietzsche, Psychology of the Self and the Treatment of Narcissism, Technique and Practice of Listening in Intensive Psychotherapy, What Constitutes the Patient in Psychotherapy,* and *A Dictionary for Psychotherapists.*

Dr. Chessick is in the private practice of psychiatry in Evanston, Illinois.